BRINGING DESIGN TO SOFTWARE

Bringing Design to Software

Edited by

TERRY WINOGRAD STANFORD UNIVERSITY

and INTERVAL RESEARCH CORPORATION

with

John Bennett, Laura De Young, and Bradley Hartfield

ACM PRESS

NEW YORK, NEW YORK

ADDISON-WESLEY

An imprint of Addison Wesley Longman, Inc.

Reading, Massachusetts   Harlow, England   Menlo Park, California
Berkeley, California   Don Mills, Ontario   Sydney
Bonn   Amsterdam   Tokyo   Mexico City

1. What is design? What happens in designing?
2. How can we improve software by applying a broad understanding of design to our practices in software design?

In communicating their different perspectives, our authors have designed their texts to address readers who have a variety of professional backgrounds and a variety of reasons for interest in software. Our natural audience is the growing group of people who consider themselves *software designers*—people who work day by day to produce new software, interfaces, and user experiences. Ultimately, their work is where, to use a popular phrase, the rubber meets the road. Effective software design requires effective software designers, and we address their concerns in both the discussions and the software-design examples given in brief profiles throughout the book.

The individual designer, however, does not represent the whole story of software design. Software designers work in (and with) organizations that include people who manage software development, market software, develop hardware, write documentation, and perform all the other activities needed to get software to users. A deeper understanding of the design process and of the goals of software design can be valuable to everyone engaged in the software enterprise. Many of our chapters and examples have as much to say to the *people who manage design organizations* as to the people who work within those organizations.

Looking further outside of the immediate design environment, we have included perspectives that address *students and researchers in human–computer interaction.* Although this book is not primarily a scholarly analysis, we have included a large number of references, and each author has suggested further readings that ground the discussion in the professional literature. In this book, we raise many more questions than we answer, and the pointers to other writing may help readers to seek and develop their own answers.

Expanding our circle still further, we hope that the book will be of interest to *professionals in other design disciplines*, such as architecture, graphic design, product design, and urban design. In "bringing design to software," we have included chapters by designers from all these fields, exploring how insights from their own disciplines can be brought to bear on software design. Colleagues from these disciplines

Bringing Design to Software

Edited by

TERRY WINOGRAD STANFORD UNIVERSITY

and INTERVAL RESEARCH CORPORATION

with

John Bennett, Laura De Young, and Bradley Hartfield

ACM PRESS

NEW YORK, NEW YORK

ADDISON-WESLEY
An imprint of Addison Wesley Longman, Inc.

Reading, Massachusetts Harlow, England Menlo Park, California
Berkeley, California Don Mills, Ontario Sydney
Bonn Amsterdam Tokyo Mexico City

Text designed by Ron Kosciak.
Cover illustrated by John Gamache.
Cover designed by Meredith Nightingale.
Production supervised by Kathleen A. Manley and Sandra Rigney.

This book is published as part of ACM Press Books—a collaboration between the
Association for Computing (ACM) and Addison-Wesley Publishing Company. ACM is
the oldest and largest educational and scientific society in the information technology
field. Through its high-quality publications and services, ACM is a major force in
advancing the skills and knowledge of IT professionals throughout the world. For further information about ACM, contact:

ACM Member Services
1515 Broadway, 17th Floor
New York, NY 10036-5701
Phone: 1-212-626-0500
Fax: 1-212-944-1318
E-mail: acmhelp@acm.org

ACM European Service Center
108 Cowley Road
Oxford OX41JF
United Kingdom
Phone: +44-1865-382338
Fax: +44-1865-381338
E-mail: acm_europe@acm.org
URL: http://www.acm.org

Credits appear on page 310

Library of Congress Cataloging-in-Publication Data
Bringing design to software / Terry Winograd . . . [et al.].
     p. cm. — (ACM press books)
   Includes bibliographical references and index.
   ISBN 0-201-85491-0
   1. Computer software—Development. I. Winograd, Terry.
   II. Series
QA76.76.D47B745 1996
005.1'2—dc20   95-37554
                                                       CIP

Text printed on recycled and acid-free paper.

ISBN 0201854910

6 7 8 9 1011 MA   03 02 01 00

6th Printing   February 2000

Preface

Software is an ambiguous word. People who talk about software may be thinking about the structure of program components, about the functionality of an application, about the look and feel of an interface, or about the overall user experience of a hardware–software environment. Each of these perspectives brings along its own context of understanding about what matters, what can be designed, and what tools and methods are appropriate.

Design is also an ambiguous word. Among its many meanings, there runs a common thread, linking the intent and activities of a designer to the results that are produced when a designed object is experienced in practice. Although there is a huge diversity among the design disciplines, we can find common concerns and principles that are applicable to the design of any object, whether it is a poster, a household appliance, or a housing development.

In *Bringing Design to Software*, our goal is to improve the practice of software design, through thinking about design from a broader perspective, and exploring how lessons from all areas of design can be applied to software. We use the word *exploring* here consciously; what you will read is an open-ended foray into ideas, rather than a how-to handbook of rules and methods. Software design is still a young field, and we are far from having a clear articulation of the relevant principles. Software design is a user-oriented field, and as such will always have the human openness of disciplines such as architecture and graphic design, rather than the hard-edged formulaic certainty of engineering design.

This book brings a collection of diverse perspectives to bear on the common topic of software design. The authors include software designers, designers in other fields, researchers, teachers, software industry executives, and industry analysts. Each chapter, in its own way, addresses two key sets of questions.

1. What is design? What happens in designing?
2. How can we improve software by applying a broad understanding of design to our practices in software design?

In communicating their different perspectives, our authors have designed their texts to address readers who have a variety of professional backgrounds and a variety of reasons for interest in software. Our natural audience is the growing group of people who consider themselves *software designers*—people who work day by day to produce new software, interfaces, and user experiences. Ultimately, their work is where, to use a popular phrase, the rubber meets the road. Effective software design requires effective software designers, and we address their concerns in both the discussions and the software-design examples given in brief profiles throughout the book.

The individual designer, however, does not represent the whole story of software design. Software designers work in (and with) organizations that include people who manage software development, market software, develop hardware, write documentation, and perform all the other activities needed to get software to users. A deeper understanding of the design process and of the goals of software design can be valuable to everyone engaged in the software enterprise. Many of our chapters and examples have as much to say to the *people who manage design organizations* as to the people who work within those organizations.

Looking further outside of the immediate design environment, we have included perspectives that address *students and researchers in human–computer interaction*. Although this book is not primarily a scholarly analysis, we have included a large number of references, and each author has suggested further readings that ground the discussion in the professional literature. In this book, we raise many more questions than we answer, and the pointers to other writing may help readers to seek and develop their own answers.

Expanding our circle still further, we hope that the book will be of interest to *professionals in other design disciplines*, such as architecture, graphic design, product design, and urban design. In "bringing design to software," we have included chapters by designers from all these fields, exploring how insights from their own disciplines can be brought to bear on software design. Colleagues from these disciplines may find it valuable to see how they might apply their skills to software design, and to reflect on the nature of their own work.

Finally, a pervasive theme of this book is that one group of people is most important in software design—the *users*. Although our primary focus is on how to do software design well, the book has much to say about the selection, introduction, and use of software. If every buyer and user of software applications has a well-developed understanding of software design, the industry will be forced to respond with better-designed software. We want to reach out to this larger audience of people who care about what software can do for them, and to help make the software that is available to them become more appropriate, more usable, and more enjoyable.

Our goal is to make visible what is common and timeless to design, while looking at the world at hand—the cases and examples that make up the tradition of software design in its short history. We have written to communicate with the reflective designer—someone who is driven by practical concerns, and who is also able to take a moment to step back and reflect on what works, what doesn't work, and why.

Origins

This book developed from a workshop on software design in the summer of 1992, organized by the Project on People, Computers, and Design at Stanford University, with support from the National Science Foundation, Interval Research Corporation, and the Association for Software Design. A group of 30 software designers, graphic designers, industrial designers, researchers, and teachers got together for a lively 3-day discussion on what software design is and might be, and on what we could see emerging in each of our disciplines that would help us to define and promote new visions of software design. At the end of that workshop, several of the participants agreed to work together on a book that would merge their individual perspectives into a composite picture of software design. Since then, we have gone through an extensive process of prototyping, debugging, and user testing many versions of this book. The result is an integrated collection of essays and interviews, addressing issues and concerns that are central to the functionality, usability, and value of software.

Acknowledgments

In any project of this length and scope, many people contribute their knowledge and skills. We have been assisted by colleagues whose understanding and whose work on this volume are truly remarkable. First, and most obviously, the chapter authors have been diligent in revising their contributions, patient in following the book through its changes of direction, and insightful in their writing and comments. The experience of producing this book has been a challenging dialog, in which they have eagerly and actively engaged.

Numerous people were instrumental in creating the original workshop, including the organizing committee—Bradley Hartfield, Mitchell Kapor, David Kelley, Donald Norman, Donald Schön, Andrew Singer, and Terry Winograd—and the conference director, Cynthia Lewis, with assistance from Barry Polley. The other conference participants (in addition to the contributors of chapters to the book) were Jeanne Bamberger (MIT), Nathaniel Borenstein (Bellcore, currently First Virtual), Larry Bucciarelli (MIT), Robert Carr (Autodesk), Parvati Dev (Stanford Medical School), Laird Foshay (Tabula Interactive), Nick Flor (UC San Diego), Chris Graham (Microsoft), John Hestenes (National Science Foundation), Susan Kare (design consultant), Jason Lewis (vivid), Kyle Mashima (Objective Software), Raúl Medina-Mora (Action Technologies), Gary Perlman (Ohio State University), David Rine (George Mason University), Kurt Schmucker (Apple Computer), Lee Sproull (Boston University), Suzanne Stefanac (*Macworld*), Susan Stucky (Institute for Research on Learning), Bill Verplank (Interval Research), Patrick Whitney (Institute of Design, Illinois Institute of Technology), Sean White (Interval Research), and Kären Wieckert (Stanford University).

The workshop and much of the subsequent work on the book were supported generously by the Interval Research Corporation. Interval's president, David Liddle, deserves a special note of thanks for his consistent and persistent efforts on behalf of this work and for his support of the development of software design in many other ways. Financial support also came from the National Science Foundation, Directorate for Computer and Information Science and Engineering, grant #CDA-9018898.

Valuable editorial assistance and reviews have been provided by Robert Brunner, Allan Bush, Laird Foshay, Jonathan Grudin, Peter Hildebrand, Barbara Knapp, Donald Lindsay, Mary Miller, Barry Polley, Richard Rubinstein, Suzanne Stefanac, Howard Tamler, Bill Verplank, and Sean White. Peter Gordon of Addison-Wesley and Lyn Dupré have been active participants in the development of the book, providing the kind of editorial input that authors hope for and rarely get from a publisher.

Finally, switching from the editorial "we" to an individual "I," I can convey only a small part of the tremendous gratitude and admiration I have for my coeditors, John Bennett, Laura De Young, and Brad Hartfield. Each of them has given the kind of dedication and effort that might be expected of a solo editor. They have labored over chapters, read and commented on drafts, worked through dozens of meetings and discussions, and contributed to the manuscript in every possible way. It is a cliché to say "without them it would not have been possible," but, in this case, the assertion is decidedly true. This book is a group production, through and through.

And now the group expands to include you, the reader, whose active participation we invite. We hope that this book will inspire you to add your own perspective—to speak up in the ongoing dialog about what software is, what it can do, and how we can design it more effectively to suit human needs and concerns.

Terry Winograd <Winograd@CS.Stanford.edu>
with John Bennett <Bennett@PCD.Stanford.edu>
   Laura De Young <Laura@Windrose.com>
   Bradley Hartfield <BradleyH@HartfieldDG.com>

PALO ALTO, CA

Contents

Introduction

In today's computer-permeated world, it can be difficult to remember that only a few years have elapsed since the microprocessor revolution enabled the computer to move out of esoteric glass-walled isolation, to become an everyday part of work and play for millions of people. In that time, the software industry has grown from a minor adjunct of the computer (hardware) industry into a major economic sector, containing some of the largest companies in the world.

Now we are witnessing a second transformation in the role that computers and their software play in people's lives. Advances in hardware technology and in software design are changing the definition of a software product. We are moving from an era in which operating systems and shrink-wrapped word processors were representative products into a new phase, in which interactive multiplayer games, information webs, smart jewelry, and personal communicators will be more typical.

In step with the accelerating movement toward transcending the conventional applications of the 1980s, a new aspect of software has moved into prominence in the 1990s—one that we can associate with the term *design*.

At a major software producer's meeting in 1990, Mitchell Kapor, the designer of Lotus 1-2-3, called his fellow software-company executives to task for ignoring design. He issued a challenge in the form of his *Software Design Manifesto* (reprinted in Chapter 1).

> Despite the enormous outward success of personal computers, the daily experience of using computers far too often is still fraught with difficulty, pain, and barriers for most people....The lack of usability of software and the poor design of programs are the secret shame of the industry.

Kapor's call did not fall on deaf ears. He articulated a sentiment that was already stirring, and his concerns resonated with people in

the software-development community. In the few years since his manifesto, software design has been moving ahead:

- In 1992, a new professional organization, the Association for
  Software Design (ASD), was founded with the mission to "trans-
  form and elevate the status and quality of software design as an
  activity." It has chapters in several cities around the United States,
  and is initiating a regular program of educational activities.
- In 1994, a new publication, *interactions*, was founded by the
  Association for Computing Machinery (ACM), in conjunction
  with the ASD and the ACM Special Interest Group on
  Computer–Human Interaction (SIGCHI). In the inaugural issue
  (January 1994, p. 88), the editors, John Rheinfrank and Bill
  Hefley, stated:

  We seem to have moved well beyond the idea that making a computer
  "useful" is simply to design a good interface between "man and
  machine." Our ideas have evolved to the point where the richness of
  human experience comes to the foreground and computing sits in the
  background in the service of these experiences.

- The entire first 1994 issue of the journal *Human–Computer
  Interaction* was devoted to a dialog about an article by John Seely
  Brown and Paul Duguid on the role of context in design.
- At the 1994 SIGCHI conference (CHI'94), Kapor gave the
  keynote address, in which he argued for the primacy of design as
  an approach to human–computer interaction. There were an
  unprecedented number of papers and sessions devoted to design
  issues. The CHI'95 conference instituted a new section called
  design briefings for presentation of notable designs and for discussion of how those designs came to be.
- Industry has increased its emphasis on the usability of software. In
  1995, Microsoft attempted to buy Intuit's money-management
  program, Quicken, for a staggering $1.5 billion, primarily because
  customers had found Quicken to be more usable and understandable than Microsoft's own software. The sale was blocked by government concerns that it would give Microsoft too great a
  monopoly in the financial-software market.
- After 25 years of development, the Internet global computer network has suddenly exploded into public view and has generated

great excitement. The popularity of the Internet is largely due to the influence of interfaces such as Mosaic, and its successor, Netscape, which have made the Internet accessible to a greatly expanded population.

It is evident that software design is coming into prominence. But that should give us a moment's pause. Just what is software design? How does it differ from programming, software engineering, software architecture, human factors, and interface design? How is software design related to other fields that call themselves design, such as industrial design, graphic design, information design, urban design, and even fashion design? It is easy to make a new label. The real work lies in generating a change of perspective that can engender new directions and new ideas.

What Is Software Design?

The Association for Software Design (ASD) delights in revealing to prospective members that they have been engaged in software design, even though their payroll records may refer to them as software engineers, as programmers, as program managers, as human-factors consultants, or as one of many other titles. The ASD membership brochure offers a definition:

> Software design sits at the crossroads of all the computer disciplines: hardware and software engineering, programming, human factors research, ergonomics. It is the study of the intersection of human, machine, and the various interfaces—physical, sensory, psychological—that connect them.

Whenever objects are created for people to use, design is pervasive. Design may be done methodically or offhandedly, consciously or accidentally. But when people create software—or any other product—decisions are made and objects are constructed that carry with them an intention of what those objects will do and how they will be perceived and used.

The education of computer professionals has often concentrated on the understanding of computational mechanisms, and on engineering methods that seek to ensure that the mechanisms behave as the programmer intends. The focus is on the objects being designed: the hardware and software. The primary concern is to implement a specified functionality efficiently. When software engineers or programmers say that a piece of software *works*, they typically mean that it is robust, is reliable, and meets its functional specification. These concerns are indeed important. Any designer who ignores them does so at the risk of disaster.

But this inward-looking perspective, with its focus on function and construction, is one-sided. To design software that really *works*, we need to move from a constructor's-eye view to a designer's-eye view, taking the system, the users, and the context all together as a starting point. When a designer says that something *works* (for example, a layout for a book cover or a design for a housing complex), the term reflects a broader meaning. Good design produces an object that works for people in a context of values and needs, to produce quality results and a satisfying experience.

What Is Software?

In the context of a book on software design, it should be obvious that we are concerned with designing software. It is far from clear, however, just what that word means. We can approach software from many different perspectives, each with its own implications for design. In this book, we emphasize software as a medium for the creation of *virtualities*—the world in which a user of the software perceives, acts, and responds to experiences.

The creation of a virtual world is immediately evident in computer games, which dramatically engage the player in exploring the vast reaches of space, fighting off the villains, finding the treasures—actively living in whatever worlds the game designer can imagine and portray. But the creation of worlds is not limited to game designers. There is also a virtual world in a desktop interface, a spreadsheet, and the Internet. The difference between interface and world was recognized by the designers of the Xerox Star—the progenitor of the modern graphical user interface—in their focus on what David Liddle (Chapter 2) refers to as the *user's conceptual model*. Later projects have used other terms—such as *conceptual model, cognitive model, user's model, interface metaphor, user illusion, virtuality,* and *ontology*—all carrying the connotation that a space of existence, rather than a set of devices or images, is being designed. The term *virtuality* highlights the perspective that the world is virtual, in a space that is neither a mental construct of the user nor a mental construct of the designer.

Today, we are all familiar with the virtuality of the standard graphical user interface—with its windows, icons, folders, and the like. Although these virtual objects are loosely grounded in analogies with the physical world, they exist in a unique world of their own, with its special logic and potentials for action by the user. The underlying programs manipulate disk sectors, network addresses, data caches, and program segments. These underpinnings do not appear—at least when things are working normally—in the desktop virtuality in which the user works.

Software is not just a device with which the user interacts; it is also the generator of a space in which the user lives. Software design is like architecture: When an architect designs a home or an office building, a structure is being specified. More significantly, though, the patterns of life for its inhabitants are being shaped. People are thought of as *inhabitants* rather than as *users* of buildings. In this book, we approach software users as inhabitants, focusing on an how they live in the spaces that designers create. Our goal is to situate the work of the designer in the world of the user.

The view of software that we adopt in this book is not the only appropriate or valuable one. Designers can master software, as they can any technology, only by understanding it from contrasting perspectives. These perspectives provide a larger context for our discussions.

Software engineering

The phrase *software design* is often used to characterize the discipline that is also called *software engineering*—the discipline concerned with the construction of software that is efficient, reliable, robust, and easy to maintain. The substantial body of literature on software design as an engineering activity (for example, Pfleeger, 1991; Rumbaugh, 1991; Blum, 1992; Brooks, 1975, 1995) is complementary to the concerns developed in this book. Blum (1996) addresses software engineering concerns explicitly from a design perspective.

Interface design

In a way, the title of this book is misleading. *Bringing Design to Software* implies that the object of design is software, leaving out considerations of the interface devices that are the inevitable embodiment of software for the user. Design cannot be neatly divided into compartments for software and for devices: The possibilities for software are both created and constrained by the physical interfaces. In today's world of computer applications, the vast majority of applications present themselves to users in a standard way—a visual display with a keyboard and pointing device. But the future of computing will bring richer resources to physical human–computer interactions. Some new devices are already in use on a modest scale—for example, pen-based personal digital assistants (PDAs), virtual-reality goggles and gloves, and computers embedded in electromechanical devices of all kinds. Researchers are exploring further possibilities, including tactile input and output devices, immersive environments, audio spaces, wearable computers, and a host of gadgets that bear little resemblance to today's personal computer or workstation. Many current textbooks and reading collections on human–computer interaction (for example, Shneiderman, 1992; Dix et al., 1993; Preece et al., 1994; and Baecker et al., 1995) include sections on interface devices. As experience with a wider variety of devices accumulates, the design of interaction based on new combinations of devices and software will be an important emerging topic in what we have—for the moment—called *software design*.

Human–computer interaction

Whenever someone designs software that interacts with people, the effects of the design extend beyond the software itself to include the experiences that people will have in encountering and using that software. A person encountering any artifact applies knowledge and understanding, based on wide variety of *cognitive mechanisms* grounded in human capacities for perception, memory, and action. Researchers in human–computer interaction have studied the mental worlds of computer users, developing approaches and methods for predicting properties of the interactions and for supporting the design of interfaces. Although it would be overstating the case to say that the

cognitive analysis of human–computer interaction has led to commonly accepted and widely applied methods, there is a substantial literature that can be of value to anyone designing interactive software (for
example, Card et al., 1983; Norman and Draper, 1986; Helander,
1988; Carroll, 1991). Practical applications of HCI research are promoted by organizations such as ACM SIGCHI, the Human Factors
and Ergonomics Society (see Perlman et al., 1995), and the Usability
Professionals Association.

Art

The experience of a person who is interacting with a computer system
is not limited to the cognitive aspects that have been explored in the
mainstream literature on human–computer interaction. As humans,
we experience the world in aesthetic, affective, and emotional terms as
well. Because computing evolved initially for use in the laboratory and
the office, noncognitive aspects have been largely ignored, except by
creators of computer games. Yet, whenever people experience a piece
of software—whether it be a spreadsheet or a physics simulation—they
have natural human responses. They experience beauty, satisfaction,
and fun, or the corresponding opposites.

As computing becomes integrated into technologies for entertainment, and as the typical user moves from the well-regimented office to
the home recreation room, software designers will need to focus more
on the affective dimensions of human response (see, for example,
Laurel, 1993). We can learn from the history of other human communication media, and can adapt the principles and techniques of novel-
ists, film makers, composers, visual artists, and many other designers
in what are loosely called *the arts*. Designing for the full range of
human experience may well be the theme for the next generation of
discourse about software design.

What Is Design?

Perhaps even more difficult than the task of defining *software* is the
task of defining *design*. A dictionary provides several loosely overlap-
ping meanings, and a glance at the design section in a library or book-

store confuses the issue even more. Although we label it with a noun, design is not a *thing*. The questions that we can ask fruitfully are about the *activity* of *designing*. The authors of our chapters did not produce a simple definition; rather, each contributes to an answer by providing a perspective on what people do when they design.

Design is conscious

People may refer to an object as being *well designed* whenever it is well suited to its environment, even if this suitability resulted from a process of unintentional evolution. In this book, we concentrate on what happens when a designer reflects on and brings focus to the design activity. Complex systems can evolve without a coherent master design—for example, cities (see Alexander, 1964) and the Internet (see Krol, 1994)—but even in these cases, conscious design is at work in creating the individual pieces and relationships that make up the whole.

Consciousness about designing does not imply the application of a formal, consistent, or comprehensive theory of design or of a universal methodology. Systematic principles and methods at times may be applicable to the process of design, but there is no effective equivalent to the rationalized generative theories applied in mathematics and traditional engineering. Design consciousness is still pervaded by intuition, tacit knowledge, and gut reaction.

Design keeps human concerns in the center

All engineering and design activities call for the management of tradeoffs. Real-world problems rarely have a *correct solution* of the kind that would be suitable for a mathematics problem or for a textbook exercise. The designer looks for creative solutions in a space of alternatives that is shaped by competing values and resource needs. In classical engineering disciplines, the tradeoffs can often be quantified: material strength, construction costs, rate of wear, and the like. In design disciplines, the tradeoffs are more difficult to identify and to measure. The designer stands with one foot in the technology and one foot in the domain of human concerns, and these two worlds are not easily commensurable.

As an example, it is easy for software designers to fall into a single-minded quest, in which ease of use (especially for beginning users) becomes a holy grail. But what is *ease of use*? How much does it matter to whom? A violin is extremely difficult for novices to play, but it would be foolish to argue that it should therefore be replaced by the autoharp. The value of an artifact may lie in high-performance use by virtuosos, or in ease of use for some special class of users, such as children or people with disabilities. There is room for the software equivalents of high-strung racing cars alongside automatic-transmission minivans.

In Chapter 5, Paul Saffo explores the dimensions of what matters to consumers of high technology. He introduces a concept that he calls the *threshold of indignation*—the point in the tradeoff curve where, for different groups of users, the perceived value is exceeded by the perceived hassle. A multidimensional understanding of what concerns users is critical to an understanding of where new software and electronics technologies will lead in practice.

Design is a conversation with materials

The ongoing process of designing is iterative at two levels: iteration by the designer as a piece of current work develops, and iteration by the community as successive generations reveal new possibilities for the medium. The cycle of an individual designer's *reflection in action* is described in detail in an interview with Donald Schön (Chapter 9), and is illustrated in Shahaf Gal's account of a student mechanical-design project (Chapter 11). As Schön and Gal point out, designing is inherently complex—every choice by the designer has both intended and unintended effects. Designing is not so much a process of careful planning and execution as it is a conversation, in which the conversing partner—the designed object itself—can generate unexpected interruptions and contributions. The designer listens to the emerging design, as well as shapes it.

Design always implies a medium of construction, and new technologies bring with them new domains for design. Architecture as we know it appeared with the technology for building with stone. Graphic design emerged with the technologies of printing, and modern product design flourished with the development of plastics that expanded the variety of possible forms for everyday products. The computer has produced the field of *interaction design*, in which new kinds of virtualities can be created and modified with a velocity that is unprecedented. The effect of new prototyping media on industries as a whole is reflected in a discussion of the *cultures of prototyping* by Michael Schrage in Chapter 10.

Design is creative

It is one thing to lay out a list of criteria for good design. It is quite another thing to do design well. Many books have been written on systematic methods for design, and in particular for the design of interfaces and interactive systems (for example, Hix and Hartson, 1993; Newman and Lamming, 1995). These texts provide useful guidance, yet designing is a creative activity that cannot be fully reduced to standard steps, and that cannot even be comprehended as *problem solving*. As David Kelley argues in Chapter 8, a designer lacks the comforting restraints of a well-organized engineering discipline, because designing is inherently messy; it includes, but goes beyond, the ability to be creative in solving problems. It begins with creativity in finding the problems—envisioning the needs that people have but do not recognize.

For the *artist–designer*, depicted by Gillian Crampton Smith and Philip Tabor in Chapter 3, interaction design is more an art than a science—it is spontaneous, unpredictable, and hard to define. The skill of the artist–designer is not reducible to a set of methods, and is not learned through the kind of structured curriculum that serves in science and engineering. On the other hand, it is not a mysterious gift. There is a long and rich tradition of education in the design fields; it draws on the interaction between learner and teacher, designer and critic.

Design is communication

Previous sections have described the interaction between the user and his world, and the interaction between the designer and her materials. What matters most is the interaction between these two interactions. A virtuality is neither just what the designer thinks it is, nor what any particular user thinks it is. It exists in the ongoing dialog between designers and users. To succeed in designing, we need to understand how designers convey meaning.

At a surface level, designed artifacts communicate content. As Crampton Smith and Tabor point out, even an object as mundane as a railway timetable conveys meanings at multiple levels. Skilled designers in every discipline know how to manage these layers of meaning. In addition, an active artifact—whether it be a computer program or a coffee maker—communicates to users about its use. A device as apparently simple as a door communicates to its users through convention. A door with a flat plate near shoulder level says "Push me!" One with a round knob says "Twist here." Although these messages are constrained by the physical mechanisms, they are also a matter of convention and learning, as every tourist finds out in trying to deal with everyday objects in an unfamiliar culture. John Rheinfrank and Shelley Evenson (Chapter 4) explain how these physical *affordances* are one constituent of a broader *design language* in which multiple meanings are being communicated, including the functional, the cognitive, the connotative, and the aesthetic. Whenever a designer constructs an object for human use, she is drawing on a background of shared design language in the community and culture.

As is true of any human language, what is visible in a statement is only a small part of the full picture. A hearer of the sentence "I'm going to kill you!" cannot interpret the intended meaning without knowing the situational context—was it said to a friend walking onto the tennis court, in an anonymous note mailed to the President, or by a parent to a child who has just left dirty clothing on the bathroom floor again? The literal meaning is but the shadow of the meaning in context.

The same is true for the artifacts that we build, including software: People do not approach them in isolation. Every object appears in a context of expectations that is generated by the history of previous objects and experiences, and by the surroundings in the *periphery*—the physical, social, and historical context in which the object is encountered. In Chapter 7, John Seely Brown and Paul Duguid describe the *border resources* that every designer draws on in creating something that is new—and that inevitably also takes meaning from what came before. They argue that widespread blindness to the periphery in software design has led to designs that may extend the literal functionality of traditional forms, but that are inappropriate in the larger human context.

Design has social consequences

Much of the discussion on software design uses examples from generic mass-distribution software, such as word processors, operating systems, spreadsheets, graphics programs, and games. Although many key concerns of software design are addressed in these applications, others are not. These highly visible applications are part of a larger picture that includes a vast number of vertical applications (for example, a medical-office billing application) and systems designed for a specific workplace setting. In these more targeted applications, the designer can see and take into account the specific effects of the design on the people who will inhabit it.

In Chapter 14, Sarah Kuhn looks at the organizational aspects of software design, which come to center stage when we build integrated computer systems for specific organizations and workplaces. The needs and concerns of the people in those workplaces can lead to complex—and, at times, controversial—design considerations, which we can address only by making the social and political dimensions an explicit part of the analysis and of the design dialog. The designer takes on a role that includes organizational as well as technical design, and can enlist workers directly in this process through techniques such as *participatory design*.

In Chapter 6, Peter Denning and Pamela Dargan introduce a technique for addressing work content as the central focus of design, which they call *action-centered design*. Their experience in working with traditional software engineering techniques has pointed out areas of failure, which designers can address by shifting attention to the structure of the work rather than concentrating on the structure of the information systems that support the work.

Design is a social activity

In concentrating on the activity of an individual designer, we can fall into the error of assuming that the overall quality of a design is primarily a result of the qualities and activities of the creative individual. As Kelley points out, the designer operates in a larger setting, which is both facilitated and constrained by interactions with other people.

In Chapter 12, Donald Norman dramatically recounts how design in a large organization is shaped by factors and forces that transcend the considerations of an individual designer. He describes two levels at which an organization constrains the space of possible designs: the explicit level of working with the differing goals and needs of the many parties in a large organization, and the tacit effect of an organization's unique culture.

Norman's saga of how organizational structures can complicate the activity of designing is complemented by Laura De Young's analysis of what a software development organization can do to facilitate customer-oriented design (Chapter 13). De Young draws examples from her work as a consultant and from the experience of Intuit—the producer of the extremely successful home financial application, Quicken—to identify the principles that designers within any organization can follow to focus the design process on the quality of the user's experience.

How Do Software and Design Fit Together?

As the preceding sections make clear, you will not find a simple definition of software design in this book. Although the book initially emerged from a gathering intended to produce such a definition, the dialog led instead to a flowering of distinct perspectives, which expanded in unique directions from a common core of issues. In developing those perspectives into a book, we have worked to enrich the dialog among them. Each chapter explores its authors' chosen concerns, in its authors' voices. Interleaved with the chapters are brief *profiles*, each describing a successful project or program that exemplifies the book's concepts in practice.

The resulting text requires work from you. It is not digested and homogenized into a single message that a software designer can conveniently summarize and apply. The integration will come as you consider how the questions that are raised here might apply to your own concerns and activities. What is common to all the authors is a concern for the situated nature of design—a sensitivity to the human context in all its richness and variety.

MITCHELL 1 KAPOR

A Software Design Manifesto

The most important social evolution within the computing
professions would be to create a role for the software designer as a
champion of the user experience....What is design?...It's where
you stand with a foot in two worlds—the world of technology
and the world of people and human purposes—and you try to
bring the two together.

1

Mitchell Kapor was one of the first people in the microcomputer industry to identify his work as *designing software*. When he began work on Lotus 1-2-3 in the early 1980s, he took on the task of designing the interactions, but he wasn't the programmer. He worked closely with a skilled programmer, Jonathan Sachs, interactively developing the design at all levels of detail—from the broad architecture to the structured organization of the command menus and the naming of the menu items.

He recounts the story of being asked by his son what he did for a living, and of being unable to come up with a good answer—he wasn't a programmer, but he was developing programs. On the other hand, he wasn't a manager, in that he was doing the detailed design work himself, rather than directing other workers. He was doing software design, but he didn't have a label for that kind of work. In his manifesto, which is reproduced here, and in a number of other talks and writings over the past few years, he has eloquently made the case that we need to think of software design as a *profession*, rather than as a side task of a manager or a programmer.

Kapor delivered his manifesto in 1990 at Esther Dyson's PC forum, a renowned gathering of microcomputer industry leaders. The response ranged from strong enthusiasm to the predictable "Why are you complaining—we're selling lots of software?" It first appeared in print 1 year later (Kapor, 1991) in *Dr. Dobbs Journal*, one of the oldest and most widely read magazines for microcomputer programmers.

This chapter is the only one in the book that is reprinted from an earlier publication. As a call to arms, it has in important place in helping us to understand the history and context of our field. The points that Kapor made are still as valid today as they were a few years ago, and the themes that he introduced echo throughout this book.

— *Terry Winograd*

THE GREAT AND RAPID SUCCESS of the personal computer industry over the past decade is not without its unexpected ironies. What began as a revolution of individual empowerment has ended with the personal computer industry not only joining the computing mainstream, but in fact defining it. Despite the enormous outward success of personal computers, the daily experience of using computers far too often is still fraught with difficulty, pain, and barriers for most people, which means that the revolution, measured by its original goals, has not as yet succeeded.

Instead we find ourselves in a period of retrenchment and consolidation, in which corporations seek to rationalize their computing investment by standardizing on platforms, applications, and methods of connectivity, rather than striving for a fundamental simplification of the user experience. In fact, the need for extensive help in the installation, configuration, and routine maintenance of system functions continues to make the work of corporate data processing and MIS departments highly meaningful. But no one is speaking for the poor user.

There is a conspiracy of silence on this issue. It's not splashed all over the front pages of the industry trade press, but we all know it's true. Users are largely silent about this. There is no uproar, no outrage. Scratch the surface and you'll find that people are embarrassed to say they find these devices hard to use. They think the fault is their own. So users learn a bare minimum to get by. They underuse the products we work so hard to make and so don't help themselves or us as much as we would like. They're afraid to try anything else. In sum, everyone I know (including me) feels the urge to throw that infuriating machine through the window at least once a week. (And now, thanks to recent advances in miniaturization, this is now possible.)

The lack of usability of software and the poor design of programs are the secret shame of the industry. Given a choice, no one would want it to be this way. What is to be done? Computing professionals themselves should take responsibility for creating a positive user experience. Perhaps the most important conceptual move to be taken is to recognize the critical role of design, as a counterpart to programming, in the creation of computer artifacts. And the most important social evolution within the computing professions would be to create a role for the software designer as a champion of the user experience.

By training and inclination, people who develop programs haven't been oriented to design issues. This is not to fault the vital work of programmers. It is simply to say that the perspective and skills that are critical to good design are typically absent from the development process, or, if present, exist only in an underground fashion. We need to take a fresh look at the entire process of creating software—what I call the *software design viewpoint*. We need to rethink the fundamentals of how software is made.

The Case for Design

What is design? What makes something a design problem? It's where you stand with a foot in two worlds—the world of technology and the world of people and human purposes—and you try to bring the two together. Consider an example.

Architects, not construction engineers, are the professionals who have overall responsibility for creating buildings. Architecture and engineering are, as disciplines, peers to each other, but in the actual process of designing and implementing the building, the engineers take direction from the architects. The engineers play a vital and crucial role in the process, but they take their essential direction from the design of the building as established by the architect.

When you go to design a house you talk to an architect first, not an engineer. Why is this? Because the criteria for what makes a good building fall substantially outside the domain of what engineering deals with. You want the bedrooms where it will be quiet so people can sleep, and you want the dining room to be near the kitchen. The fact that the kitchen and dining room should be proximate to each other emerges from knowing first, that the purpose of the kitchen is to prepare food and the dining room to consume it, and second, that rooms with related purposes ought to be closely related in space. This is not a fact, nor a technical item of knowledge, but a piece of design wisdom.

Similarly, in computer programs, the selection of the various components and elements of the application must be driven by an appreciation of the overall conditions of use and user needs through a process of intelligent and conscious design. How is this to be done? By software designers.

Design disciplines are concerned with making artifacts for human use. Architects work in the medium of buildings, graphic designers work in paper and other print media, industrial designers on mass-produced manufactured goods, and software designers on software. The software designer should be the person with overall responsibility for the conception and realization of the program.

The Roman architecture critic Vitruvius advanced the notion that well-designed buildings were those which exhibited firmness, commodity, and delight.

The same might be said of good software. Firmness: A program should not have any bugs that inhibit its function. Commodity: A program should be suitable for the purposes for which it was intended. Delight: The experience of using the program should be a pleasurable one. Here we have the beginnings of a theory of design for software.

Software Design Today

Today, the software designer leads a guerrilla existence, formally unrecognized and often unappreciated. There's no spot on the corporate organization chart or career ladder for such an individual. Yet time after time I've found people in software development companies who recognize themselves as software designers, even though their employers and colleagues don't yet accord them the professional recognition they seek.

Design is widely regarded by computer scientists as being a proper subpart of computer science itself. Also, engineers would claim design for their own. I would claim that software design needs to be recognized as a profession in its own right, a disciplinary peer to computer science and software engineering, a first-class member of the family of computing disciplines.

One of the main reasons most computer software is so abysmal is that it's not designed at all, but merely engineered. Another reason is that implementors often place more emphasis on a program's internal construction than on its external design, despite the fact that as much as 75 percent of the code in a modern program deals with the interface to the user.

More Than Interface Design

Software design is not the same as user interface design.

The overall design of a program is to be clearly distinguished from the design of its user interface. If a user interface is designed after the fact, that is like designing an automobile's dashboard after the engine, chassis, and all other components and functions are specified. The separation of the user interface from the overall design process fundamentally disenfranchises designers at the expense of programmers and relegates them to the status of second-class citizens.

The software designer is concerned primarily with the overall conception of the product. Dan Bricklin's invention of the electronic spreadsheet is one of the crowning achievements of software design. It is the metaphor of the spreadsheet itself, its tableau of rows and columns with their precisely interrelated labels, numbers, and formulas—rather than the user interface of VisiCalc—for which he will be remembered. The look and feel of a product is but one part of its design.

Training Designers

If software design is to be a profession in its own right, then there must be professional training that develops the consciousness and skills central to the profession.

Training in software design is distinguished from computer science, software engineering, and computer programming, in that its principal focus is on the training of professional practitioners whose work it is to create usable computer-based artifacts—that is, software programs. The emphasis on developing this specific professional competency distinguishes software design on the one hand from computer science, which seeks to train scientists in a theoretical discipline, and on the other, from engineering, which focuses almost exclusively on the construction of the internals of computer programs and which, from the design point of view, gives short shrift to consideration of use and users.

In architecture, the study of design begins with the fundamental principles and techniques of architectural representation and composition, which include freehand drawing, constructed drawing, presentation graphics, and visual composition and analysis.

In both architecture and software design it is necessary to provide the professional practitioner with a way to model the final result with far less effort than is required to build the final product. In each case specialized tools and techniques are used. In software design, unfortunately, design tools aren't sufficiently developed to be maximally useful.

Hypercard, for instance, allows the ready simulation of the appearance of a program, but is not effective at modeling the behavior of real-world programs. It captures the surface, but not the semantics. For this, object-oriented approaches will do better, especially when there are plug-in libraries, or components, readily available that perform basic back-end functions. These might not have the performance or capacity of back ends embedded in commercial products, but will be more than adequate for prototyping purposes.

A Firm Grounding in Technology

Many people who think of themselves as working on the design of software simply lack the technical grounding to be an effective participant in the overall process. Naturally, programmers quickly lose respect for people who fail to understand fundamental technical issues. The answer to this is not to exclude designers from the process, but to make sure that they have a sound mastery of technical fundamentals, so that genuine communication with programmers is possible.

Technology courses for the student designer should deal with the principles and methods of computer program construction. Topics would include computer systems architecture, microprocessor architectures, operating systems, network communications, data structures and algorithms, databases, distributed computing, programming environments, and object-oriented development methodologies.

Designers must have a solid working knowledge of at least one modern programming language (C or Pascal) in addition to exposure to a wide variety of languages and tools, including Forth and Lisp.

The Software Design Studio

Most important, students learn software design by practicing it. A major component of the professional training, therefore, would consist of design studios in which students carry out directed projects to design parts of actual programs, whole programs, and groups of programs using the tools and techniques of their trade.

Prospective software designers must also master the existing research in the field of human–computer interaction and social science research on the use of the computer in the workplace and in organizations.

A design is realized only in a particular medium. What are the characteristic properties of the medium in which we create software?

Digital media have unique properties that distinguish them from print-based and electronic predecessors. Software designers need to make a systematic study and comparison of different media—print, audiovisual, and digital—examining their properties and affordances with a critical eye to how these properties shape and constrain the artifacts realized in them.

Design and the Development Process

Designers must study how to integrate software design into the overall software development process—in actual field conditions of teams of programmers, systems architects, and technical management.

In general, the programming and design activities of a project must be closely interrelated. During the course of implementing a design, new information will arise, which many times will change the original design. If design and implementation are in watertight compartments, it can be a recipe for disaster because the natural process of refinement and change is prevented.

The fact that design and implementation are closely related does not mean that they are identical—even if the two tasks are sometimes performed by one and the same person. The technical demands of writing the code are often so strenuous that the programmer can lose perspective on the larger issues affecting the design of the product.

Before you can integrate programming and design, each of the two has to have its own genuine identity.

A Call to Action

We need to create a professional discipline of software design. We need our own community. Today you can't get a degree in software design, go to a conference on the subject, or subscribe to a journal on the topic. Designers need to be brought onto development teams as peers to programmers. The entire PC community needs to become sensitized to issues of design.

Software designers should be trained more like architects than like computer scientists. Software designers should be technically very well grounded without being measured by their ability to write production-quality code.

In the year since I first sounded this call to action, there has been a gratifying response from the computing industry and academic computer science departments. At Stanford University, Computer Science Professor Terry Winograd has been awarded a major National Science Foundation grant to develop and teach the first multicourse curriculum in software design. And in Silicon Valley and elsewhere there is talk of forming a professional organization dedicated to advancing the interests of software design.

Suggested Readings

Nathaniel Borenstein. *Programming as if People Mattered: Friendly Programs, Software Engineering, and Other Noble Delusions.* Princeton, NJ: Princeton University Press, 1991.

Paul Heckel. *Elements of Friendly Software Design.* Berkeley, CA: Sybex, 1994.

Bruce Tognazzini. *Tog on Software Design.* Reading MA: Addison-Wesley, 1995.

About the Author

Mitchell Kapor was the founder of Lotus Development Corporation and the designer of the Lotus 1-2-3 spreadsheet. Presently, he is an adjunct professor in the Media Laboratory at MIT, developing courses on software design, and is chair of the advisory board of the Association for Software Design. He is also a cofounder and board member of the Electronic Frontier Foundation.

1. SOFTWARE DESIGN AND ARCHITECTURE

Mitchell Kapor's Software Design Manifesto (Chapter 1) draws an analogy between software design and architecture. Kapor characterizes software design in terms of the theories of the Roman architect and architectural theorist Vitruvius, who proclaimed that well-designed buildings were those exhibiting the virtues of *firmness*, *commodity*, and *delight*.

Since the manifesto was originally presented, the architecture–software analogy has been repeated many times in the literature on human–computer interaction and software design. We in the software profession may have much to learn from the ancient and rich tradition of architectural practice and architectural theory. At the same time, in drawing such a broad analogy, it is possible to fall into superficiality, finding attractive but misleading guidance. This profile identifies some of the issues that the architectural analogy highlights about software design, relating them to the content of the subsequent chapters.

Roles in Design and Construction

In trying to understand the boundaries that distinguish software design, software engineering, interaction design, and the many other professional categories in our field, we can draw an analogy to the different roles in creating a building. In the simplest projects, designer, builder, and artisan are one. A single person or a small cooperative group sets out to build a structure. In contrast, developing a large software system,

Profile Authors: Terry Winograd and Philip Tabor

designs, usually fairly recent, whose analysis and appraisal provide the raw material for theory and future practice. These designs may be classics, but they are not necessarily so: Students—and all practitioners—often learn more from disasters.

Kapor proposes a curriculum with courses such as the *History of the Word Processor*, just as an architecture student might study the history of the town square. Students would examine the different periods and genres (Figure 1.2), analyzing the development of the timeless concepts and seeing how those concepts have led to implementations in different architectural media (platforms and operating systems). Perhaps it is too early to base a software-design education on classics and precedents, as Kapor suggests; the field is so young, and is changing so rapidly. Or perhaps not, since the design-cycle times are so

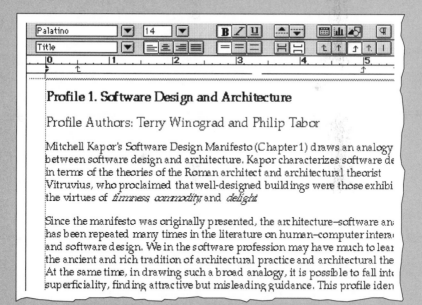

FIGURE 1.2   Genres in Software The graphic-interface word processor represents a software genre, with established conventions and styles that cut across the individual products. Elements such as toolbars, rulers, and pull-down menus for styles are as conventional in this genre as are the characteristic arched windows and buttresses of the cathedral. (*Source:* Microsoft® Word for Macintosh 5.0.)

13

much shorter than are those of buildings. Students can begin by studying the *design languages* discussed by John Rheinfrank and Shelley Evenson (Chapter 4) and the emerging *genres* that carry social meaning, as described by John Seely Brown and Paul Duguid (Chapter 7).

The second component of architectural education is the *studio*. Students tackle design projects in an environment where experienced professionals review and critique their work. The spirit of teaching is not "Let me tell you all you need to know about how to design," but rather "Let me help you to understand and improve what you've done." Donald Schön (Chapter 9) has studied this kind of teaching extensively, and describes it as *reflection in action*. Although studio-based teaching is not a part of traditional engineering and computer-science education, it is a component of newer proposals for human–computer interaction curricula, such as the National Science Foundation study on new directions in human–computer interaction and research (Strong, 1995) and the interdisciplinary student design projects sponsored by Apple, as described in Profile 9.

Architectural education also includes a more traditional body of instruction on the practical issues of building: structures, economics, materials, and the many details of construction. This component is analogous to the current education in *software engineering*, as distinct from computer science, which focuses on the technical engineering aspects and their theoretical foundations, often to the exclusion of practical concerns of management, economics, and the design process. As Donald Norman demonstrates in his tale of the Macintosh power switch (Chapter 12), all these dimensions can be relevant to the designer in surprising ways.

Style and Function

Architecture, like fashion, is a public art form. We are constantly exposed to new styles, each of which is a response to what came before. In architecture, a shared style develops over a long time; people know what a church or a house looks like, and each new instance develops a little from its predecessors. Software design, like architecture, is a cultural phenomenon, and therefore is subject to the forces of taste, fashion, and desire. Software is still much younger and less well developed, but we can see the development of styles—the IBM 3270-display mainframe style, the Microsoft style, the Nintendo style—on which a designer can build.

Theoretical Framework

Just as Vitruvius' virtues of firmness, commodity, and delight can be mapped onto the software world, it is interesting to examine other conceptual structures that have been applied to architecture as well. For example, a work of architecture can be seen in terms of three interlocking domains: material components, spaces, and experiences. So an architect might conceive of a building primarily as (1) an assembly of walls, floorplates and columns; (2) a cluster of spatial volumes, some squat, some lofty; or (3) a sequence of feelings induced in the user—of welcome, awe, constriction, and release. Renaissance architectural theory tended to focus on the material components of architecture. Twentieth-century Modernism, with its emphasis on abstraction, immateriality, and expression, has stressed architecture's spatial and experiential components (widely influential texts were Giedion (1941) and Rasmussen (1959)).

Obvious parallels can be drawn to software, which traditionally has been designed with a focus on the computing itself: algorithmic form, function, and implementation. The software-design field is now turning to understand the nature of the human–computer interactions— the metaphorical spaces that people inhabit—and to the experience that software offers the user. Peter Denning and Pamela Dargan (Chapter 6) argue for a shift away from software design that is focused on the computer to software design that begins with the domain of action for the users. Crampton Smith and Tabor emphasize the ways in which interfaces communicate and shape the user's experience, rather than seeing interfaces as representations of underlying function.

Also, in considering the experience of the user as a basis for design, an issue of frequent concern to architects is that their client—the customer whom they have to satisfy with the design—often is not the end user. We are all familiar with buildings that are impressive monuments to the companies that commissioned them, but are *inhabitant unfriendly.* As Sarah Kuhn points out (Chapter 14), the same phenomenon is frequent in software systems: They are designed to meet needs of the client who commissions them, without being suitably designed in consideration of the end-user experience.

Beyond the Analogy

Having laid out the many areas of similarity, we could equally well point out substantial differences that distinguish software design from architecture—every comparison could be the starting point for a debate. The point, however, is not whether we can find a fit for every aspect of architecture in our understanding of software design. As with all metaphors and analogies, the value of looking at software design as architecture lies not in finding precise answers, but in raising provocative questions.

Suggested Readings

Christopher Alexander. *Notes on the Synthesis of Form.* Cambridge, MA: Harvard University Press, 1964.

Sigfried Giedion. *Space, Time, and Architecture: The Growth of a New Tradition.* Cambridge, MA: Harvard University Press, 1941.

William J. Mitchell. *City of Bits.* Cambridge, MA: MIT Press, 1995.

Peter Neumann. *Computer-Related Risks.* Reading, MA: Addison-Wesley, 1995.

Steen Eiler Rasmussen. *Experiencing Architecture* (Second United States edition). Cambridge MA: MIT Press, 1959.

An interview with DAVID LIDDLE

Design of the Conceptual Model

Software design is the act of determining the user's experience with
a piece of software. It has nothing to do with how the code works
inside, or how big or small the code is. The designer's task is to
specify completely and unambiguously the user's whole
experience....The most important thing to design properly is the
user's conceptual model. Everything else should be subordinated to
making that model clear, obvious, and substantial. That is almost
exactly the opposite of how most software is designed.

17

In 1978, David Liddle was asked to head Xerox's new System Development Division, to create products based on the research being done at the Xerox Palo Alto Research Center (PARC). Over the next few years, Liddle and his group developed the Star system, which was the forerunner of today's graphical user interfaces (GUIs), such as the Macintosh, Microsoft® Windows®, NEXTSTEP, and Motif. Although the Star did not have the commercial success of its later derivatives, its innovations were the model for consistent integration of now-familiar mechanisms for windows, icons, menus, drawings, and onscreen formatted text.

To a degree that was unusual at the time, and that has been matched only rarely since then, the Star development proceeded in a reflective way, with a good deal of attention to the development methods and to the role of those methods in defining the product. The design methods emphasized the user's experience, as reflected in the conceptual model the user had of what the system was and of what it could do. In this way, the Star was as much an innovation in the design process as in the product itself. Rather than deciding what the system would do, then figuring out how to produce interfaces, the developers engaged psychologists and designers from the beginning in an extensive set of mockups, prototypes, and user tests to see what would work, and how it could work.

This interview of Liddle by a group from the Association for Software Design offers insights into the nature of software design, and into the specific ideas that were generated by the Star's programmers, psychologists, and designers, who pioneered a new kind of interaction with the computer.

— Terry Winograd

Association for Software Design: You were instrumental in the design and development of the Xerox Star, one of the first systems to use a graphical user interface. What was the overall context in which the Star work got started?

David Liddle was interviewed by a group from the Association for Software Design, consisting of Barry Polley, Andrew Singer, Suzanne Stefanac, and Terry Winograd.

David E. Liddle: By the mid-seventies, developers were beginning to move away from the distributed model of computing, in which an employee sat at a terminal and shared processor time. IBM's entry-level division was promoting the idea of individual computers, almost like tiny mainframes, for small businesses. But connectivity was not part of that picture.

Xerox had been thinking about an individual, self-contained unit that would be connected to a laser printer and to other self-contained units on a network. This concept was based on ideas coming out of the Palo Alto Research Center (PARC). Inspired by Alan Kay's vision of the Dynabook, we had built the Alto, which was the first personal computer with a bitmap screen, graphical interface, pointing device, and many other features that we now take for granted. Other groups at PARC were developing the original Ethernet and the first laser printers.

We were also familiar with and impressed by the work done by Doug Engelbart's Human Augmentation group at the Stanford Research Institute (SRI), where they had created the first on-screen editor, had integrated it with a unified hypertext system, and had built new interface devices such as the mouse and the chording keyset. Although theirs was still a time-sharing system built around a mini-computer shared by a workgroup of expert users, it set a new standard for the kinds of interactions that were possible, such as spatial editing, pointing, and a command language different from text typed in a command mode.

The PARC environment fostered an important collision of ideas: interconnected peer computers controlled by individuals; spatial, gestural, and nonverbal interaction techniques; and extremely high-quality typographical text and graphics.

ASD: What did it take to move this collision from the research laboratory into a product?

DEL: Within PARC, there had been no attempt to see that applications were integrated. With the Star, we were intent on identifying a single model that would work across all the different capabilities. In early 1975, I was asked to start a development project to produce a basic system platform to support future image-processing products. This platform included a new processor architecture, an operating system called Pilot, and a development environment called Mesa. That summer, I was asked to move the work out of the pure research realm of PARC, and to help start the System Development Division. We were charged with building products based on PARC's work—getting the ideas out of the laboratory and into commercial practice.

In the summer of 1978, we were commissioned to build a product line on this platform, including the first file and gateway servers; small-scale laser printers; the Ethernet; and the first graphical, bitmap-display, iconic user-interface product—the 8010 Star. The Star was launched in May of 1981. We had started on it in earnest in summer 1978, so there were 3 years of head-down, pick-and-shovel work, building Star, preceded by about 2 years of system development on the processor family and underlying software.

ASD: Given the novelty of the ideas, the development must have called for going beyond the standard process. How did you envision your task?

DEL: We tackled it in a very different way from most software development groups. Before we designed the Star, I commissioned a study that produced a document on methodology for the design of the user interface. We borrowed additional people from PARC to help us work on it. It laid out an approach—a thorough approach—to doing software design. That document and that methodology were the basis for the whole Star design process. It began with task analysis, looking at a fairly wide range of users. Next came the job of developing scenarios for uses of the imagined product based on the task. Then, it proposed a model for a graphical user interface, carefully distinguishing three aspects: the display of information, the control or command mechanisms, and the user's conceptual model.

The first component—information display—deals literally with what appears on the screen. It encompasses all those relatively minor aspects, like what window borders and buttons should look like, what fonts are used and where, what icon shapes are used, and so on. This component is important, but is not the crucial concern from the standpoint of usability. Information display is the least important of the three separate components.

The second component is the control mechanism—the machinery used to invoke commands. It is extremely important that command invocation be designed consistently across different applications. In terms of usability, this component is much more important than information display.

The most important component to design properly is the third, the user's conceptual model. Everything else should be subordinated to making that model clear, obvious, and substantial. That is almost exactly the opposite of how most software is designed.

ASD: Just what do you mean by a *user's conceptual model?*

DEL: This model represents what the user is likely to think, and how the user is likely to respond. For example, one of the events that changed civilization in the past decade was Dan Bricklin's choice of the spreadsheet metaphor and its underlying conceptual model (see Profile 11). Neither the information display (limited by the machines that were available, and by how much space his program, VisiCalc, required), nor the command invocation were great. However, that conceptual model was exceptionally durable. The *desktop metaphor* for managing objects—for filing and printing and mailing and the like—is another widely applicable metaphor.

ASD: Is the metaphorical connection to the physical world the key element of a user's conceptual model?

DEL: No. It is a mistake to think that either spreadsheets or desktops were intended to imitate accounting pads, office furniture, or other physical objects. The critically important role of these metaphors was as abstractions that users could then relate to their jobs. The purpose of computer metaphors, in general, and particularly of graphical or icon-oriented ones, is to let people use recognition rather than recall. People are good at recognition, but tend to be poor at recall. People can see objects and operations on the screen, and can manage them quite well. But when you ask people to remember what string to type to perform some task, you are counting on one of their weakest abilities.

ASD: How did you apply your analysis of the users' model in developing the specification for the Star?

DEL: We ended up writing a 400-page functional specification before we ever wrote one line of code. It was long, because it included a screen view of every possible screen that a user would see. But we did not just sit down and write it. We prototyped a little bit, did some testing with users to decide what made sense, and then wrote a spec for that aspect. Then we prototyped a bit more, tested it, and then spec'd it again, over and over until the process was done.

I got Bill Verplank, who had done human-factors work at MIT, to work with the testing. Verplank was in our Los Angeles development center, where he would bring in the users and make accurately time-stamped videos that superimposed a view of the screen, a view of the user, and a view of the user's hands. Verplank and his crew did 600 or 700 hours of video, looking at every single feature and function. From all these video recordings, we were able to identify and eliminate many problems. For example, we chose a two-button mouse because, in testing, we found that users demonstrated lower error rates, shorter learning times, and less confusion than when they used either one-button or three-button mice.

ASD: You were presenting the test users with new concepts, right? The ideas of icons, windows, and menus were not familiar to them.

DEL: Yes. The term *menu-driven* had been used prior to our work, but its meaning was different from what you and I think of today. Most mainframe applications were starting to switch from command lines to menu-oriented screens. Initially, software had to work on Teletypes, which were linear—the typewritten stream just moved down the page—so you couldn't have menus. Generally, you could hit a question mark and it would list all the commands you could give. You typed one of those commands and the system told you whether the command was acceptable. With the advent of the IBM 3270 terminal, you could display a whole field of text on the screen, could use control keys to move around, and could enter text anywhere on the screen. So the display could present a set of commands and let you choose one by moving the cursor over it. People already recognized the benefit of menus for making the possible commands more easily visible.

We did not call any of the mechanisms in the Star *menus*. Apple always called them menus; we never did. But the idea was there nonetheless, tied to the objects on the screen. Instead of being in command space, where you were always asking, "Okay, what's the next command?" you sat there with a restful screen full of icons. You pointed to one of them, and then you hit *properties* or *options*, and you were presented with all the operations that you could do with the object, as well as its characteristics (Figure 2.1).

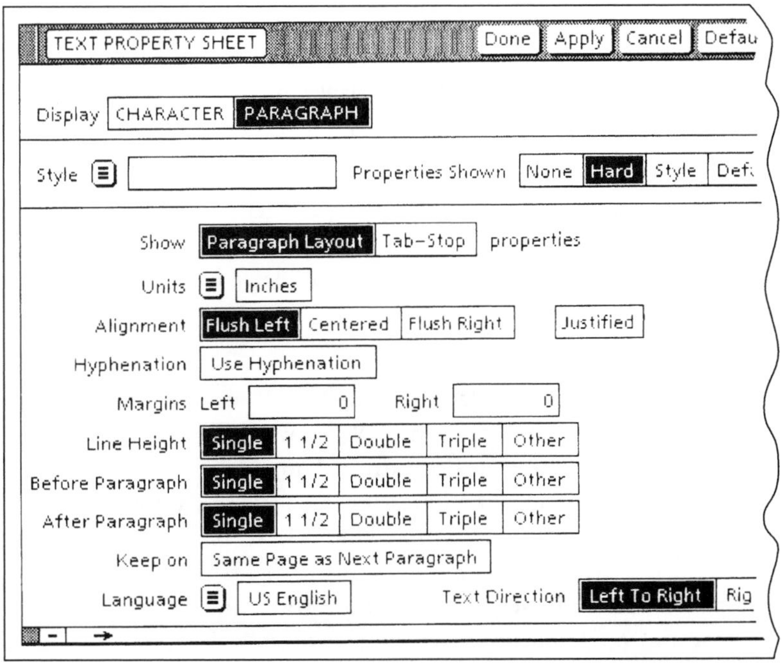

FIGURE 2.1   Property Sheets   The new flexibility that the Star provided by allowing users to manipulate objects directly on the screen required its designers to invent ways for users to examine and modify the properties of those objects. The property-sheet mechanism was applied uniformly to every kind of object; users could select any object, hit the PROPS key on the keyboard, and see a window displaying all the properties and options relevant to that particular object. (From Jeff Johnson et al, "Xerox Star, a retrospective," *IEEE Computer* 22:9 (September, 1989), p. 17. Copyright © 1989 *IEEE*. Reprinted with permission.)

So we had an early object-oriented approach, the idea being that you inspect the particular icon and it displays to you the messages that it will accept. It does not accept anything else: It tells you what you can do relative to that object, in that particular context. You could never see a command alternative in a context in which you could not use it. This idea of *progressive disclosure*—providing a great deal of context for everything you did, and evaporating the context when you were finished—was extremely important.

In later systems, such as the Macintosh and Windows, people did strange things with icons, such as using them to represent an application program. The user should never need to operate directly on programs. An icon should represent a document of some kind—you double-click on it, and you are automatically in the right program for dealing with it. That was not what happened, because the later designers were retrofitting the Star's concepts over existing ideas. In the Macintosh, they just missed it; in Windows, they were retrofitting it over DOS.

ASD: What do you think in general of the later interfaces that were based on the Star?

DEL: The structure and design of NeXT's Interface Builder was great, but the user interface of the NeXT machine is not that good. They did with Unix what Windows did with DOS—they didn't have the courage to break from Unix, so as a result you see lots of things that look like limestone tablets, but when you open them up, you have to deal with a Unix file or process, with all its intrinsic ugliness. Instead of designing good, new, useful metaphors and end-user illusions, they took the simple design of the Star and made all the property sheets look like pre-Raphaelite frescos (Figure 2.2). That's distracting. The graphics suffer from this Muscle Beach phenomenon—they're not harmonized with the task that you have at hand. When you're typing a humble business memo, and up pops a carved monument, it is out of all proportion, and is disruptive.

ASD: You clearly were focused on how the software that you developed could create what is now often called the *user experience*. How did all that user involvement go over with programmers, who would be likely to enjoy designing limestone obelisks?

DEL: Development using real testing was not all that smooth. Sometimes, an idea would seem to be settled. We would all agree on a prototype; then, Bill would try it out with real users, and we would find out that they had trouble with it. People on the team sometimes got upset. We'd have to go in and renegotiate something we had all thought was settled. Still, all in all, people did agree to be responsive, within all possible reason.

Although most of the individuals on our team were technically programmers, they were first and foremost software designers. Many were

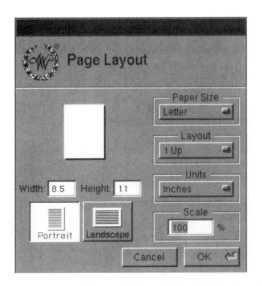

FIGURE 2.2   **Evolution of the Graphic Interface**   Interfaces that followed the Star, such as NEXTSTEP, adopted many of the conceptual elements of the Star, embellishing them with elaborate graphics. (From *NeXT User's Reference*, 1990, p. 119. Reprinted by permission of NeXT Software, Inc.)

researchers in computer science, who saw their activity as distinct from programming. Within our group, you were viewed as a philistine if you wanted to argue too much about implementation before the design was done. Our attitude was always, "Wait a minute, let's make this work for the user. If we find we can't implement something, then we'll go back to the drawing board. But we're not going to pick things that we think will be small or fast to build, and then bully the user into accepting them."

ASD: Didn't your approach lead to specifications that were difficult to fit into the capacities of the machines you had? Most applications developers focus on taking advantage of the specific power of the platform, but you were concentrating on the user.

DEL: That's where we parted company, in my view, from many development projects. For example, at around the same time, Charles Simonyi and his team at PARC were developing a text editor (or, as we would now call it, a word processor) named Bravo—the direct predecessor of Microsoft® Word, which was developed when Simonyi went to Microsoft. Bravo was very, very carefully and cleverly designed around what would run fast and be small and easy to implement on the Alto. Its designers took the view that the users should be willing to learn more, so that they could take advantage of a program's functionality. That was okay—it was a good balancing act. We, on the other hand, always worried more about the functionality than about implementation.

One consequence of our emphasis on the user was that, when Version 1.0 of Star was first released, it was too slow. We couldn't reach the performance levels that we wanted. The operating system, Pilot, ran fast, but the Star application software that ran on top of it created a bottleneck. We couldn't just speed up the machine. We were already pushing the limits of the hardware that we could produce at a viable cost.

ASD: How did corporate management respond to the project?

DEL: We were treated with benign neglect the whole time we were developing Star. Xerox's executives really weren't prepared to deal with the Star as a product, even when we had it almost finished. The Star was almost done, and we had no division willing to manufacture or market it! The staff in El Segundo were ready to make the boards; we could get the electronics done; but we couldn't convince Xerox to put it in a box and package it. Every 3 months, there would be an attempt to kill the project.

Just when things were looking pretty bad, I met Don Massaro, who was president of the Office Products Division. He thought that dedicated word-processing systems of the kind on the market in those days were unbelievably boring, and he didn't believe that they would last. He already knew about PCs, and he had helped to get Apple financial credit when it started up. The top brass at Xerox had told him, "We've been trying to figure out what to do with this Star stuff. Why don't you take a look at it: If it's no good, we'll kill it." So I showed it to Massaro. All his people said to get rid of it, but he said, "No, this idea is great, I've got to have the product." So suddenly, at the last minute, we were working with someone who had a whole division, with a factory in Texas and a sales crew.

ASD: How did the Star fare as a product?

DEL: Nearly 100,000 Star systems were eventually shipped (later under the name *Viewpoint*), but obviously we didn't capture the market that was opened by the Macintosh, PCs, and so on. The people who used the Star liked it, but the market and Xerox's positioning in that market weren't right to take full advantage of the package we had put together.

ASD: One critique I've heard is that Star didn't include a book-keeping mode, in the vein of our present-day spreadsheets, and that this omission impaired its acceptance. Is there any validity to that story?

DEL: Well, it is true in a way. Spreadsheets didn't come out until a year after the Star was born. The Star actually did have smart forms in it, so you could do many tasks that are now done with spreadsheets, by interconnecting these forms and fields. But the smart forms were more difficult to use than spreadsheets, because they didn't offer a consistent metaphor.

The Star's data management was simple—it managed linear, typical records well. The problem was that we couldn't anticipate and develop all the different kinds of functions that people wanted. We didn't have a platform for third-party applications, which is what operating systems offer today. Everything had to be built by Xerox: the hardware, the operating system, the development environment, the servers, the system for creating and managing files, and the user applications. The Star was a highly integrated, user-oriented system—but a closed one. Its development, of course, was before the PC, and before there was any microcomputer software industry.

ASD: Was it ever part of the game plan to open up the system—to invite other companies to develop applications?

DEL: There was no option back then other than totally proprietary systems. There weren't any open systems. No software ran on any two brand names, so that alternative just didn't occur to us. The ultimate weakness of the Star as an overall system was our failure to provide an opening for the kind of diverse, robust application-software–development industry that we see today.

ASD: What do you think were the main strengths and contributions of the Star?

DEL: Two different dimensions of what we did still have had loud echoes in today's world of software design. The first was the set of ideas embodied in the Star interface itself (see Profile 2): the physical desktop metaphor, direct manipulation, a general way of dealing with property sheets for objects within a consistent user model, what-you-see-is-what-you-get (WYSIWYG) editing, generic commands (such as *Move* and *Copy*), and so on. Later systems have improved on these ideas, although in certain aspects I still think that Star was a great advance over its successors.

The second dimension was the design methodology. We put the user's experience in the forefront, and developed our design principles from what we saw users doing. These principles were a significant part of the Star legacy.

Many people ask, "Why worry about specific principles of user-interface design? Why not regard design as an artistic process, with each product a fresh expression?" But that view isn't realistic. The repeated, serial use of products having gratuitously different user interfaces produces cognitive dissonance. The abrupt switching back and forth between the abstractions of your job and the abstractions of computing can be dispiriting and debilitating, reducing productivity and satisfaction significantly. Designers make their greatest user-interface errors when they don't think about users in terms of what those users are doing in their jobs.

We articulated specific principles, which later found their way into documents such as the Macintosh Human Interface Guidelines (see Profile 4). We applied them to each of the design elements in the Star, to get maximal unity and simplicity.

For example, we had to identify the core control mechanisms for commands. It was clear that these mechanisms had to be consistent across different applications. We ended up with a small set of generic commands that we built into the hardware of the Star keyboard. They were the basis for the idea of standard menu commands in the Macintosh. The uniformity of these commands across applications gave users a consistent interface—one of the features that gave the Macintosh platform a jump start.

ASD: You mentioned that your user-based approach included many prototyping cycles. Was that a new idea?

DEL: The Star development was the first project I know of that used a systematic and extensive prototyping cycle to develop the interface. It wasn't dominated by the code jockeys, as most projects were.

ASD: Do you recommend, then, that prototyping always precede any writing of code?

DEL: Absolutely, provided you can make prototypes that are good enough for users to test. If you cannot, then you can show the users screen views and other visual representations, so at least you can start with thoroughly specified user functionality.

ASD: What do you see happening in software design and development in the future?

DEL: The situation today is different from what we were tackling in the days of the Star. The industry is entering a new phase of development of computer products, following a cycle of technological maturity—one that has been repeated for many new technologies, such as the radio, the automobile, and the telephone.

In the first phase, the new technology is difficult to use, and its benefits are not yet obvious. It appeals mainly to those people who are fascinated with it for its own sake—the early adopters. You'll see clubs of enthusiasts who love to share stories on how they fought and overcame the trials and tribulations. They see most people as not worthy of using the technology. Ham radio is a good example, and, in the same vein, the legends of Silicon Valley are full of stories of the brave pioneers who tackled the MITS Altair or the Osborne.

In the second phase, the economic benefits are developed to the point where the hard-headed business managers will adopt that technology for practical uses. Their interest is in the bottom line—not whether the technology is fascinating or easy to use, but whether it will promote greater efficiency, productivity, and profits. (To continue with the radio metaphor, everyone is familiar with radios for truck and taxi dispatch, police, military, and so on.) This business class covers most of the major microcomputer applications sold today (except for the games market). In designing for it, the main consideration is cost effectiveness. If better design can speed up use, cut training time, or add to efficiency in any other such way, then it is important. If the new technology doesn't produce a measurable difference in one of these dimensions, then it is a frill.

The third phase reaches the public—the discretionary users who choose a product because it satisfies a need or urge. They don't care about cost–benefit analyses, but they do care about whether the product is likable, beautiful, satisfying, or exciting. Cellular telephones have reached this level in the radio market. Computer games have been there since the beginning—a game succeeds because people like to play it. They enjoy the experience that they get from the design of the graphics, the sounds, and the flow of play. An increasing portion of the computer market is shifting to the consumer end of the spectrum (see Chapter 5). The huge new markets of the future—the successors to the productivity markets dominated by IBM and Microsoft in the past—will be in this new consumer arena. Design that focuses on the user, rather than on the mechanisms, will move to center stage.

ASD: How would you describe software design in general?

DEL: Software design is the act of determining the user's experience with a piece of software. It has nothing to do with how the code works inside, or how big or small the code is. The designer's task is to specify completely and unambiguously the user's whole experience.

That is the key to the whole software industry, but, in most companies, software design does not exist as a visible function—it is done secretly, without a profession, without honor. I hope that this situation will be changed by organizations such as the Association for Software Design and by the new teaching programs that are springing up in universities (see Profile 9).

When the Wright brothers first flew an airplane, or when Benz drove the first automobile, the wonder was not that people could drive or fly easily, but that they could do so at all. These machines eventually left the enthusiast realm and became forces of change in society, because the principles of their use became more important than the technology of their construction. We have not yet piloted computers and software to that point, but we have made a good start. If we can keep our eye on the user, we can keep moving ahead in the right direction.

Suggested Reading

Jeff Johnson, Terry Roberts, William Verplank, David C. Smith, Charles Irby, Marian Beard, and Kevin Mackey. "Xerox Star, a retrospective." *IEEE Computer* 22:9 (September, 1989), 11–26. (Reprinted in Baecker et al., 1995, 53–70).

About the Author

 David Liddle is president of Interval Research Corp., in Palo Alto, California. He was a founder of Metaphor Computer Systems and was a vice-president at IBM. He is Consulting Professor of Computer Science at Stanford University, where he teaches courses on human–computer interaction and on the computing industry. He is also on the board of directors of a number of prominent software companies, is chair of the advisory board of the Santa Fe Institute, and serves on the engineering advisory committees at Stanford University and the University of Michigan.

2. THE ALTO AND THE STAR

In 1970, the Xerox Corporation established the Palo Alto Research Center (PARC), to invent the future of the electronic office. In PARC's first decade, a stream of innovations emerged that set the stage for today's computer industry. Among other technologies, laser printing, local-area networking, and desktop publishing software were first developed at PARC. Many of the prominent companies in the computing industry, such as 3COM, Adobe, and Apple Computer were started or were heavily influenced by PARC graduates.

PARC's most notable innovation was the personal computer, which grew out of earlier concepts by Alan Kay for what he called a *reactive engine* and a *Dynabook*. The progenitor of the modern personal computer, the Alto, was developed in 1972 by Kay's Learning Research Group (LRG) and a number of researchers in PARC's Computer Systems Laboratory (CSL), under the direction of Robert Taylor. Just as the Model-T contained the fundamental elements of a modern automobile, the Alto included the central elements of today's personal computer: a bitmapped graphic display, which enabled it to display text in multiple fonts, combined with graphics; a mouse as a pointing device; removable magnetic storage; and an operating system designed for a single user who alternates among multiple applications. Although the Alto's cost at the time was high (at standard industry markup, it would have sold for more than $75,000), the PARC strategy was to act as though the Alto was a personal computer—to put one on every desk and to see what people would do with it.

The result of this bold strategy was a proliferation of experimental software for writing, drawing, communicating, teaching, and comput-

Profile Author: Terry Winograd

ing in many domains. The Smalltalk language and programming environment, developed by Kay's LRG, pioneered uses of the graphic interface. Other software developed in CSL included the Bravo text editor, which developed many of the sophisticated features of today's word processors and was the predecessor of Microsoft Word; Draw and Markup, the ancestors of MacDraw and MacPaint, and the many drawing programs that later followed their lead; and programs that made it possible for personal-computer users to make use of networked facilities for file storage and laser printing.

The Xerox Star was born out of PARC's creative ferment, designing an integrated system that would bring PARC's new hardware and software ideas into a commercially viable product for use in office environments. The Star drew on the ideas that had been developed, and went further in integrating them and in designing for a class of users who were far less technically knowledgeable than the engineers who had been both the creators and the prime users of many PARC systems (one of PARC's favorite mottoes was "Build what you use, use what you build.") As David Liddle describes in Chapter 2, the Star designers were challenged to make the personal computer usable for a community that did not have previous computer experience.

From today's perspective, the Star screen (Figure 2.4) looks rather unremarkable, and perhaps a bit clumsy in its graphic design—a boxy Model-T when compared to the highly styled look of today's Taurus or Jaguar. What is notable from a historical perspective, of course, is how much the Star does look like current screens and how little it looks like the character-based and vector-drawing screens that preceded it.

The visible mechanisms on the Star display were backed up with a set of design principles that grew out of a user-oriented design methodology and by a great deal of empirical testing, as described by Liddle in Chapter 2. Several principles were central to the Star design:

1. *Direct manipulation.* The core concept that distinguished Star (and other Alto programs) from the conventional computer interfaces of their time was the use of a bitmapped screen to present the user with direct visual representations of objects. In the Star's *desktop metaphor*, documents, printers, folders, collections of fold-

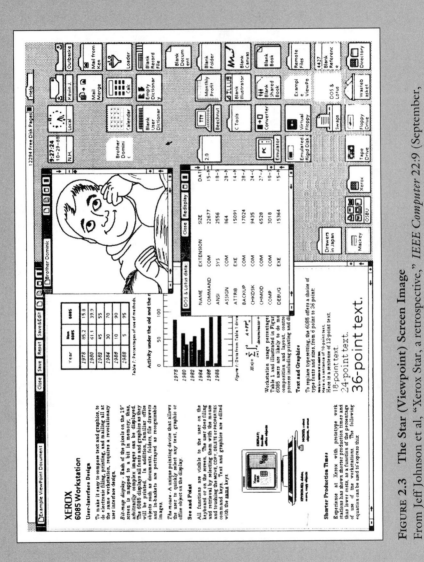

FIGURE 2.3   The Star (Viewpoint) Screen Image

From Jeff Johnson et al, "Xerox Star, a retrospective," *IEEE Computer* 22:9 (September, 1989), p. 13. Copyright © 1989 *IEEE.* Reprinted with permission.

ers (file drawers and cabinets), in and out boxes, and other familiar office objects were depicted on the screen. To print a document, for example, the user could point (using the mouse) to the icon for the document and the icon for the printer, while using a key on the keyboard to indicate a Copy operation.

2. *WYSIWYG (what you see is what you get).* In previously available programs for producing sophisticated graphical output—such as drawings or page layout with multiple fonts—the user created and edited a representation that looked like a programming language, and then compiled the resulting program into a visible form. Alto programs pioneered a new style that Star unified, in which the user works directly with the desired form, through direct manipulation. The user makes changes by operating on a direct representation of what will appear on the printed page. As shown in Figure 2.3, the Star user could intermix text, tables, graphs, drawings, and mathematical formulas. In fact, most of the popular microcomputer applications of today have not yet reached the degree of integration that Star offered more than a decade ago.

3. *Consistency of commands.* Because all Star applications were developed in a unified way by a single development group, it was possible to adhere to a coherent and consistent design language (see Chapter 4 for a discussion of design languages). The Star keyboard embodied a set of *generic commands*, which were used in a consistent way across all applications: *Move, Copy, Delete, Open, Show Properties,* and *Same* (copy properties). Evoking one of these commands produced the same behavior whether the object being moved or copied, for example, was a word of text, a drawing element, or a folder of documents. Through the use of property sheets (Figure 2.1), the user could manipulate the aspects that were specific to each element, such as the font of a text character or the brush width of a painted line. The *Open* command was the basis for applying a technique of *progressive disclosure*—showing the user only the relevant information for a task at hand, and then providing a way to reveal more possibilities as they were needed.

In addition to these three key concepts, many specific design features made the Star unique, including its attention to the communicative aspects of graphic design, its integration of an end-user scripting language (CUSP), and its underlying mechanisms for internationalization—from the very beginning, Star versions were developed in several languages, including non-European languages with large character sets, non–left-to-right orthography, and so on.

Some of the aspects that led to the Star's design quality may have also hampered its commercial success—in particular Xerox's dependence on development groups within a single company to produce all the applications software. But the result was one that supports Liddle's assertion that "In some aspects, I still think that Star was a great advance over its successors."

Suggested Readings

David Canfield Smith, Charles Irby, Ralph Kimball, Bill Verplank, Eric Harlslem. Designing the STAR user interface. *Byte* 7:4 (April, 1982), 242–282.

William Bewley, Teresa Roberts, David Schroit, and William Verplank. Human factors testing in the design of Xerox's 8010 "Star" office workstation. *Proceedings of CHI'83*, New York: ACM, 1983, 72–77.

GILLIAN CRAMPTON SMITH *and*

PHILIP TABOR

The Role of the Artist–Designer

Interaction design cannot dispense with scientific method and engineering knowledge; indeed, familiarity with computing technology is as essential to an interaction designer as familiarity with building technology is to an architect.... [but] interaction design is more of an art than a science. Its ultimate subject matter—human experience and subjective response—is inherently as changeable and unfathomable as the ocean.

One of the key issues in creating a discipline of software design is determining the scope of concerns—the boundaries within which software design differentiates itself from other areas of design. Gillian Crampton Smith and Philip Tabor bring a particular perspective to the design of software, from their backgrounds in other design fields. Crampton Smith trained as a philosopher and art historian, then worked as a typographer and graphic designer for books, magazines, and newspapers. Philip Tabor trained as an architect and teaches architectural theory at the Bartlett School in London.

They have both been deeply involved in the interactions between their disciplines and computing. Crampton Smith set up the computer studio at St. Martin's School of Art in London, started a postgraduate course for practicing graphic designers to learn about the potential of computers for their work, and, in 1989, initiated the Computer Related Design course at the Royal College of Art (see Profile 9). Tabor did his doctoral research on computer-aided design in architecture. His primary focus is on how the meaning of architecture is shifting in the light of developing electronic media.

Crampton Smith and Tabor view the software-design enterprise from a position on the border—balancing a technological and an artistic perspective, with a focus on how people and designs communicate. In this chapter, they describe the role of the *artist–designer*—a person whose focus is not on *software design* as traditionally conceived, but rather is on *interaction design*. Software is a medium for the actions and experiences of the people who use it. Interaction design, then, has the characteristics of the traditional design areas in which the authors have worked—in which issues of form, function, and communication are inextricably entwined.

—Terry Winograd

THE WORD "DESIGN" IS often associated with the visual, affective qualities of objects. Aesthetics certainly play a central role in fields such as fashion, product, interior, and graphic design, and increasingly in software design as well. But that does not mean that the job of *artist–designers* (graphic designers and so on, as opposed to *engineer–designers*) is primarily decorative.

Of course, artist–designers try to make things look good. Pleasure in the sensuous qualities of surface look is what probably drew them to design in the first place. But the vague shorthand of approbation that they often use (*cool, neat,* and so on) indicates a response that is not purely sensuous. It is mediated through sets of values and meanings currently at large in the world. The artist–designer's skill, developed by training, is to design things that not only fulfill a utilitarian purpose, but that also speak to the user through messages that are implicit as well as explicit. Some implicit messages are social: How do we tell the difference between the *Sun* and the London *Times,* or between a Harrods bag and one from Tesco? (United States readers may wish to substitute the *National Enquirer* and *The New York Times,* Saks Fifth Avenue and K-Mart, respectively). Other messages convey function and operation. Which way is up? Where do I open it? What *is* it?

The focus of this chapter is *interaction design*—designing the way people interact with objects and systems, especially with computer software. The product, therefore, is almost entirely experiential: It creates an alteration in the mind of the user. So the customary (originally Platonic) assumption, that substance—the *real* thing—is separate from, and is privileged over, appearance, is misleading. As far as the user is concerned, WYGIWYS: What you get is what you see. The interface *is* the product.

The permeation of semiotics into psychology and the social sciences has left its mark on everyday common sense and conversation. Although sometimes a cigar is just a cigar, as Freud warned, we have become accustomed to looking behind things for their significance— for the role they play in the economy of signs (see Baudrillard, 1981). It is only recently, however, that this aspect of our mentality has become important to software design. One reason is the increasing affordability of richer visual and auditory displays, and the computing power to support them—and thus, potentially, of more nuanced representations. A second reason is that users have changed: Fifteen years ago, computers were the specialized tools of technological professionals. Today, however, they are used by people in all (well, many) walks of life for work and entertainment.

Information technology is becoming an environment within which people operate, rather than a device that they pick up and use. It is part of everyday culture. People buy products, including software, not only for what those products ostensibly do, but also for what they represent. Consumers buy into a symbolic world that both differentiates them from other people *and* reinforces their sense of belonging. A third reason is that, in an information-rich society, competition for attention is huge and discriminating. Distinctions of iconography and style are increasingly important to retain the attention of an audience.

This chapter argues the following:

- The effectiveness of the structure of a piece of software, and of its interface, depends on how they are interpreted by users.
- This interpretation by users is not independent of context. It depends on the cultural codes, shared sensibilities, emotional responses, and habitual prejudices that users bring to it.
- Recent advances in display technology allow richer and more expressive communication at the human–computer interface.
- Decreasingly useful, therefore, is the idea that the functionality of a piece of software is separable from, and takes precedence over, its appearance.
- Decreasingly useful, too, is the idea that the main task of artist–designers is to beautify already-designed products.
- The fundamental training and skills of artist–designers lie in detecting, creating, and controlling cultural and emotional meanings.
- If we are to make full use of these skills, we need to have the input of artist–designers from an early—if not the first—stage in any design project.

Nowadays, in short, the habitual model of software design—engineering first, visual representation later—makes less and less sense.

The Artist–Designer

Software design in today's changing environment increasingly requires the input of designers who can predict and control how users will react to a piece of software. Fortunately, suitable skills are already available—in artist–designers whose experience and training are in areas such as graphic design, film making, product design, architecture, painting, and illustration. The graduate program in Computer Related Design at London's Royal College of Art brings together these skills to exploit developing technologies and media (see Profile 9). The training emphasizes

- *Invention.* Divergent thinking; innovation; new forms for new purposes
- *Empathy.* Putting yourself in the users' shoes; imagining what they are like; how they live, love, and have their being
- *Evaluation.* Juggling and balancing incommensurable factors, such as cost versus performance, and timelessness versus fashionability
- *Visualization/representation.* Imagining objects, ideas, processes, structures, scenarios, and so on; thinking them through in spatial or visual form; vividly communicating them to team members, users, and clients

There is no logical reason why the skills of artist–designer and engineer–designer cannot be combined in one person. A few people are totally ambidextrous in this way, and many are partly so. But the time needed to gain education and experience in either domain, not to mention the differences in temperament suited to the two domains, means that most designers specialize in one or the other. It is therefore through teamwork that the domains converge.

The effectiveness of this teamwork is diminished by misunderstandings created by habits of mind that exaggerate the distinctions between content and form, substance and appearance, function and aesthetics. We shall explore these distinctions, first defining more clearly what artist–designers do, using graphic design as our exemplar.

The Example of Graphic Design

The field of human–computer interaction came of age when the monitor replaced the Teletype printer. Since then, and at least for the foreseeable future, the dissemination of information through a two-dimensional combination of images and alphanumeric characters has been central to software design. For most of the Gutenberg era, however, this task fell to the typographer. Recently—since the invention of offset lithographic printing has allowed cheap reproduction of images as well as of text—it has fallen to the graphic designer as well. So graphic design, which includes typography, is an apt illustration of more general artist–design theory, practice, and procedure.

Graphic designers find structure in information that is useful to the intended audience, and they give that structure form (in text and pictures) to communicate its meaning. Structure and communication are as central to designing a poster for a rock concert as they are to designing a maintenance manual. So graphic design describes the means, not the end. The end of a piece of graphic design is meaning—a rich interplay of implicit and explicit messages, understood by the viewer and transmitted graphically (see Crampton Smith, 1994).

Formally, the graphic designer has remarkably few dimensions of freedom. There is the frame: the perimeter, usually rectangular, of a page, for instance (or, in the case of interaction design, of a screen or window). Within the frame may be disposed blocks of text, abstract objects such as lines and geometrical shapes, and iconic or pictorial images. To this scant trio may be added the space left when these items have been disposed. That is the cast of the play.

The stature and dress of these characters may vary within limits. Text is inflected by size, font, weight, and color, for instance. But the number of possible and distinguishable point sizes is usually small; fonts are basically either with or without serifs; a given typeface usually comes in roman or italic, and two or three weights, and there are only so many basic hues to mix.

Graphic design's relative lack of formal means has three consequences. First, intense attention is focused by both designer and audience on small distinctions, which are delicate and difficult to control—in the case of type design, they are difficult for the untrained eye even to distinguish. Second, each combination of distinctions is recognized as having predecessors—as constituting a style. Third, each style soon accumulates—if it does not already have—a set of associations or conventional meanings (as discussed by Brown and Duguid in Chapter 7). These associations change over time: Asymmetric, sansserif typography once exuded the uncompromising and unfamiliar aura of the avant-garde; now it advertises bubble-gum.

The Inseparability of Content and Form

There is a commonly held assumption that content is somehow separate from form. (See, for example, the discussion of the *conduit metaphor* by Reddy, 1993). We think that this assumption is mistaken. Content cannot be perceived without form, and the form of a message affects the content. For instance, an obvious aim of graphic design is explicitly to inform: that the 0905 train to Cambridge goes from platform 3, say. For this purpose, clarity, legibility, predictability, and economy of means are essential. These characteristics, however, are not only useful, but also affective—the timetable shown in Figure 3.1

Table 2 *East Coast*   *INTERCITY*®

There are other non-InterCity trains London — Stevenage — Peterborough.

Mondays to Fridays	✗	✗	🅿🅂 N	🅿🅂 K	✗	✗	✗	✗	✗	D
London Kings Cross	0610	0700	0730	0750	0800	0820	0900	0910	0930	1000
Stevenage	0629	0719	0749u	0809u	—	—	—	—	0949	—
Peterborough	0706	0751	—	—	0845	0905	0945	0955	1019	1045
Grantham	0725	0809	—	—	—	0925	—	1014	—	—
Newark Northgate	0737	0821	—	—	—	0936	—	1026	—	—
Lincoln	—	—	—	—	—	1012	—	1103	1201	—
Retford	0751	0836	—	—	—	—	—	1040	—	—
Doncaster	0807	0852	0901	—	—	1004	1032	1056	1107	—
Grimsby Town	0944	—	1049	—	—	—	1145	—	1249	—
Cleethorpes	0954	—	1100	—	—	—	1155	—	1300	—
Hull	0923	—	1035	—	—	1127	—	—	1227	—
Wakefield Westgate	0854	0908	—	0933s	—	1020	—	1113	—	—
Leeds	0914	0928	—	0953	—	1041	—	1134	—	—
Shipley	0949b	1017q	—	1049	—	1117	—	1217	—	—
Bradford Interchange	0952b	1009	—	1036	—	1122	—	1206	—	—
York	0833	—	0927	—	0952	—	1100	—	1133	1153
Harrogate	0943	1033	—	—	1103	1043	1133	1143	1233	— 1243
Scarborough	0926	—	1032	—	—	1050	—	1200	—	1232
	✗	✗	✗	✗	✗	✗			✗	✗

FIGURE 3.1   **Graphic Communication**   The graphic design of a railway timetable does more than simply inform—its form conveys a message that the rail company is dependable, efficient, and trustworthy. The same words, written in a flowery hand script, would not convey the same message. (*Source:* British Railways Board, 1995.)

evokes an emotive response—a congenial *feeling* of clarity, predictability, and so on. The graphic design implies, whether or not intentionally and truthfully, that the rail company is dependable, efficient, and trustworthy.

Thus, the form of a design (almost any design of any kind, we claim) is inseparable from the content. How a design conveys a message is an important part of the message itself. Moreover, every piece of design carries an aesthetic charge, whether or not it has been consciously attended to; even inattention will be interpreted by the audience as meaningful. Marshall McLuhan (1964) went further: form and content are identical, the medium is the message.

We emphasize this point to crush the hope that there exists in graphic or interaction design a universal form into which any content may always be poured with optimal effect. The assumption that content and form are separable tends to encourage forms (designs) that, supposedly neutral and content independent, are instead simply bland and spiritless.

We do not mean to deny the utility of templates, interface guidelines (see Profile 4), and all those rules of thumb on, say, text size and line length, which are listed in desktop-publishing how-to books. That is the kind of craft lore that—as Einstein is alleged to have said of Le Corbusier's proportional system—makes the good better and the bad difficult. Nor do we deny the validity of the more general taxonomic strategies and perceptual–psychological principles codified by artists and designers of the Bauhaus (hierarchy, enclosure, unity, contrast, and so on) that appear to have always governed graphic activity.

The difficulty with these taxonomies and rules is that a design that serves well both the particular material and the particular audience cannot be adduced from principles alone: It requires a leap of invention. Moreover, although individual principles may hold good, competition between mutually contradictory requirements must be resolved pragmatically, according to the specific audience, material, and context.

The notion that content and form are separable also encourages the idea that content must be devised and specified completely before it can be dressed in form, or that in some way form emerges naturally from use (form follows function). But the opposite (function follows form) is often, acceptably, the case. In certain artist–designer tasks, in fact, no precise intention may be specified in advance—it may be recognizable only when it is achieved. A client might ask an architect simply to design a beach house, for example, relying on the designer to create a house that is exhilarating and life enhancing. A detailed performance specification will come later, if at all.

The Indivisibility of Function and Aesthetics

The railway timetable of Figure 3.1—a simple and straightforward information-design problem—demonstrates that any design inevitably carries an affective charge. The fulfillment of function inevitably generates, and is generated by, an aesthetic. Yet, closely related to the notion that content and form are separable is the myth that function and aesthetics are divisible.

This idea has several lamentable aspects. One is that it usually comes bundled with the puritan assumption that function takes precedence over aesthetics—a view we have shown to be illogical. Another is that this precedence tends to be temporal; that is, artist–designers are invited to only the final stages of a design's development, to apply a final coat of spray-on aesthetics. That this perception annoys artist–designers, we stress, cannot be entirely attributed to volatile bohemian temperaments. Marketeers and accountants are equally frustrated by the waste of their wisdom when they are not consulted on a product's design until it is almost launched, and normally mild structural engineers become sullen when architects haul them in at the last minute to make visions stand up.

Aesthetics, moreover, are concerned with more than visual appearance. There is a delight in a program that is rigorously consistent, elegantly clear and lean, where sound and vision are perfectly at one, or where the representation chosen neatly fits the ways that users think about what they are doing. These qualities cannot be added on at the end: They are integral to the design and engineering of the product.

The Component Activities of Interaction Design

Of all the activities necessary for the development of any design, five comprise the inventive core of the process:

1. *Understanding.* What is going on here? What is the underlying problem to be solved? Photographs, videos, sketches, and notes can be used to aid designers in observing and analyzing the information or the problem. Designers talk with people, especially clients and users, and look at the information to be communicated.

2. *Abstracting.* What are the main elements? What kind of information is being conveyed? What do people want to do with it? What is important? What is irrelevant? Lists, sketches, and diagrams are the usual tools here.

3. *Structuring.* What are the relationships among the elements? What different ways can the elements be ordered to be useful for users? What are the users interested in? How much can they take in? The designers' assumptions will be checked with the users and the clients.

4. *Representing.* How can this structure be represented in visual and auditory form? What representations does the material suggest? What representations might the designer glean from thinking about the users' world? Should the representation be concrete or abstract? Is metaphor appropriate? Here, the designer typically uses sketches on paper and interactive sketches in a medium such as Macromedia Director (see Profile 10), which may be evaluated with colleagues or users.

5. *Detailing.* Exactly what color should this element be? What style of depiction should be used? How is the picture plane handled? How do the elements move? Should an illustrator be hired? Some designers work directly in a paint program such as Adobe Photoshop. Others start on paper, and move to the computer later.

These five processes are not executed sequentially. Designers circle among them as activity in one throws light on another. When considering the structure of the information, for instance, a designer might also be thinking about how much text can be put on the screen, or how this particular audience might most intuitively interact with the information. So the stage at which interaction designers are admitted to the design process determines the extent to which the full range of their skills can contribute to a software product's success.

Three Projects

To illustrate the process of interaction design, we shall describe briefly three occasions at the Royal College of Art in which interaction designers were involved:

1. When the basic engineering design was complete, so only detailed interaction design remained to be done (the accounts project)
2. At an earlier stage, when the performance specification of the application had been established, but not the model that was to represent the purpose of the application and how to interact with it (the Suitcase project)
3. Still earlier, when the users' needs were first discussed, so the purpose and representations could be designed together, each contributing to the other's development (the fashion project)

1. The accounts project

Imagine that an application is almost finished, but performs disappointingly. An experienced engineer is called in to optimize the code, but finds that the problems are more fundamental—they lie in the data structures. Optimizing the code would make superficial improvements, but the basic flaws remain. In the real world, this scenario should be rare, because software engineers are involved from the start. An important part of the product, however, is a coherent model that tells users what the product is and how they operate it—its central organizing model. Yet interaction designers, who have much to contribute to this model's invention and representation, are seldom called in sufficiently early.

47

Two of the College faculty (Gillian Crampton Smith and Martin Locker) were involved in the attempted rescue of an accounts package, one month before the project had to be finished. The original designers—an accountant and software engineer—had modeled the code's underlying structure on traditional paper-based work, without sufficiently considering how shifting tasks to the computer would change everyday accounting procedures. When the screens at last came to be designed in detail, it became apparent that the conceptual model—now hard-wired into the structure—was obsolete. By then, the timetable only allowed screens to be designed that were neat and presentable but did little more than list the functions provided. An inventive model, relating better to the users' future world and work, would have required the application to be fundamentally restructured (see Denning and Dargan's discussion of action-centered design in Chapter 6).

2. The Suitcase project

A more productive time for interaction designers to enter stage left, then, is when the application's performance has been specified, but there is not yet a specification of how that performance is to be fulfilled. An example is a project for students to redesign the desk accessory Suitcase, a mini-application that allows Macintosh users to install and de-install fonts in their system folder. The existing interface allows users to access all the functions, but gives little clue about what the application is, what it does, how you use it, or what, after you have used it, has been done. You must either remember or check the manual.

The students started by analyzing the context in which the application would be used and the kinds of tasks that its users would be doing. They found that the basic communication problem was to distinguish easily between fonts available in a library and fonts already installed. Possible solutions used more descriptive phrases such as *available types* versus *loaded types*, or *library* versus *in use*. Other solutions animated the movement of fonts from a list of those available to a list of those installed.

The most successful solutions, by Robert Girling and Sally Grisedale, totally recast the users' conceptual model of the application

FIGURE 3.2   The Suitcase Problem   The desk accessory for moving fonts in older versions of the Macintosh Finder allows users to access all the functions, but gives little clue about what the application is, what it does, how you use it, or what, after you have used it, has been done. The challenge posed in a student project at the Royal College of Art was to improve the interface. (Courtesy of Fifth Generation Systems. Reprinted by permission of Symantec Corporation.)

by abandoning the desk-accessory approach and incorporating the tool into the application's font menu. Through layout, terminology, and animation, the purpose of the application—to install and de-install fonts—was communicated to the user, and the state of the system was shown explicitly (Figure 3.3).

An interaction designer who thinks about information in terms of what users do with it, and the context in which they use it, may imagine approaches different from those suggested by the way that the system is engineered. If interaction design is considered only at the end, software is driven by engineering design, of which users are rightly unaware, rather than by the representations with which they interact.

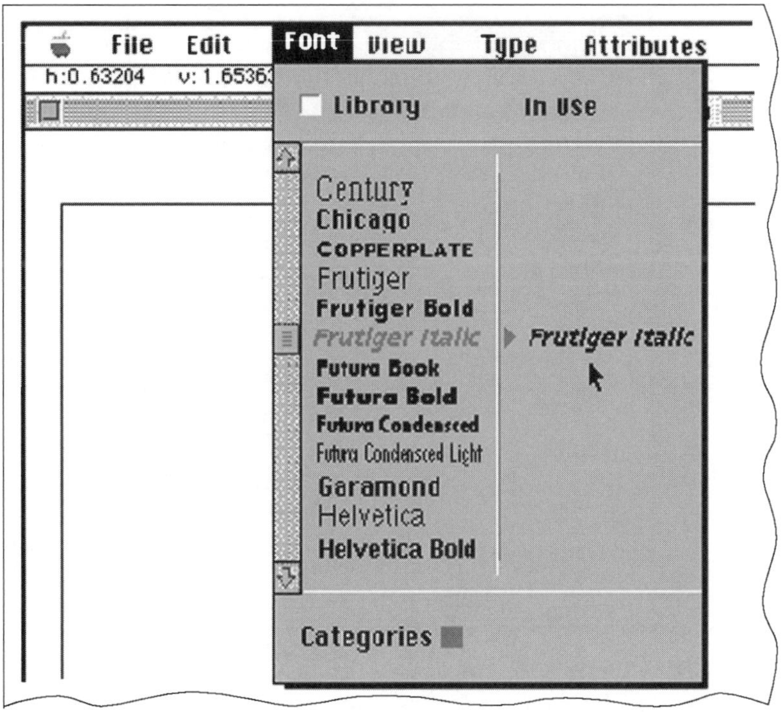

FIGURE 3.3   The Font Mover   One solution to the Suitcase problem was to recast the users' conceptual model of the application by abandoning the desk-accessory approach and incorporating the tool into the application's font menu. (© Royal College of Art. Reprinted with permission.)

3. The fashion project

In the fashion project, interaction designers were involved from the beginning. A consortium of clothing manufacturers asked the College to see how computers could help in the fashion-design process. A research and design team was assembled, comprising interaction designers from engineering, product, and graphic-design backgrounds (Gillian Crampton Smith, Charlie Hill, and Philip Joe), as well as cognitive scientists Ellie Curtis and Michael Scaife from Sussex University. We went through the five design stages just described, cycling back through them more than once:

- *Understanding.* One of the cognitive scientists spent several months at the factories and design studios, watching what was done and asking people what their work was and how they viewed it. The team began their design investigation as a graphic designer would: by considering the existing paper file compiled for each *garment* type. This file, containing some 50 different forms, had evolved to enable the manufacturers to keep track of each stage of the garment's production. The researchers could see from the file the information that already had to be provided, and they hoped to provide additional amenities.

- *Abstracting.* The paper file was used to keep track of every garment type in the production process. It contained information about the garment's geometry, its materials, the trimmings to be used and the company that supplied them, the garment's critical path, and test reports on sample garments. The file's fundamental purposes were to ensure that all the season's garments got to the shops in time, and to avoid costly errors. The file was not active: It did not, for instance, alert the users to emerging problems. It offered no overview of progress—how many garment types were delayed, say, or were ahead of schedule.

- *Understanding.* The researchers discovered that people involved in different parts of the manufacturing process held vastly different views about what the process was and what was important. They concluded that, to make sense to all users, the central organizing idea of the software model should be the garment, rather than the departments, work stages, techniques, or data flow.

- *Structuring.* One of the interaction designers with a graphic-design background looked in detail at the types of information represented and how they might be categorized. One approach that turned out to be productive was to divide the information according to how it could be manipulated: pick from a list, choose from a range, tick off something finished, and so on. The aim was to see whether there were a few underlying regularities that could be represented similarly, to reduce the apparent complexity of the information.

- *Representing.* The team brainstormed with lists and sketches, searching for metaphors to represent the information. Could deadlines be shown as milestones or hurdles? Might the different seasons' designs be represented as clothes rails, with garments hanging on them? Although there were useful metaphors for different elements, none seemed satisfactorily all-encompassing.

- *Abstracting.* Surveying the range of different representations that they had devised, the researchers were forcibly reminded that each provided a different handle on the process. One of the cognitive scientists mentioned John Searle's (1969) concept of speech acts: Propositions are not simply true or false, but rather have purpose—are exhortations or supplications, for instance. The team realized that the fashion information was useful only if it promoted action. This realization helped them to escape from the mindset associated with the existing data structure—the paper file—and from the assumption that their task was simply to represent the information.

- *Representing.* One demand, clearly, was that every garment should be ready on time and without problems. Managers had to be alerted to difficulties that arose, so that they could minimize the consequences (a stitch in time). The researchers therefore sought ways to communicate a feel for how schedules were progressing, and whether there were problems ahead. The next need was remedial action. So the team designed a system whereby faults—a wrinkled zip on a sample, say, or an inaccurate dimension—would be flagged on the image of the garment itself, and notified directly to the computer desktop of the staff involved.

- *Understanding.* The team returned to the factory to check the assumptions so far, and asked people further about the purpose of the information—what they did with it and what they might like to know that the existing systems did not tell them.

- *Structuring and representing.* To keep in mind all the ideas that had emerged, and to discard those that they did not find useful, the researchers took pages from all the sketchbooks and photocopied, cut them up, and assembled them into a large map of all the different approaches. This map prompted them to make suggestions: "If you represented each garment on the timeline like a bar, you could also show how far ahead of or behind schedule it is." "You could highlight this flag in color, to make the problems jump out." "If you represented problems as Post-It notes, you could see at a glance where there had been problems and whether they were still there; you could use the same representation as a message to the person who had to deal with the problem."

- *Detailing.* Only now—well over halfway through the design work—did screen and interaction design begin. The work done up to this stage on structure and design strategy is almost invisible to anyone looking at the final result. Indeed, it becomes obvious only if it has not been done well: The more skillfully it is achieved, the more transparent it is.

The detailed design, done by one interaction designer with the help of a second, involved decisions such as the exact screen layout, the colors and type to be used, a consistent logical and visual style for the representations, the management of transitions between screens, the feedback to be given, the users' means to navigate the information, and the hundreds of other details that make software effortless and pleasurable to use.

The two designers had decided that each garment type should have two views: a *portfolio* (information about the item itself) and a *timeline* (information about its schedule)—two conceptual models, or central organizing ideas, to make the huge range of information coherent and easy to grasp. This decision came from considering both how this particular information could be represented within the limitations of the medium, and how it could be made to fit the conceptual world of the users. So using the image of a portfolio with tabs for different sections, for instance (Figure 3.4), both suggested the original file and referred to the world of fashion designers. In terms of representation, it had the advantage of encouraging direct manipulation and allowing problems to be shown clearly on the image of the garment.

As the garments were measured, any deviations from specification would be marked in red. Any problems, such as a wrinkled zip or

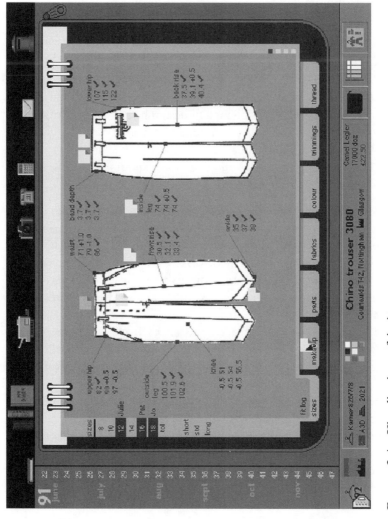

FIGURE 3.4 Visualizations of Action
(© Royal College of Art. Reprinted with permission.)

poorly finished pocket, would also be flagged. In addition to indicating the faults on the image of the garment, the system would notify the relevant staff directly via their desktop machines. The shelf at the top of the display is for tools: rule book, diary, printer, scanner, autodial phone, calculator, and an envelope (for posting changes in the database to other users).

In this kind of design process, few individual design decisions are startlingly innovative; the creative task is to forge a coherent and consistent whole, in terms of logic, representation, and the users' world.

The process of detailing the representation was the most problematic in terms of tradeoffs among competing requirements. For instance, the designers wanted to represent simultaneously the timeline of each of about 30 garments—the responsibility of one department. Time could be represented as a vertical or a horizontal axis. If they used the best-understood—horizontal—orientation, however, they could not get enough garments on screen from top to bottom. They tussled with ways of shrinking, scrolling, and so on, but none seemed successful. They particularly resisted turning the representation through 90 degrees, because the labels would have to read from top to bottom. But they finally accepted the vertical orientation, because nobody referred to a garment by its name: People used only its number. More important than the legibility of the labels was an overall grasp of which garments were slipping behind schedule.

There were also problems of pictorial logic and coherence. Generally, pictorial icons were used to represent objects; a coat hanger, for instance, represented a season's collection of garments. Clicking on the hanger, however, did not reveal further icons representing each garment, but rather revealed just a bar, colored to show whether the garment's production was behind or ahead of schedule. Pictorial consistency was sacrificed for relevance and compactness.

Two people worked full-time for four months on this project, and three worked part-time—roughly one person-year in all. Over this period, the 50 different representations in the original paper file were compacted into two basic views, showing the information in a way that allowed users to grasp it much more intuitively. The look and feel of the tool were designed to avoid the character of computer-controlled bureaucracy and to resonate with the visual sensibilities of fashion designers. An important part of the system's function was that it be stylish and enjoyable to use.

Interaction Design: More Art Than Science

Interaction design involves three interlocking elements to which the skills of artist–designers are particularly germane:

1. The design of what the software *does*—its purpose for people
2. The design of a model of what the product *is*, and its *representation* to users in the terms of their world, through vision, touch, and sound
3. The detailed design of the software's *look and feel*—the exact number of pixels, their color, how fast or smoothly they move, and so on

Interaction design cannot ignore scientific method and engineering knowledge. Indeed, familiarity with computing technology and psychology is as essential to an interaction designer as familiarity with building technology is to an architect. After all, no science breeds more theories than do the human ones such as psychology and sociology—or than does art itself. But because interaction design deals primarily with values, preferences, and meanings—with, if you like, aesthetics and semantics—it can have neither a universal *predictive* theory nor always-reliable methods to generate solutions. You can say, for instance, that a certain color of type will be legible to most readers, but you cannot say with the same degree of certainty that readers will or will not like it. So informed instinct (hunch) is as important as is principle in interaction-design practice, and osmosis (the largely intuitive absorption of skills and values) is as important in interaction-design education as is factual information transfer.

This level of ambiguity and subjectivity is not a result of interaction design's relative youth. It is intrinsic to all the artist–designer disciplines; it gives them their power, subtlety, and robustness. Interaction design is evolving rapidly. Like all artist–designer disciplines in the industrial and electronic ages, it must constantly reinvent itself to respond to changing situations and sensibilities. The interaction designer needs to break rules and to overturn precedents, as well as be able to follow them.

In the end, interaction design is more of an art than a science. Its ultimate subject matter—human experience and subjective response— is inherently as changeable and unfathomable as the ocean.

Suggested Readings

Carl Dair. *Design with Type.* Toronto: Toronto University Press, 1952, 1967.

Maurice de Sausmarez. *The Dynamics of Visual Form.* London: Studio Vista, 1964.

Gyorgy Kepes. *Language of Vision.* Chicago: Paul Theobold, 1969.

Kevin Mullet and Darrell Sano. *Designing Visual Interfaces: Communication Oriented Techniques.* Englewood Cliffs, NJ: Prentice-Hall/SunSoft, 1995.

Emil Ruder. *Typographie.* Teufen, Switzerland: Arthur Niggli, 1967 (text in German, English, and French).

Edward Tufte. *The Visual Display of Quantitative Information.* Cheshire, CT: Graphics Press, 1983.

Edward Tufte. *Envisioning Information.* Cheshire, CT: Graphics Press, 1990.

About the Authors

Gillian Crampton Smith, originally a graphic designer, is the Professor of Computer Related Design at the Royal College of Art in London. She consults on interaction design for companies such as Interval Research, Apple, and Philips.

Philip Tabor teaches at the Bartlett School of Architecture, University College, London, where he has served as director. He has worked in architecture studios in the United States and in England, for 10 years as a partner in Edward Cullinan Architects. He is editor of the *Journal for Architectural and Planning Research* and on the editorial board of *Architectural Research Quarterly.*

Profile

3. KID PIX

Broderbund's Kid Pix is one of the most popular computer programs that has been designed for children—at one time, it was the best selling Macintosh application. Simply described, it is a drawing program for the crayon and finger-paint crowd, providing a variety of tools to produce colorful, playful drawings. What makes it interesting to the rest of us (besides the fact that adults enjoy using it as well) is the dramatic change of viewpoint that it represents on what a drawing program is supposed to do.

From a functional point of view, Kid Pix is a descendant of widely used programs such as MacPaint and MacDraw, which had their predecessors in the early bitmap drawing and painting programs that were developed for the Alto computer at Xerox PARC (see Profile 2). Like these adult products, Kid Pix provides the user with a canvas on which to draw, and with a palette of tools, each of which can be used to create or modify objects in the drawing.

From a graphic-design viewpoint, Kid Pix loudly and consistently declares its underlying attitude—this is a fun program for kids. Its design is in stark contrast to that of the timetable that Gillian Crampton Smith and Philip Tabor presented in Figure 3.1, which portrays its publisher as dependable, efficient, and trustworthy. The Kid Pix interface avoids the neat precision and minimalist graphics of a traditional drawing application, conveying instead the construction-paper-and-crayons look of children's art. The fonts, colors, and drawing styles in the interface were chosen to attract children and to convey a feeling of light-hearted enjoyment (Figure 3.5).

Profile Author: Terry Winograd

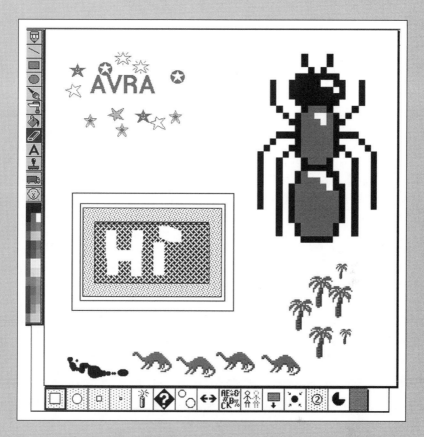

FIGURE 3.5 **Kid Pix** In designing this tremendously popular children's drawing program, Craig Hickman (an art teacher who wanted a program for his own children to use) set out to create an interactive experience, rather than to decorate the interface of a conventional drawing program. The icons at the bottom represent many different ways to erase the entire drawing. (*Source:* Brøderbund Software, Kid Pix.)

The significant innovation of Kid Pix, however, lies deeper than its choice of graphics and screen design: Its basic functionality is not oriented to producing drawings, even though it is a drawing program. A striking clue is the fact that Kid Pix offers eight different tools for the purpose of erasing the entire drawing. At first glance this seems like bad design. Why so many? Why more than one? Doesn't this violate the principles of redundancy, consistency, and simplicity that guide interface design?

Of course, the eight eraser tools are not all the same. Even though each tool produces the same end effect, each does so with a unique style. One tool produces a loud explosion, blasting the drawing in expanding ripples outward off the screen. Another tool plasters large alphabet letters all over the drawing, then divides the screen in two and marches everything off to the sides, accompanied by the sound of a rusty elevator door. Another tool initiates a countdown from 5 seconds to 0 (with real voices doing the counting) while showing the numbers in circles with sweeping lines, as on old-fashioned film leaders. At the end of the countdown comes more action and sound. And so on through a variety of creative and amusing options.

Kid Pix designer, Craig Hickman, made a fundamental shift when he recognized that the essential functionality of the program lay not in the drawings that it produced, but in the experience for children as they used it. The fun of doing a Kid Pix drawing lies partly in seeing the evolving result on the screen, but it lies more in the action that accompanies the drawing activities. Figures and colors twirl and dance on the screen; a little round-mouthed face says "Oh-oh!" when you undo an action; paint spots are splotted down at random with a pop-corn-popping sound; GUI paint drips down the screen in oozing blobs; and on and on. In fact, a relatively small number of Kid Pix creations ever reach the computer's printer, and by the time most Kid Pix users finish making changes to a drawing, they will have completely obliterated and reconstituted the picture many times. The animations, the sounds, and the playful look of the results all combine to create a drawing experience that attracts and engages the intended audience.

Kid Pix highlights the points made by Crampton Smith and Tabor in Chapter 3:

- The effectiveness of the structure of a piece of software design and of its interface depend on how they are interpreted by users.
- This interpretation by users is not context independent. It depends on the cultural codes, shared sensibilities, emotional responses, and habitual prejudices that users bring to it.
- Recent advances in display technology allow richer and more expressive communication at the human–computer interface.
- Decreasingly useful, for these reasons, is the idea that the functionality of a piece of software is separable from, and takes precedence over, its appearance.

Computer and video-game designers have, of course, recognized these points for years. It would make little sense to separate the interface from the functionality for PacMan or Doom. Kid Pix occupies an interesting middle ground—half game, half productivity software (it does, after all, produce drawings). But as Crampton Smith and Tabor point out, all kinds of software are subject to users' context-dependent interpretation. Just as the effectiveness of Kid Pix depends on the message it conveys about fun, the effectiveness of business software depends on conveying a coherent message about taking care of the user's work in a dependable and understandable way. A spreadsheet with a cute cartoon interface would not be sucessful as a business spreadsheet, any more than Kid Pix with a precise draftsman-oriented interface would be Kid Pix.

Suggested Reading

Mollie Bang. *Picture This: Perception and Composition.* Boston: Little Brown, 1991.

JOHN RHEINFRANK *and*

SHELLEY EVENSON

Design Languages

Design languages have been used to design things as diverse as
products, buildings, cities, services, and organizations. They are
often used unconsciously, arising out of the natural activity of
creation and interaction with created things. Yet, when consciously
understood, developed, and applied, design languages can build on
and improve this natural activity, and can result in dramatically
better interactions, environments, and things of all kinds.

During the years when the Xerox Star was being developed, John Rheinfrank was part of a design team at Xerox, but he was not working on computer systems. Along with Arnold Wassermann, William Hartman, and a joint team from Xerox and the design firm of Fitch RichardsonSmith, he was engaged in a top-down redesign of the entire Xerox line of copiers (Rheinfrank et al., 1992). The project was guided by two fundamental principles:

1. Understand how people use the machines in real settings.
2. Think of the machine as a medium in which the designer communicates to the users. See it not just as an object with mechanical functions, but also as a statement in a design language.

The phrase *design language* can be interpreted many ways, but in the sense that Rheinfrank and Shelley Evenson (a prominent graphic designer) describe it in this chapter, it denotes the visual and functional language of communication with the people who use an artifact. A design language is like a natural language, both in its communicative function and in its structure as an evolving system of elements and of relationships among those elements.

Drawing on their extensive design experience with products such as copiers, industrial control rooms, and computer interfaces, as well as traditional applications of graphic design, Rheinfrank and Evenson reveal fundamental issues that are highly relevant to software design. The plasticity of software interfaces—the ease with which the look and feel can be changed at will—makes them especially amenable to the conscious development and use of design languages, as discussed in the accompanying profile on the Macintosh Human Interface Guidelines.

— *Terry Winograd*

AT THE SIMPLEST LEVEL, natural (spoken or written) language is a means for communication. It is a tool through which we create the phrases and sentences that make up our conversations with other people. At a higher level, communication—and language—is inseparably assimilated into our daily lives and activities. We talk to one another to get things done. We comment on the world around us, trying to develop a shared understanding that will help us to make better decisions. We communicate to build and maintain our relationships with people around us. We do not just *use* our language: We *live* with it. The generation and interpretation of phrases and sentences can be understood only when language is seen within the larger context of everyday activities and experience.

Just as natural (spoken or written) languages are the basis for how we generate and interpret phrases and sentences, so *design languages* are the basis for how we create and interact with things in the world. And, like spoken or written language, design languages are assimilated into our everyday activities, mediating our experiences with the world (often tacitly), and contributing to the perceived quality of our lives. Design languages can be used to design things that are small or large, tangible or intangible. Design languages have been used to design things as diverse as products, buildings, cities, services, and organizations. They are often used unconsciously, arising out of the natural activity of creation and interaction with created things. Yet, when consciously understood, developed, and applied, design languages can build on and improve this natural activity, and can result in dramatically better interactions, environments, and things of all kinds.

The power of using design languages consciously has been recognized and described by other design theorists, such as Christopher Alexander (1979) for architecture and urban design, William J. Mitchell (1992) for architecture and media, Edward Tufte (1990) for visualization, and Terry Winograd (Adler and Winograd, 1992) for software design.

Design Languages in Use

Design languages are present everywhere in our constructed environment.

Most design languages have evolved through unconscious design activities. For instance, houses in Nantucket have been designed with a language of form, materials, and structure that derives its substance from the local environment, and that arose in response to physical, social, and economic influences on early settlers (Figure 4.1).

FIGURE 4.1   The Language of Houses   The elements of this Nantucket house convey a design language that derives from the environment, the inhabitants' needs, and the ongoing evolution of the construction materials and methods. (*Source:* Courtesy of John Rheinfrank and Shelley Evenson.)

Nantucket—an island with a relatively harsh climate—was settled by people who planned to make their fortunes from the sea, such as whaling and fishing. They began by building small houses, with cedar shingles placed over a wood frame. The cedar trees that have evolved to thrive on the island are small, rugged conifers. The early settlers learned that cedar wood had water-repellent and insect-repellent properties. The shingles made from them are also small; when overlapped over the house frame, they cause water to run off the roof and sides of the house. To take advantage of the beautiful views, people built houses with large windows. To protect against the elements, they built shutters to cover those windows. Beach houses had storm fences to keep water and sand at a distance. As the original settlers made their fortunes, they added on to their homes in a piecemeal fashion, often planting gardens in the enclave created by the multiple wings. The design language of houses in Nantucket arose from necessity and was adopted by convention. The resulting style of architecture

has been recognized as appropriate to the area. It has since been codified, and it is now imposed on any new buildings, even though the
necessities of the overall design intent have been supplanted.

Design languages can also be created to accelerate the assimilation
of a new technology into everyday activity. For example, recent Xerox
photocopiers have been designed with a language of form and graphics that communicates to users how they can be used (Figure 4.2).
This language includes elements from other design languages that are
familiar to users. Doors on these copiers have obvious handles that
indicate how they are to be opened. Color and value coding distinguish various areas of the product. For example, areas where originals
are to be fed in to the machine are green, areas where paper is loaded
are blue, and copy-output areas are red. Although users are not taught
these colors explicitly, the consistent use of color and shade throughout a line of copiers produces tacit recognition, much in the way that

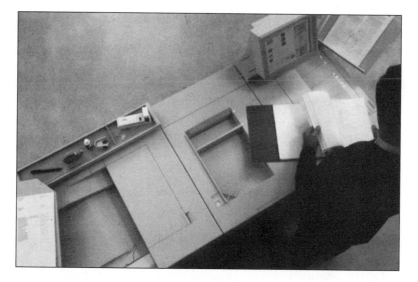

FIGURE 4.2   **The Language of Photocopiers**   The Xerox photocopier
shown here was designed with explicit attention to the design language that
would convey its functionality most effectively. The designers used elements of
color, form, and labeling in a consistent way across a full line of products, creating a language and identity that was readily recognized and understood by
the users. (*Source:* Courtesy of John Rheinfrank and Shelley Evenson.)

we learn most of our native language through using it, rather than through having its structure pointed out.

In addition, like other machines with which users are familiar, copiers have an overall frontal orientation. A language of graphic elements offers information at the point of need, with links to more detailed information elsewhere. Users do not need to be trained, nor do they need to refer to complex instructions. They quickly recognize handles, focus on colored areas as points of important interaction, and come to rely on informative graphics to orient them and to provide resources for understanding the intended interaction.

Design Languages and Meaning

Design languages are central to how designers contribute to experiences; they play a significant role in people's everyday experience of the world.

Natural languages consist of words and rules of grammar, and are used to create meaningful utterances. By analogy, design languages consist of design elements and principles of composition. Like natural languages, design languages are used for generation (creating things) and interpretation (reading things). Natural languages are used to generate expressions that communicate ideas; design languages are used to design objects that express what the objects are, what they do, how they are to be used, and how they contribute to experience. People's knowledge of natural language is the basis for their interpretations of what other people say; similarly, a design language can be the basis for how people understand and interact with a product. The best design languages create experiences of use that are simple and straightforward—then they go one step further, to make interactions between people and objects pleasant and continuously meaningful in the context of everyday life.

Design languages play an important role in the expression of the *unfolding of meaning* of objects. Essentially, design languages are the means by which

- Designers build meaning into objects, so that objects express themselves and their meanings to people.

- People learn to understand and use objects.
- Objects become assimilated into people's experiences and activities.

Traditional conceptions of language have seen meaning as strictly associated with form and style, relatively independent of context. Design languages can be used most effectively when meaning is seen not just as the built-in sense of an object, but also as the quality of *sense making* that objects have and can produce, especially with respect to their surroundings. In other words, doing design requires more than making meaningful objects; it requires crafting whatever it is about objects that lets them participate in the creation of meaningful experiences. According to this view of meaning, the sense of an object cannot be separated from the experience that the object simultaneously sits in and helps to create (see Rheinfrank and Welker, 1994, and the discussion by Brown and Duguid in Chapter 7).

Typically, design languages consist of

- *Collections of elements.* Building blocks that designers and users employ to communicate, such as shapes, textures, colors, actions, and metaphors
- *Sets of organizing principles.* Descriptions of how the elements might be composed to build things that have meaning
- *Collections of qualifying situations.* Examples of how elements and principles of composition might change based on the context

Designers can use all these components to generate new uses of the language (products or services) that are meaningful in particular contexts of use, and that honor a particular set of underlying assumptions about people and people's uses of the product or service. Design languages are not fixed formal languages. They are generative: They contain an imperative (an underlying intent or need for interaction) and social mechanisms for their own revision through ongoing interaction. Users of objects respond to the resources given to them by designers. By using (or failing to use) these resources, users provide the basis for the revision of the language. As the expectations of designers and users change, the language evolves through invention, accident, and other events that create an impetus for transformation. By consciously developing the language, we can dramatically accelerate the process through which a new design language is naturally and meaningfully assimilated into activities and experience.

Design languages usually evolve gradually. They become a deeply held tradition, are difficult to challenge, and are even more rarely questioned. People tend to assume that they are valid, and to continue to work through them, rather than to think about them and their appropriateness. This habit is particularly dangerous in a time of accelerating change. A business might be using a language that no longer allows it to produce products that make sense to customers; thus, it becomes particularly vulnerable to a competitor whose product line suddenly addresses a more appropriate set of needs.

Digital cameras that use a design language of professional 35-mm film-based cameras either will be uncompelling—interpreted as nothing new or special—or will be overly constrained by the behavior of light-lens optics, and will therefore fail to take advantage of the primary innovations possible with digital technology. In another way, cellular telephones now emulate the form and features of wired telephones, rather than shifting to a design language that is grounded in the diverse communication needs of people who are mobile. We are just beginning to see the breakdown of this rigidity with the introduction of products such as Sony's MagicLink and Motorola's Envoy and Marco. These *personal communicators* embrace a person's need to deal with the complexity inherent in mobile work styles. In addition to the primary communication functions, they include personal organizers and tools for managing communications, and they support the use of images and data during communication.

Taking advantage of design-language innovations, we can produce the core elements of successful corporate design strategies (Rheinfrank et al., 1993). Companies can consciously consider and design new design languages, with the intent of creating new product paradigms. Sony developed the *My First Sony* line of consumer electronics for children a few years ago. Each product has a balance of elements that suggest "cool audio devices" with elements that suggest "childlike and playful." The products in the line that express these attributes most obviously have established a clear benchmark for products in this category.

Benefits of Design Languages

Explicit use of a design language is beneficial from the three essential perspectives of interpretation, generation, and assimilation into everyday life.

Interpretation: Design languages and learning

Designers can use a design language to give people strong cues and powerful resources for learning by using. They can do so by shaping their designs to take advantage of what people already know and have the potential to do. For example, a designer of photocopiers who understands the design language of door handles and applies this understanding to the design of "opening things" can provide people with physical cues for how to open things by using handles that correspond to the contexts of the artifacts being designed and that clearly communicate "open here" in those contexts.

One thing that designers can do to help people learn is to reveal functionality through *transparent-box design,* rather than to conceal it through *black-box design* (Lave and Wenger, 1991). In a black box, all functionality is opaque, or hidden from view, and people accomplish their goals by pushing buttons that signify nothing whatsoever about the inner workings of the object. The technology is made *foolproof.* (Note the degrading reference to the assumed competence of the user.) Point-and-shoot cameras that take care of everything and produce acceptable photographs are black boxes, even when they are sold in bright colors. From one perspective, they de-skill users and lead to impoverished communities of practice. From another perspective, they make picture taking easy, freeing the user to attend to the scene and to capture an event without struggling with settings and technical adjustments. As users, we both gain and lose when we are highly constrained by the point-and-shoot limitations of the camera.

In a *transparent box,* functionality is revealed, and people are provided with the opportunity to comprehend the inner working of the artifact that they are using. A camera with more flexibility can enhance the capabilities of the user to capture events in a variety of ways, even using specialized features to enhance the sensory capacities of the picture taker and to create special effects. Rather than foolproofing, we can create a transparent control space, designed so that the depth and breadth of options are clear to the user when they are appropriate. A well-designed transparent object selectively reveals to people just enough information about how to use the artifact and how the artifact works for people to accomplish their goals or to do tasks. A transparent camera could be optimized for certain situations of use (family gatherings, sporting events, and so on) and could reveal technical functionality and suggestions for use that would allow users to enhance the quality of their photos and to develop their skills at a pace of their own choosing. We can arrange this selective revelation to allow the *meaning* of the full experience of using the artifact to unfold gradually according to need, over time, as the artifact is used.

Design languages also make it easier for people to learn, by allowing patterns of use to be transferred from one artifact to another. Designers can help users to transfer patterns of use by consciously and consistently understanding and applying a design language across a family of product offerings. People can then take advantage of the resulting similarities in how products are used, often without any conscious relearning.

The members of product families resemble one another with respect to their forms and interaction styles. Thus, when people learn about one family member's form and interaction style, they can transfer this learning to other members of the same product family, adding to the overall usability of the entire product offering. Most consumer power-tool manufacturers have employed a simple language across their products. The trigger on a drill is the same color as the switch that starts the belt moving on a sander. The highlight color means *tool on* and is used consistently across the product range. The standard Apple Macintosh user interface (see Profile 4) is another good example of this consistent use of language: Users can easily learn new applications, because they take advantage of their understanding of similar and familiar objects, and the associated conventions of interaction.

Generation: Design languages and business

Businesses can use design languages explicitly to create coherent ways that customers form a consistent—and increasingly more positive—impression of the corporation. This impression becomes stronger as customers are repeatedly exposed to a corporation's products. In the end, this impression plays a large role in determining future customer purchases, thereby also determining the success of the corporation. Nike uses its communication design language to target its messages to its various audiences, (youth, women, sports enthusiasts), yet its overall impression is unified and coherent: Everyone can "Just do it." This powerful message is then confirmed by Nike's product array.

The most effective design languages do more than create coherence; they also create relevance. They ensure that the product line meets customer needs, and that it plays a crucial role in customers' everyday activities. Thus, the leading design languages set an industry standard for coherence, relevance, and quality. Once adopted by customers, they force competitors either to adopt the same standards or to produce equally strong alternatives. If a design language that is appreciated by customers becomes dominant in a market, it may take rival corporations years to make the changes necessary for effective competition. Nike's products are designed with the user's context in mind. Not so many years ago, we used only sneakers. Taking up the language pioneered by Nike, we now use specialized shoes for aerobics, the water, walking, running, hiking, and even cross-training (sneakers revisited?). Reebok tried to compete by applying similar principles in another niche, to street shoes (the BOKS line), but has never been able to challenge the cultural dominance of Nike.

When a new or recast product line appears and convinces customers that it will meet their needs in a fundamentally better way, then customers move toward it steadily and irreversibly. This observation holds especially true when design languages are used to influence the whole spectrum of ways that a company communicates with its customers (advertising, customer service, literature, purchase experience, merchandising, and so on).

Assimilation: Design languages and meaningful innovation

One quality of design languages makes them potentially dangerous in an environment of accelerating change: They are most effective when they acquire presence over time, through their *assimilation* into people's lives. Design languages typically are most influential when they have become deeply embedded, when people can unconsciously assume that they are valid and can continue to act through them, rather than think about them and their appropriateness. A reflective corporation can build on traditional assumptions and then identify, develop, and implement a new design language quickly and effectively as part of the movement toward a dramatically improved market position. For example, the first cellular radios were *wireless telephones*, in much in the same way as we referred to the first automobiles as *horseless carriages*. In both cases, a primary innovation was attached to the past, through a prevailing design language. Its early development was constrained by the reference until enough momentum was achieved for the interactive evolutionary process to modify the design language. The potential of cellular communication almost certainly has as little to do with today's telephone as today's automobile has to do with buggies and buggy whips. We will one day look back at today's personal computers (TV sets with typewriter keyboards) and software as historic curiosities of the same ilk.

The Design-Language Approach

In our design projects through the years, we have identified the following five steps in the development of design languages:

1. Characterization
2. Reregistration
3. Development and demonstration
4. Evaluation
5. Evolution

We shall describe each of these steps in detail.

Characterization

Characterization is a process of describing the existing underlying assumptions and precedent-setting design languages. In many cases, when designers design, they unconsciously accept current underlying assumptions about the nature of the object that they are designing, without challenging those assumptions. For example, for many years, offices were made of traditional building materials. The difficulty of reconfiguring spaces constructed of these materials created a long tradition of closed offices and broken up spaces that required extensive (and expensive) remodeling to accommodate the natural variety of uses. In the mid-fifties, modular office systems were developed. They introduced an entirely new language for the production of offices. Along with the language came assumptions about openness and flexibility, and radically new building economies. A new industry formed around this primary innovation and the attached set of assumptions.

The office-building industry today faces the challenge of readdressing its assumption base. The original design language was deeply grounded in the productivity of single individuals during a time when the prevailing work tools were calculators and typewriters. Current work practices seem to be evolving toward conditions that call for collaboration, communication, geographically distributed work teams, and organizations with fluid structure. None of these conditions can be addressed effectively with the current office design language.

As an example of characterization, we shall describe a design-language–development program that we conducted for FRS, a division of Emerson Electric. FRS produces equipment that digitally controls and monitors complex process manufacturing facilities, such as paper, chemical, or pharmaceutical plants and refineries. When these types of plants were first built, operators used controls tied to individual aspects of the process, and monitored the production process using strip charts, sight, and sound. As analog and digital controls were introduced, operators moved to control centers and control rooms, where they continued to perform similar functions remotely. This arrangement was desirable, because the production process was usually messy, noisy, and dangerous.

The interface to early digital control systems mimicked the readouts from the dials and face plates and the information from the strip charts. A larger span of control simply meant more discrete pages of information, reflected in separate screens. An interface for process control today could have 250 pages of electronic information and abstract representations of physical objects. The role of the operator in a plant is to watch these pages of information, to spot problems, to respond to alarms, and to intervene in the process as necessary. The control-room physical environment is dominated by furniture and equipment consoles that have an industrial ruggedness, clearly related to the equipment present on the plant floor. This view of the plant, operators, and control-room regime has remained unchallenged since the introduction of the first system.

Every design-language–development project should start with a clear characterization of these current assumptions. It is only from this explicit understanding that a designer can challenge—then recast—the current set of assumptions. At the end of this first step, assumptions such as the ones that we just described should be part of the conscious awareness of the designer.

Reregistration

Reregistration is the creation of a new assumption set and design framework. During this step of design-language development, designers use a variety of methods to explore emerging trends and needs. Market and technology surveys are conducted. Latent or masked user needs are identified through a variety of (ethnographic) field-research techniques, such as observing current use situations, interviewing users, and surveying activity in related situations.

Designers then consciously create new design assumptions by constructing alternative design–conceptual frameworks, then *acting out* these frameworks inside *idealized* situations of use.

In our process-control project, after we had assessed the situation, we challenged the assumptions surrounding the role of the operator in the plant community. Observing practice, we saw that operators were the hub of communication in the plant. They supported a number of other functions, such as engineering, maintenance, quality control, operations, planning, and scheduling. We also observed that operators were familiar with the physical layout of objects in the plant. Many operators performed routine maintenance and troubleshooting functions on alternating shifts. Through our observations, we identified specific patterns of activities and interactions that either were unsupported, or were supported ineffectively by the products and services provided by the vendors in the industry. We then began to define a new design direction. We realized that the control room was the primary center of a business, rather than a place to keep a big control panel.

Creating a new set of assumptions fosters creativity by allowing a design team to move away from designing according to preframed and preanalyzed sets of assumptions, and by encouraging members to move toward designing according to the patterns that they construct collaboratively from current contexts of use. Results are best when customers, users, engineers, salespeople, and executives can all participate in this reregistration process, since each brings unique and relevant domains of knowledge and experience (see Profile 14 on participatory design). The creation process is symmetric: As usage changes, the language is modified. Seen from another perspective, the developers and users coevolve, with the language as the mediator of meaning.

Development and demonstration

Designing the language begins when the team gives concrete visible form to the assumptions and to the design framework. In our example, a designer might suggest that more representational process objects would help operators to orient themselves to the plant. Instead of taking the physical plant with which operators are familiar and abstracting it, why not just represent objects more like the objects are in the real world? Following this line of thought, elements in the design language for a process-control interface would be representational images of boilers and other objects in the plant.

At the same time that the language elements are being *developed*, they are being *demonstrated*, in scenarios, sketches, or prototypes. These embodiments act to create tangible *stories of the future* that can be compared and contrasted with stories gleaned from the field during the characterization stage. This simultaneous demonstration of the elements as they are being conceived is crucial. Although it is not difficult to picture a concept such as "more representational boilers," concepts such as "communication support for the plant community" may be difficult to imagine without tangible examples.

Demonstrations also allow designers to evaluate how elements interact with one another, to make sure the meaning of one does not confuse or negate the meaning of another. Another purpose for iterative demonstration of the language is to test the reframing hypothesis. For example, is there enough carryover from existing process-plant practice to support the quick adoption of this new technology?

Demonstrations also help organizations to make development assumptions explicit. Specifications come to life in the design language, and misconceptions can be discussed and resolved quickly. The interactive coconstruction of a design language is facilitated by the concreteness of the demonstrations and prototypes (see Schrage's discussion of prototyping cultures in Chapter 10).

Evaluation

The *evaluation* stage places the design language in context. After the demonstrations have been developed, they are placed within real or hypothetical situations of use. Ideally, this evaluation starts as soon as the first demonstrations are produced, to see whether the language resonates with its users. Refinements are made to the language as necessary. In an evaluation of our process-control interface, we found that an element such as "people buttons" for direct dialing to a coworker, which made perfect sense to the design team, were confusing to a user when they were placed next to buttons for powering on an object. Both were perceived as buttons by the user, yet they had completely different functions, which were not revealed by their appearance.

The design team develops a stable set of demonstrations, constructing several composite objects, based on the design language, that cover the range of expected future work situations. These new expressions can also be evaluated and iterated on, so that they further contribute to the richness of the language. Applying the process-control language to portable (small-scale) and wall-sized (large-scale) products can lead to new language elements, such as process abstractions (used to create an overview of the entire process) in a tablet or on a wall, or modifications to existing elements (less representational boilers that scale well on a portable.)

Evolution

No matter how good the design, there will be further additions and changes to the language once it is in use. The best design language is still appropriate for only the needs of its time. Needs and practices change constantly. Designers must be sensitive to such changes, and must continue to extend the design language. Where possible, design languages should be constructed to support users in developing new forms of interaction, based on their own activities in their own situations. One of our goals for the process-control design language was to support members of the plant community in developing custom-tailored interfaces specific to their needs, giving them the power to create new elements as they need those elements.

Conclusion

Design languages are powerful expressions of what we know and share about the world around us. Henry Ford invented a design language for automobiles in a way that allowed him to mass produce cars and to reach customers. Innovations in the car language were fast and furious in those early days. Sadly, the language of the car has evolved slowly since then, and most of the changes have been merely of form, rather than of substance. Software design seems to be poised at the edge of a similar era of innovation. Just as running boards on cars were part of the assumption set of the car language for years, windows, icons, menus, and pointing (the WIMP interface) seem to be a part of the unchallenged assumption set for computer interfaces. Yet, games and more play-oriented activities implemented on CDs use different languages for interaction. We propose that explicitly creating software design languages based on their contexts of use, and according to the steps we have outlined, will provide new suggestions for evolution or revolution of the WIMP language, and will move us into an era of more meaning-full interaction with computers.

Suggested Readings

William J. Mitchell. *The Reconfigured Eye*. Cambridge, MA: MIT Press, 1992.

John Rheinfrank. The technological juggernaut: Objects and their transcendence. In Susan Yelavich (ed.), *The Edge of the Millennium: An International Critique of Architecture, Urban planning, Product and Communication Design*. New York: Watson-Guptill, 1993.

John Rheinfrank, William Hartman, and Arnold Wassermann. Design for usability: Crafting a strategy for the design of a new generation of Xerox copiers. In Paul Adler and Terry Winograd (eds.), *Usability: Turning Technologies into Tools*. New York: Oxford University Press, 1992, pp. 15–40.

John Rheinfrank and Katherine Welker. Meaning. In Michael Bierut et al. (eds.), *Looking Closer: Critical Writings on Graphic Design*. New York: Allworth, 1994.

About the Authors

 John Rheinfrank is a senior strategist at Doblin Group, in Chicago, where he directs programs that focus on decision strategy and on breakthrough product and service development. Prior to joining Doblin Group, he was a Senior Vice-President at Fitch, an international design consulting firm, where he was cofounder of the Exploratory Design Laboratory (EDL), an interdisciplinary team conducting project-based design research.

Shelley Evenson is a design strategist at Doblin Group. Originally trained as a graphic designer, she has worked in interaction design for the past decade, with a focus on creating compelling user experiences. Prior to joining Doblin Group, she was a Vice-President at Fitch and was cofounder of EDL. Her work has been published by the ACM, the American Institute of Graphic Arts, and the American Center for Design.

4. MACINTOSH HUMAN
INTERFACE GUIDELINES

The greatest reason for the early success of the Macintosh was the perception by potential buyers that it was easy to use. This perception was not an accident; it was the result of Apple's conscious strategy in creating "the computer for the rest of us."

What was different about Macintosh applications? Most visibly, they were among the first consumer software to make use of the graphic user interface (GUI) that was pioneered by the Xerox Star (Profile 2), with its windows, icons, menus, and pointing device (leading to another commonly used acronym: WIMP). There has been much debate over the benefits and limitations of such interfaces, yet it is clear that, in the large, GUIs enhance usability for many applications, especially for novice users.

Ease of use comes from more than what you see on a single screen. A more subtle, but critical, aspect of the original Macintosh interface was consistency across applications. Applications for different purposes, built by different developers, all followed a common style of providing GUI elements and using those elements to communicate with users. This commonality was the result of a concerted campaign by *Apple evangelists*, such as Bruce Tognazzini (see Tognazzini, 1992). The job of an evangelist was to convince applications developers to structure their interface in *the Macintosh way*, rather than in their own way, even if they thought their own way was prettier or better. The evangelists carried their bible, later published as the *Human Interface Guidelines* (Apple, 1987), illustrated in Figure 4.3.

Profile Author: Terry Winograd

Profile 4: MACINTOSH HUMAN INTERFACE GUIDELINES

Document windows

Because a document may contain more information than a window can display at one time, the window provides a view of a portion of a document. Document windows also provide a graphic representation of opening, closing, and other operations performed on documents. Windows are usually, but not necessarily, rectangles. Figure 3-3 shows a standard document window and its components.

Close box ──────────────────────
Title bar ──────────────────────
Zoom box ──────────────────────
Scroll bar ──────────────────────
Size box ──────────────────────
Scroll bar ──────────────────────
Scroll box ──────────────────────
Scroll arrow ──────────────────────

Figure 3-3
Standard document window

Opening and closing windows

Windows appear on the screen in different ways as appropriate to the purpose of the window. The application controls at least the initial size and placement of its windows.

A standard window has a **close box.** When the user clicks the close box, the window goes away. (In the Finder, this is animated—the window shrinks into the folder or icon from which it was opened.) If an application doesn't support closing a window with a close box, it shouldn't include a close box on the window.

FIGURE **4.3** Macintosh *Human Interface Guidelines* These guidelines specify how each design element (in this case, a document window) should look, and what behavior it should exhibit. The correspondence of look and behavior is the key to a working design language. (From Apple Computer Inc., *Human Interface Guidelines: The Apple Desktop Interface,* © 1987 Apple Computer Inc. Reprinted by permission of Addison-Wesley Publishing Co., Inc.)

The evangelists' achievement was that any user who was familiar with a few Macintosh applications could approach a new application with a reasonable sense of what it could do and how to make it perform. This sense of familiarity led to the feeling that the Macintosh was easy to use. The guidelines defined a comprehensive design language, as described by Rheinfrank and Evenson in Chapter 4, and were supported by the availability of a *programmers' toolbox*, which facilitated developers writing programs that followed the guidelines. In many cases, extra programming was required if the developer wanted to violate a guideline.

The Macintosh interface design language included visual and syntactic details, such as the names of standard menu items, and deeper functional elements, such as the use of a clipboard with universal *cut*, *copy*, and *paste* commands to be provided in a standard way in every application. In the early days of the Star, the Lisa (Macintosh's predecessor), and the Macintosh, there was a raging debate about whether the moving and copying of documents, text, and drawings should be done via cut and paste from a clipboard, or via *move*, *copy*, and *delete*, commands, which were dedicated keyboard buttons on the Star. The differences were not just in the names, but also in the underlying conceptual model. The Macintosh designers may have chosen a less functional alternative (there are many people who still argue that they did so), but they did choose, and that choice led to consistency. Every application provided the same clipboard commands, making it possible for users to move text and drawings from one application to the other, regardless of the application. It was many years before this seemingly elementary form of consistency was available in either PC systems or Unix workstations.

A quick browse through Apple's *Human Interface Guidelines* reveals dozens of language elements, such as the organization of commands into menus; consistent use of dialog boxes for parameters, warnings, and errors; and standard ways of organizing and managing windows. Equivalent style guides now exist for every major interface. It is interesting to see the variations that have emerged from what is fundamentally the same interface, as illustrated in Figure 4.4. The differences are reminiscent of the relationships among simple corresponding vocabulary words from French, Spanish, and Italian. The common Latin origins lead to a basic similarity, but each language has its own consistency. Also, as is true of natural languages, there is little room for argument about which communicates more effectively. There are minor variations, but, for the most part, what is important is that, within any one language, there is a consistent way of using words that is understood by everyone who speaks that language.

In all human languages, rules are made to be broken—creative innovation violates previous conventions. Design languages continue

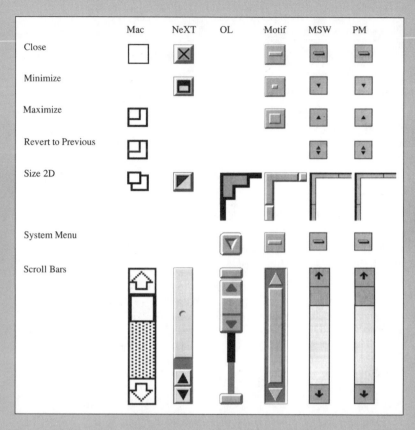

	Mac	NeXT	OL	Motif	MSW	PM
Close						
Minimize						
Maximize						
Revert to Previous						
Size 2D						
System Menu						
Scroll Bars						

FIGURE 4.4   **A Cross-Linguistic Comparison**   Each of the common GUI interfaces has its own variant of the GUI design language, expressed in a style guide. All the widely used interface styles are similar in functionality, and each offers a coordinated set of conventions for representing functions visually. (Reprinted with permission of Aaron Marcus Associates. Aaron Marcus, *Graphic Design for Electronic Documents and User Interfaces.* New York: ACM/Addison-Wesley, 1992, p. 153.)

to change and evolve, just as natural languages do. The language of the Macintosh was a replacement for a long-standing and well-known language based on character-terminal interfaces, such as the IBM 3270, for mainframe applications, such as airline reservation and forms entry systems. As Liddle describes in Chapter 2, the designers of new GUI applications had to break loose from the tacit assumptions that had been effective for their design of screen fields, layout, and interaction sequences. The designers of interfaces yet to come will have the same difficulty in breaking away from the WIMP language in which they are now so fluent. The WIMP GUI is not the ultimate user-interface design, any more than Latin was the ultimate language. It has been hardy and useful, but it is tied to the hardware and systems tradeoffs that prevailed in the 1980s.

Suggested Readings

Lauralee Alben, Jim Faris, and Harry Saddler. Making It Macintosh. *interactions* 1:1 (January, 1994), 11–20.

Apple Computer. *Human Interface Guidelines: The Apple Desktop Interface.* Reading, MA: Addison-Wesley, 1987.

Apple Computer. *Making it Macintosh: The Macintosh Human Interface Guidelines Companion* (CD ROM). Cupertino, CA: Apple Computer, 1993.

Aaron Marcus. *Graphic Design for Electronic Documents and User Interfaces.* New York: ACM/Addison-Wesley, 1992.

Microsoft Corporation, *The Windows Interface: Guidelines for Software Design.* Redmond, WA: Microsoft Press, 1995.

Bruce Tognazzini, *Tog on Interface*, Reading, MA: Addison-Wesley, 1992.

PAUL SAFFO

The Consumer Spectrum

We are a frighteningly adaptable species. A good tool should adjust itself to the user, but good tools are scarce, and so we have learned to adapt ourselves to all but the most awkward of gizmos.... Of course, there are limits to what computers can expect their human companions to put up with. We do not use tools simply because they are friendly. We use tools to accomplish tasks, and we abandon tools when the effort required to make the tool deliver exceeds our threshold of indignation.

The software designer approaches a design task with a background of concerns and assumptions. She may, for example, want to make the software obvious and easy to use for novices. Or she may want it to be compatible with a well-known application, or maximally effective and efficient for the skilled user who is tackling a complex and specialized task. Much of the discussion in this book, and in the literature on human–computer interaction that preceded it, addresses one or another of these concerns.

There is a prior question, however, in designing a product for consumer use. What does the consumer care about? It is easy to let slogans such as *user friendly* and *easy to learn* blind the designer to the diversity of the software marketplace. Different people have different concerns. It takes a broader kind of perspective—that of an industry observer—to interpret the complex and often conflicting demands and forces in the market.

Paul Saffo began his career as a lawyer, specializing in technology law. He soon decided that the technology was more fun than the law, and spent his free moments as a software designer. Eventually, he gave up his law practice and joined the Institute for the Future, a consulting firm that tracks the long-term trends of technology. Saffo is particularly noted for his analysis of the current and future developments of *cyberspace*—the networked communication, computing, and information world that is rapidly expanding and is entering our everyday lives.

Saffo's perspective cuts across the usual boundaries between developer and user and between technology concerns and business concerns. He offers insights into how different aspects of software design are relevant in determining what will succeed in the software world. He argues that the traditional software-design concerns of functionality and ease of use are not always positive in a given product, but rather play a complex role in a larger tradeoff space of consumer concerns.

— *Terry Winograd*

CONSUMERS ARE NOTORIOUSLY FICKLE when it comes to purchasing high-tech products. So much so, in fact, that computer and consumer-electronics industries attach great importance to user friendliness as a critical success factor. Yet even the most cursory glance at the last two decades of hits and failures suggests that this characteristic is only part of the whole user equation. Consumer history is littered with multiple instances of user-friendly products that were market duds, including RCA's DiscoVision (an early laser-disk system), numerous home computers, and a host of early consumer-electronics gadgets, such as voice-controlled telephones, smart appliances, and pocket-sized photocopiers.

At the other extreme, there is no shortage of instances of complex products that have gone on to market success. The majority of consumers today have no clue how to use even a fraction of the features on their VCRs, or to navigate the maze of buttons on the average TV remote control. The most glaring exception is the personal computer itself. If ease of use is so important, then how did the first DOS-based PCs—notoriously cranky, unfriendly, and arbitrary devices—ever establish themselves in the market? If ease of use and user friendliness were all important, DOS would have been abandoned in favor of the Macintosh or some other operating system long before Windows was finally ready to ship.

DOS flourished because user friendliness encompasses only part of the usefulness equation, not only in computing, but also in the entire high-tech product sector. DOS PCs persisted in the face of easier-to-use alternatives because we are a frighteningly adaptable species.

A particularly dramatic example of our adaptability comes from the early years of Douglas Engelbart's research at the Stanford Research Institute (SRI). His team was testing multiple input devices, including a gizmo comprising a stylus at the end of a sliding rod that in turn rotated around a central pivot. Engelbart reminded one of his programmers to write a polar-to-xy coordinate conversion program before setting out this gizmo for other people to try. The programmer forgot, but set up the demo, which his teammates began to use on a walk-up basis. The omission was discovered by Engelbart a few days later when, walking past, he noticed a user staring at the screen, drawing an arrow-straight line by unwittingly pulling the stylus through a perfect arc!

A good tool should adjust itself to the user, but good tools are scarce, so we have learned to adapt ourselves to all but the most awkward of gizmos. Computers are especially ungainly devices, so manufacturers count on users to meet their incomplete inventions more than halfway. The happy captives are said to be *computer literate*—

tame and tractable, and expert at making up for the manufacturers' design failings.

Of course, there are limits to what computers can expect their human companions to put up with. We do not use tools simply because they are friendly. We use tools to accomplish tasks, and we abandon tools when the effort required to make the tool deliver exceeds our *threshold of indignation*—the maximal behavioral compromise that we are willing to make to get a task done.

The Threshold of Indignation

This measure of threshold of indignation completes the usefulness equation, capturing both the importance of the task that we are trying to complete and the user friendliness of the tool with which we are trying to complete it. In the case of the PCs in our offices, computers do not have to be friendly at all if the task is important enough and we have no alternative. Knowledge workers suffering from CRT eye strain and repetitive-motion syndrome understand intuitively that this extreme is the unfortunate norm in the business world. Our business culture forces on office workers relatively high thresholds of indignation. Businesses often have the luxury of being able to provide training that can do much to turn annoying techarcana into acceptable business tools.

In contrast, individual consumers have extremely low thresholds of indignation. Even the friendliest of information appliances will gather dust if the task bores us. The majority of VCR owners never venture beyond the play and record buttons on their machines, because the fancy features offer little benefit when weighed against the inconvenience of the fiddly command sequences. Similarly, the market for home computers before 1993 was confined largely to students and businesspeople overworking at home in the evenings—individuals who were bringing home their high business thresholds. And hobbyist early adopters have even higher thresholds yet!

The threshold-of-indignation measure also has more general application beyond information technologies. Experience with other devices can help us to understand the full range of potential consumer behavior. For example, cultural familiarity with a technology also influences the threshold. Automobiles are even more user hostile than are PCs. They are complex to maintain and hazardous to operate, regularly killing and maiming scores of innocent citizens. Yet automobiles seem user friendly, because we have spent a lifetime assimilating a host of automobile skills, including pumping gas, conversing with mechanics, learning the intricacies of the vehicle code, and understanding automotive-loan financing. Similarly, our telephone system has become steadily more complicated since divestiture, yet we have barely noticed, because our learning curve has kept pace, raising our collective threshold of indignation. We have all become operators, internalizing the complexities of direct dialing, calling cards, and access codes.

As this latter example suggests, thresholds of indignation can change over time. A 1920s time traveler would be lost in the touchtone complexities of our 1990s telephone system. Yet, if we traded places, we would be equally confused and infuriated by endless and time-consuming transactions with human operators.

Also, generational responses to technologies differ markedly, with different-age cohorts exhibiting differing levels of comfort with distinct systems. Baby boomers prefer the efficiency and anonymity of bank automatic-teller machines, whereas their parents avoid these banking robots to conduct their transactions through a human teller. More recently, younger users have taken to cyberspace environments such as World Wide Web, while their elders are left watching from the sidelines. Eventually, some portion of the laggard elders will follow, but only after the younger generation has blazed the trail.

Reinventing the function of the device can alter thresholds of indignation. PCs became a consumer hit when CD-ROMs reached critical mass, and faster modems combined with a growing Internet to deliver applications that are more exciting than mere word processing and spreadsheets. In short, the PC was reinvented from an original role of standalone processing tool to a new role of access window on a larger information world.

The Universe of Tools and Users

One additional dimension completes the consumer-adoption equation: ability and willingness to pay. As depicted in Figure 5.1, we can model the entire consumer universe with willingness and ability to pay on one

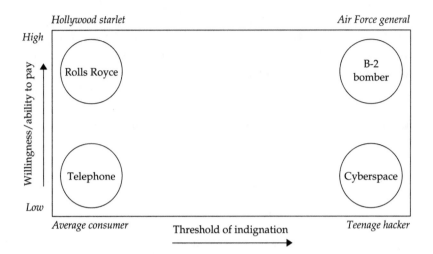

FIGURE 5.1   The Consumer Universe   The range of consumer behavior in purchasing products can be bounded by two dimensions: *threshold of indignation*, and *willingness to pay.* Each of the extremes in the four corners has its natural purchasers and archetypal products.

axis, and threshold of indignation along the other. The full range of consumer responses and the products that consumers are willing to purchase are indicated in each of the four corners, described next:

- *The Air Force general—infinite wealth, matched only by an infinitely high threshold of indignation.*   Imagine a device that is infinitely expensive and infinitely complex, and you have described the B-2 Stealth bomber, with all the latest in high-tech trickery, pound-for-pound costing *more* than its weight in gold. There is only one consumer with both the cash and the requisitely high threshold of indignation to own one of these. Even NASA cannot match the buyer or the product with its nearly as complex high-tech gizmo, the Space Shuttle.

- *The teenage hacker—a general's love of complexity, but no cash.*   Now imagine a device that is as impenetrably complex and confusing as a B-2, but is accessible to someone who has no money at all. Until the early 1990s, the Internet was the quintessential technology for this quadrant by virtue of the nerdy complexity of the access tools of the time. Back then, the Internet was so confusing that only two kinds of individuals were willing to commit the time to understand its intricacies—computer scientists and teenage hackers. For the latter, the Internet's sheer mind-numbing complexity made the environment an irresistible electronic playground accessible with a small investment in a PC and modem. Even though new tools have made the Internet ever more accessible, cyberspace remains a license for teenage obsession. Teenagers explore its nether reaches even as other consumers await the Holy Grail of the "Internet in a box."

- *The Hollywood starlet—lots of cash and utterly no patience.* Who has endless wealth, but no patience with even the simplest of devices? Zsa Zsa Gabor's on-screen persona nicely matches this intersection, so we generalize this quadrant as that of the Hollywood starlet. The perfect consumer toy for such bored rich people is, of course, a Rolls Royce. And if it is too complex to drive, then so much the better. Just throw in more cash for a chauffeur, at once simplifying the interaction with the device and adding to the price! High-end home theater systems today are the Rolls Royces of consumer electronics.

- *The average consumer—limited cash and limited patience.* Finally, there are the rest of us, the average consumers with limited cash and limited patience. Consumers love novelty as much as do the other three, but a combination of cash and time constraints limits our purchasing flights of fancy. If a product delivers benefits (either functional or entertainment) without too much work and does not cost too much, we will make it an integral part of our lives. The telephone is the model product for this quadrant: it is cheap (as low as $10); it is easy to use (just plug it in); and it delivers real, immediately understandable benefits. The challenge for consumer manufacturers is to tame their products and to drive down costs to the point at which their products sell into this corner.

A Snapshot of High-Tech Products Today

By filling in the matrix with an assortment of products sold today, we can quickly get a sense of where one zone makes a transition into another. Figure 5.2 shows such a high-tech spread for the

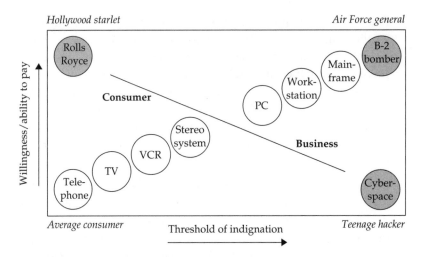

FIGURE 5.2 The High-Tech Spread   Products can be arrayed within the matrix, revealing a continuum of information devices suitable to a variety of populations. A distinct—but permeable—line in the center divides consumer-oriented devices from business devices.

world of the consumer (left half of diagram) and business (right half of diagram).

On the business side, PCs are the simplest and cheapest of the devices depicted, and are the ones most easily understood by the individual worker. Workstations are slightly more expensive and complex, because they must be connected into a network managed by system professionals. Mainframes are more remote and complex yet, whereas cyberspace until recently (when new tools made it radically more accessible) was all but invisible to everyone except the anointed few. In fact, we can describe each of these products along purely functional lines that have nothing to do with the technology. A PC is a device that an individual user can turn on and off, to which she can add and remove software at will. With a workstation, the user can control the on–off switch, but must ask someone else's permission before messing with the software. And a mainframe is a device that she can approach only through bureaucracy.

The same principles apply on the consumer side. A telephone is solidly in the consumer quadrant by virtue of its low cost, clear benefits, and ease of use. TVs are a bit farther out on both axes: They are more costly and difficult to use, because we must hook them to AC power and an antenna or cable, and then navigate through an ever-growing number of channels. VCRs fall yet farther out. Although VCR prices are about the same as TV prices, a VCR's complexity falls well beyond the few features that most viewers actually use. Component stereo systems fall at the edge of the consumer quadrant. Not only are the pieces expensive, but also setup involves figuring out a tangle of wires, setting custom preferences, and then learning how to use obscure and confusing remote controls. Fortunately, many consumers live in families that typically include individuals farther along one axis than the other members. As a team, they can make product desires a reality. Mom and Dad do the purchasing, and their more technology-tolerant children install the stereo or perform the intricacies of VCR programming.

The model in Figure 5.2 can help to explain consumer trends, and, in specific instances, can even predict a product's chances of success or failure. Note a few of its specific implications:

- *High-tech products tend to move downward and left over time.* It is axiomatic that the cost of high-tech components drops rapidly over time, and the performance of new components increases. For example, Moore's law (named after Intel cofounder Gordon Moore) states that the cost of a given unit of processing power on a chip decreases by a factor of 10 every 2.5 years, whereas the number of circuits that can fit in a given space (an indirect measure of performance) increases at the same rate. The dropping cost factor means that high-tech products will move downward on the map over time. The rising performance factor tends to push products left along the indignation curve, because it takes extra power to make devices user friendly.

- *Consumer thresholds tend to rise over time.* As mentioned earlier, consumers become accustomed to particular technologies, and their threshold of indignation rises. Newfangled telephones once frustrated our grandparents; today's more complex systems rarely annoy us. In short, we evolve with our technologies, our rising sophistication matching the new capabilities of technology. Generational factors play a role here—children raised with Ataris and Nintendos have little difficulty grokking the complexities of Windows-based PCs and Internet gateway services. This factor

95

adds some force to the leftward motion of products on the map—time and rising sophistication alone will make devices more user friendly.

- *Product manufacturers tend to be tuned to particular zones on the map—and moving is remarkably difficult.* We can also place industries on this map. For example, the consumer-electronics industry is focused on the lower-left (consumer) quadrant, whereas the computer industry centers on the upper-right quadrant. Each industry—and often each segment within each industry—is finely tuned to the specific threshold of indignation of its core customers, and to the price point of its mainline products. This orientation makes it extremely difficult for companies to move out of their habitual areas, because doing so requires acquiring new understandings about unfamiliar levels of indignation thresholds, and reorienting entire manufacturing and sales processes to a different price granularity of product.

In this latter regard, companies are like villages that hunt different kinds of game for their food. One village might hunt mammoths, depending on one kill every 6 months. Another might depend on weekly deer hunts; a third might be inhabited by rabbit eaters, who must come home with game every day to survive. In high-tech industry today, aerospace firms are mammoth hunters, personal-computer companies are deer hunters, and consumer-electronic firms are rabbit hunters. Just as mammoth hunters might find rabbit hunting demeaning and exhausting, aerospace companies are unlikely to invent the consumer-electronic successor to the VCR, even though they pioneered many of the components that VCR makers incorporate into the products.

- *It is easier for companies to move right or up than down or left.* All things being equal, it is easier to move into customer populations that have higher indignation thresholds than to move in the opposite direction. Selling more expensive products, although difficult, is far easier than selling cheaper products. IBM's woe-filled attempt to dominate the PC market is a case in point.

Moving down or left is like trying to swim to the bottom of a pool while wearing a life vest. By paddling furiously, you can get part way down; eventually, however, you will bob back to the surface. A few highly aggressive companies can move down one level, but they rarely get farther. IBM's move into PCs in the 1980s represented a heroic—but ultimately futile—attempt. Although IBM made "big iron"—mainframes and the like—the infant PC sector was a close neighbor that the company was able to greet by virtue of good executive decisions and visionary managers. But IBM's next step down—into home PCs, with the PC Jr—was a singular disaster because the consumer-level prices and threshold of indignation were too alien to the men in gray suits.

- *Adaptive interfaces are an important opportunity.* User friendliness is profoundly relative: What is friendly and helpful to a novice user may be highly intrusive to a seasoned expert. Given that users progress through stages of mastery, it is only logical that interfaces should be capable of identifying a user's skill level, matching to it, and then systematically revealing more capabilities in a way that encourages the user to learn. Of course, this matching of interface to levels of skill is even more important outside the consumer environment, where professional effectiveness depends on having the right tool for the job, and moreover a tool matched to its user's evolving skills. As the Japanese craftsperson Sōetsu Yanagi (1972) once observed, "The craftsman is most free when his tools are proportionate to his needs."

- *Ads and hype are important influencers of consumer thresholds of indignation.* "It's new and I don't like it." The sentiment was that of a change-weary 6 year old, and it echoes the sentiment of most of us at one time or another. Advertising and hype—overenthusiastic, often credulous enthusiasm for a new product—can be a potent weapon in moving us all into a frame of mind open to new ideas. Far from being an impediment, this sort of excitement is an essential feature in the technology-diffusion process.

- *The most important product opportunities are the gaps immediately adjoining a company's core markets.* New companies can look anywhere on the matrix that seems to fit their capabilities, but established companies should seek gaps close to home—a pattern reflected by Apple's and IBM's respective entries into personal computing. Success is most likely when a company is following

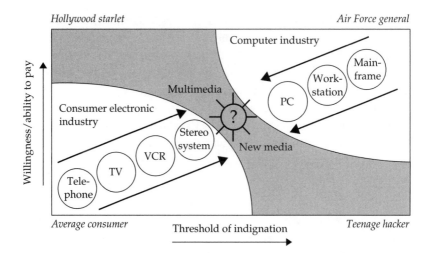

FIGURE 5.3 Where Industries Fit In The gap between the zones of the computer and consumer-electronics industries is becoming ground zero for competition in the 1990s. Consumer-electronics players are trying to grow up into it, while computer players, such as Apple and Microsoft, are trying to reach down.

already-familiar customers, or is leveraging already-understood technology. Moving into an area where both factors are unfamiliar amounts to playing corporate Russian roulette. The biggest gap in the high-tech sector today lies in the center of the matrix, as depicted in Figure 5.3. That is where the new media industries in the making are appearing.

When we view this matrix, it becomes apparent that new media are not merely an extension to personal computing, but rather provide the obvious collision point between upward- and rightward-moving consumer-electronics companies and downward- and leftward-moving computer manufacturers. If the model has any predictive value, it is a sure bet that the consumer-electronics players are the most likely to grab most of the action in the long run, although the ultimate winners will have to understand and master the needs from both sides of the gap if they are to succeed. The players who find creative ways to team up across this gap are likely to dominate these new industries in the decade ahead.

Suggested Readings

Ivan Illich. *Tools for Conviviality*. New York: Harper & Row, 1973.
Jun'ichiro Tanizaki. *In Praise of Shadows*. New Haven: Leete's Island Books, 1977.
Sōetsu Yanagi. *The Unknown Craftsman: A Japanese Insight into Beauty*. Tokyo and New York: Kodansha, 1972, 1989.

About the Author

 Paul Saffo is a director of the Institute for the Future in Menlo Park, California. He writes about the social and economic aspects of emerging digital technologies for numerous magazines and newspapers. A book of his essays, *Dreams in Silicon Valley*, has been published in Japan.

5. MOSAIC AND THE
WORLD WIDE WEB

When Paul Saffo wrote the original business-intelligence report on which Chapter 5 is based, he selected cyberspace as an example of a high-indignation, low-cost technology. In 1993, you needed to be a dedicated computer expert to make use of the tantalizing functionality of the national and international computer networks. The late-night teenage hacker was the epitome of the network user, and the Internet was known only by the technical cognoscenti.

1994 saw a dramatic shift, largely due to the rapid spread of a program named Mosaic, which gave people quick and easy access to the network as part of the World Wide Web (WWW). Suddenly, the Internet blossomed into the image for the information super-highway; it began to become a part of everyday life for millions of people.

The WWW was initially developed in the early 1990s by Tim Berners-Lee and his colleagues at the CERN nuclear research laboratory in Geneva, intended for communication among researchers in high-energy physics. Its goal was to make *hypertext* available on the Internet. Hypertext—a structure of interlinked on-line information—had been advocated as early as the 1960s by visionaries such as Ted Nelson and Douglas Engelbart (see Bieber and Isakowitz, 1995). Hypertext augments information on the computer by providing *links* that make it possible for a user to jump immediately to some document, or place in a document, that has been selected by the author. Although many versions of hypertext have been implemented in the past few decades, the WWW was the first system that allowed links to

Profile Author: Terry Winograd

cross from a document on one network server to another document on another server. Anyone with a workstation on a network can write documents in a simple specialized format (the HyperText Markup Language, or HTML), which can include links to any other document on any server on the network.

Mosaic is a *browser* for the WWW, initially developed by Marc Andreessen and colleagues at the National Supercomputing Center at the University of Illinois. A browser is a program that displays documents (text and graphics) on the screen, making it easy for users to follow hypertext links by simply clicking on the corresponding piece of text with the mouse. Figure 5.4 shows a page from the WWW, displayed in Mosaic.

Mosaic was easily and widely available. It was distributed free of charge, because it had been developed as part of a federally funded research project. A user could download it directly on the Internet, rather than having to go through a physical software-distribution channel. With this new kind of computer application, everyone from art teachers to companies that wanted to sell goods online saw the potential for quick, easy interaction, and the WWW began to take off.

The design lessons to be learned from Mosaic are not specific to its interface, but rather they reflect general phenomena in a larger domain of social design:

The critical-mass phenomenon

As is true of many startling advances, we can see in hindsight that Mosaic and the WWW did not require any major technical breakthroughs. The innovation was the culmination of a long and complex development of the underlying computer network and graphics technologies. Mosaic combined the right degree of functionality and ease, moving the network technology over a threshold that enabled a larger population to participate in networking. As more people in turn began to use the WWW, more people saw it and wanted to be able to participate, beginning a spiral that will culminate in widespread everyday use, as similar spirals did in earlier decades with the telephone and television, and more recently, the office fax.

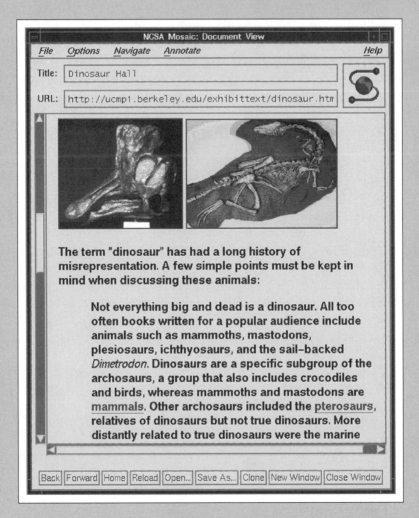

FIGURE **5.4**   **A Page from the World Wide Web**   Mosaic made it possible
for its users to display both text and graphics from the WWW. The underlined
sections of text are *anchors*, indicating links to other documents or parts of
the page. The user can display the linked material by simply clicking on the
anchor. (From Lawrence Hall of Science, University of California at Berkeley.
Reprinted with permission.)

Simplicity as the key design principle

One reason for Mosaic's success was that the protocols on which the software was based (HTML and the HyperText Transfer Protocol, HTTP) were extremely simple. They did away with many of the sophisticated features of other word-processing and networking protocols, including apparently necessary features, such as security (the ability to control who can read or write documents) and basic document formatting (for example, the ability to indent paragraphs). The key insight was *less is more*. A minimal system made it easy for a wide population of developers to experiment, to build their own versions, and to discover possibilities that the original designers never envisioned. Of course, as later versions and new browsers have been developed, many new features have been added, and the protocols are becoming more complex. At some point, they may even bog down in the weight of unplanned growth, and may need to be replaced by new standards. In the meantime, however, simplicity of structure and operation gave a tremendous boost to the initial spread of the WWW.

Open development

The Internet as a whole has undergone explosive growth and rapid development, in large part due to a philosophy of distributed open development, of which the WWW is one example. Instead of relying on a managed development project, the community lets a set of standards emerge through a kind of bubbling up from the grassroots. In general, a standard is adopted because one or more groups have used it to make something work. It is then modified and evolved through a decentralized process in which anyone can propose changes, invent extensions, and build new layers on top if it. Although the results are often chaotic and may later need to be reengineered for robustness (or *firmness*, as Vitruvius would have said—see Profile 1), the vitality of the unplanned development process leads to rapid innovation, and the pragmatic "take what works and build on it" ethic of the community leads to rapid evolutionary selection.

The power of distribution networks

The fact that Mosaic was a network application led to another benefit. The Internet made it possible for new versions of the software to reach thousands or even tens of thousands of users within a short time after a release. Users could download a newer version of Mosaic, using Mosaic, with just a click of the mouse. When Netscape Communications (then called Mosaic Communications) released its first version of Netscape, an improved browser for the WWW, the new browser swept through the community within days, and established a de-facto standard within weeks. In traditional software-distribution channels, the preparation, packaging, and sales of a new release take months. Of course Netscape, like Mosaic, spread quickly in part because it was available without charge. As mechanisms for payment over the Internet develop, it will become possible to distribute software for a fee. The role of networking as a software-distribution mechanism will increase in importance as we begin to fulfill the promises of commerce on the net that were fueled by Mosaic and the WWW.

Suggested Readings

Robert Horn. *Mapping Hypertext.* Lexington, MA: Lexington Institute, 1989.

Ed Krol. *The Whole Internet User's Guide & Catalog* (Second edition). Sebastopol, CA: O'Reilly, 1994.

Jakob Nielsen. *Multimedia and Hypertext: The Internet and Beyond.* Boston: Academic Press, 1995.

James Nyce and Paul Kahn (eds.), *From Memex to Hypertext: Vannevar Bush and the Mind's Machine.* Boston: Academic Press, 1991.

PETER DENNING *and*

PAMELA DARGAN

Action-Centered Design

The standard engineering design process produces a

fundamental blindness to the domains of action in which the

customers of software systems live and work. The connection

between measurable aspects of the software and the satisfaction

of those customers is, at best, tenuous. We propose a broader

interpretation of design that is based on observing the repetitive

actions of people in a domain and connecting those action-

processes to supportive software technologies.

Peter Denning has led a distinguished career in the computer-science profession. In addition to holding several prominent teaching and research-management posts, he has been the president of the Association for Computing Machinery (ACM), the head of the ACM Publications Board, and Editor-in-Chief of the *Communications*, ACM's most widely read publication. He has spearheaded national computing curriculum taskforces, including one that produced a milestone document on principles for revising the computer-science curriculum, known widely as the "Denning report" (Denning et al., 1989).

From this background, we might expect his perspective to be close to the conventional wisdom of computer science, and his advice about design to be tied closely to the methods and slogans of software engineering. But the chapter included here reflects a different direction—one that brings to the center people and their practices, rather than the technologies of computing.

Working with Pamela Dargan, an experienced software designer as well, Denning set out to find out how successful software designers had managed to create software that users found usable and well suited to their needs. Denning and Dargan did not simply study the systems; they asked the systems' designers and developers what had led to achieving a good design. As Denning and Dargan report, the answers were surprisingly consistent—and were surprisingly far from the conventional wisdom on software engineering.

— *Terry Winograd*

THE SOFTWARE LANDSCAPE is a mixed field of successes and failures. Along with notably successful software packages for every task from payroll to party invitations, we find notable failures, some of them spectacular. As one measure, a 1979 U.S. Government Accounting Office review of nine software projects for the Department of Defense showed that about 2 percent of the allocated funds was spent on software that was delivered and in use; about 25 percent was spent on software that was never delivered; and about 50 percent was spent on software that was delivered, but was never used (Neumann, 1995). This example may represent an extreme case, but everyone in the software industry knows that such problems are widespread and are of large magnitude. Software engineering—a discipline invented in the 1960s to address the so-called *software crisis*—has unwittingly created an illusion that a rigorous process of transforming requirements into systems is the key to reliable design. With this illusion comes a false sense of security that the solution to the crisis is at hand—and that we will obtain it faster by throwing more research dollars at the problem.

The shortcoming is not due to a lack of effort or intelligence among software practitioners. The problem is of a different kind: The standard engineering design process produces a fundamental blindness to the domains of action in which the customers of software systems live and work. The connection between measurable aspects of the software and the satisfaction of those customers is, at best, tenuous. We propose a broader interpretation of design that is based on observing the repetitive actions of people in a domain and connecting those action-processes to supportive software technologies. We call this activity *action-centered design*, and we propose it as the basis of a discipline of software architecture.

Approaches to Software Design

Various English dictionaries that we have consulted list no fewer than 10 different senses of the verb *design*. The primary meaning is "to make or conceive a plan." Software design is concerned with the form and function of a software system and with the structure of the process that produces that system. Two principal approaches are practiced. *Software engineering*, which dates to the mid 1960s, is based in the engineering tradition, where design is seen as a formal process of defining specifications and deriving a system from them. *Human-centered design* is more recent, dating to the late 1980s. In this approach, designers immerse themselves in the everyday routines and concerns of their customers. These approaches have complementary strengths and weaknesses. We believe that the two can be brought together into a new discipline: *software architecture.* The central practice of software architecture, *action-centered design,* produces maps that serve as blueprints, uniting system-oriented engineers and customer-oriented designers.

Let us begin with software engineering. Software engineers believe that most of their work lies in the process that generates a system having the form and function specified by the customer. They refer to this process as the *software-lifecycle model.* The most common varieties of the software-lifecycle model are the *waterfall model* (Figure 6.1) and the *spiral model* (Figure 6.2). Vivid descriptions of how this process is organized can be found in the works of Andriole and Freeman (1993), Boehm (1976), DeGrace and Hulet-Stahl (1990), and Dijkstra (1989).

Unlike other engineers, however, software engineers have not achieved success in the engineering design process. They have not developed a systematic method of producing software that is easy to use, reliable, and dependable: They have not developed a discipline of software production.

Many explanations have been proposed for this anomaly. The most popular ones posit the notion that software is complex and violates the continuity laws that pervade most engineering disciplines—changing a single bit in a program can produce drastic changes in behavior. In this view, software is seen as a *radical novelty,* for which our customary engineering analogies are misleading (see Dijkstra, 1989; Parnas, 1985). However comforting they might be, none of these explanations has produced a practical means for systematically producing usable, dependable software.

The engineering design process operates from three assumptions:

1. The result of the design is a product (artifact, machine, or system).
2. The product is derived from specifications given by the customer. In principle, with enough knowledge and computing power, this derivation could be mechanized.
3. Once the customer and designer have agreed on the specifications, there is little need for contact between them until delivery.

The software crisis is usually seen as a breakdown in the application of this methodology, especially due to faulty input in the form of incomplete or incorrect specifications.

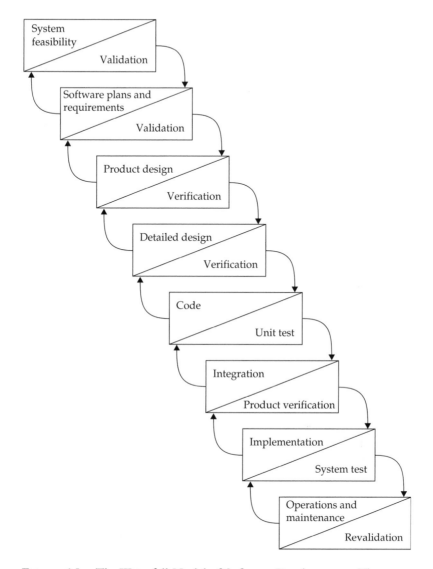

FIGURE 6.1   The Waterfall Model of Software Development   The traditional waterfall model emphasizes the structured relationships between adjacent stages in an idealized process that moves from abstraction to implementation. It does not take into account the realities of iterative design, such as the prototyping cycle described by Schrage in Chapter 10. (*Source:* Adapted from Barry Boehm, "A spiral model of software development and enhancement," *IEEE Computer* 21:2 (May 1988), p. 62. Copyright © 1988 *IEEE.* Reprinted with permission.)

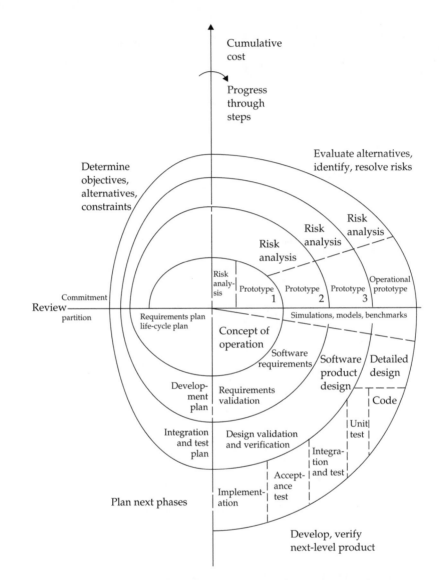

FIGURE 6.2 **The Spiral Model** The spiral model improves on the water-fall model of Figure 6.1 by emphasizing the iterative nature of the design process. It introduces a cycle of iterative prototyping, but it is still designer and product centered, rather than user and action centered. (*Source:* Adapted from Barry Boehm, "A spiral model of software development and enhancement," *IEEE Computer* 21:2 (May 1988), p. 64. Copyright © 1988 *IEEE*. Reprinted with permission.)

The school of human-centered design emerged in Europe in reaction to the shortcomings of *product-centered design* as practiced in the standard engineering design process (Floyd et al., 1992). One approach to human-centered design (see Kuhn's description in Chapter 14) focuses on workers using computer-based systems in industrial settings, emphasizing the role of human judgment and experience in work. Another approach focuses on the interaction and coordination among people and organizations, arguing that the software crisis is fundamentally a failure of customer satisfaction (Denning, 1992a).

The standard engineering design process offers little to connect the actions of designers with the concerns of users; the interaction between these two groups is limited to the requirements and specifications documents and to the final signoff. Donald Norman (1993) argues that the product-centered design process focuses primarily on the machine and its efficiency, expecting humans to adapt. In contrast, he says, the human-centered design process leaves to humans the actions that humans do well, such as empathizing, perceiving, understanding, solving problems, listening for concerns, fulfilling commitments, satisfying other people, and serving interests. It leaves to machines what humans do not do well, such as performing repetitive actions without error, searching large data sets, and carrying out accurate calculations.

Human-centered design of computer systems is based on understanding the domain of work or play in which people are engaged and in which they interact with computers, and programming computers to facilitate human action. Anthropologists play a significant role in this work. Human-centered design operates from three assumptions:

1. The result of a good design is a satisfied customer.
2. The process of design is a collaboration between designers and customers. The design evolves and adapts to their changing concerns, and the process produces a specification as an important byproduct.
3. The customer and designer are in constant communication during the entire process.

A New Interpretation of Design

A discipline of software design must train its practitioners to be skilled observers of the domain of action in which a particular community of people engage, so that the designers can produce software that assists people in performing those actions more effectively. The phrase *domain of action* is meant to be broad; it includes specialized domains, such as medicine, law, banking, and sports, as well as general domains such as work, career, entertainment, education, finance, law, family, health, world, dignity, and spirituality. Software engineers must reframe design from a process of deriving a software system from specifications to a process of supporting standard practices in a domain, through software that enables more effective action.

The assessment of whether software is useful, reliable, and dependable is made by the people who act in a domain. By focusing on a system and its specifications, the traditional engineering process loses sight of those people—of their common concerns and of their actions. The process cannot offer a grounded assessment of quality, because many of the factors influencing quality are not observable in the software itself (Denning, 1992a). Human-centered design, at least, does not lose sight of the community. As presently constituted, however, human-centered design lacks formalisms and is not capable of making connections systematically between user concerns and the structure of software.

There is an increasing number of software engineers today who are using *object-oriented design* as a way to frame the requirements-analysis stage of the engineering design process, and are using *object-oriented programming* as an approach to implementation. Having observed this trend, we asked a number of prominent software engineers this question: "What is the concern that makes people find object-oriented programming so attractive?" Their answers were instructive. Most saw object-oriented programming as another fad, rather than as the silver bullet that will end the software crisis. Most thought that object-oriented programming appeals to some intuitive sense about how the software will be used, and thereby reduces the apparent complexity of the software.

We then asked the designers of the following award-winning software packages, "What does it mean for a design to be intuitive and judged as complexity-reducing?"

- Quicken (by Intuit): A personal financial-accounting system (see Profile 13)
- MeetingMaker (by On Technologies) and Synchronize (by Crosswind Technologies): Systems for scheduling meetings and managing calendars in groups
- Topic (by Verity): A system for retrieving documents from a database based on their text content
- Macintosh user interface (by Apple Computer) (see Profile 4)

We asked the designers of these software packages what they had done to achieve a good design. There was a surprising level of unanimity in their answers:

- Pick a domain in which many people are involved and that is a constant source of breakdowns for them. (For example, the designer of Quicken chose personal finance.)
- Study the nature of the actions that people take in that domain, especially of repetitive actions. What do they complain about most? What new actions would they like to perform next? (In personal finance, the repetitive actions include writing checks and balancing the checkbook; the most common complaints include errors in arithmetic and discrepancies between bank statements and personal balance sheets; and the most-sought new action is to generate reports automatically for income-tax purposes.)
- Define software routines that imitate familiar patterns of action. Users will have little to learn to get started, because the software merely helps them do what they find obvious. Include functions that permit actions that most users have wished they could do, but could not do manually. (In personal finance, these functions include presenting screen images of template checks, allowing electronic payments, and providing a database that records transactions by income-tax type.)
- Deploy prototypes early in selected customer domains. Observe how people react and what kinds of breakdowns they experience. Because the customers frequently shift concerns, especially after they are seasoned users, the software designer must have means of observing shifting concerns and of taking these shifts into account in the next version of the design. Thus, there are beta-test sites, individual follow-up sessions, hot lines, highly attentive technical and customer support staff, suggestion boxes, bug advisories, and

the like. It is of central importance to stay in communication with customers (see Chapter 13 for an account of how Intuit creates and maintains customer communication).

All the designers said that they did not pay much attention to standard software-engineering methodology. Several said that the internal structure of their code is ugly and is not well modularized. When fixing bugs, they made patches; when the system got too patchy, they declared the next version and redesigned the software completely.

One way to summarize these findings is this: Software systems have customers. Quality means customer satisfaction. Customers are more likely to be satisfied by software that is transparent in their domain of work, because it allows them to perform familiar actions without distraction, and to perform new actions that previously they could only imagine. Customer satisfaction is not static: Customers change expectations, and software must evolve to track their shifting expectations.

We also reviewed the published papers of people who had designed software systems that were given the Best System award by the Association for Computing Machinery (ACM). We found a similar set of concerns expressed here, even though the initial users of these systems were typically technical specialists (see Denning and Dargan, 1994).

Pattern Mapping as a Basis for a Discipline of Design

A discipline of software design should be capable of training its practitioners so that they can systematically fulfill promises to build and install software systems that are judged useful and dependable by their customers. The key to transforming software design and engineering into a customer-centered discipline is the development of a method of mapping from human actions to software functions in a way that is intelligible to clients, designers, and engineers simultaneously.

The field of architecture is rich in useful analogies and practices. Architect Christopher Alexander (1979) says that the job of an architect is to give expression to the patterns in the use of space that permit the building's occupants to carry out their daily actions effectively. He says that surprisingly few patterns are needed to describe and generate

In any public place where people loiter, add a few steps at the edge where stairs come down or where there is a change of level. Make these raised areas immediately accessible from below, so that people may congregate and sit to watch the goings-on.

Public place

Stair seats

❖ ❖ ❖

Give the stair seats the same orientation as SEAT SPOTS (241). Make the steps out of wood or tile or brick so that they wear with time, and show the marks of feet, and are soft to the touch for people sitting on them—SOFT TILE AND BRICK (248); and make the steps connect directly to surrounding buildings—CONNECTION TO THE EARTH (168)....

FIGURE 6.3   **Element of a Pattern Language**   An architectural pattern language, as described by Alexander, consists of a vocabulary of design patterns, each of which links an observation about the human uses of a structure with a sketch and a guideline for building.(From Christopher Alexander, *A Pattern Language*, 1977, NY: Oxford University Press. Reprinted with permission.)

buildings—a dozen or so suffice for a typical home, and three or four dozen serve for a typical office. The immense variety of buildings arises from the infinite number of ways that these basic patterns can be combined. Alexander says that these patterns are not objects, such as bricks, beams, boards, floors, or ceilings, but instead are relationships among simpler patterns and the environment. An example of a simple architectural pattern is shown in Figure 6.3.

When everyone involved knows the pattern language of the building, Alexander says, it is easy for the builders to construct an edifice that is harmonious with the lives and work of the building's users. The patterns constitute a kind of *design language* for communication between builder and inhabitant (see Rheinfrank and Evenson's discussion of design languages in Chapter 4).

The architect's blueprint is a map (actually, an interrelated set of maps) that expresses the patterns and their relationships, and that provides a common language across architect, builder, and client. Although Coplien and Schmidt (1995) have proposed a set of patterns for software construction, the fields of software design and engineering have no generally accepted method of mapping that is analogous to the blueprint—no agreement on the basic patterns of human action that will be composed in a software system. Although we do not yet have a formal method to construct such maps, we do know what we would want from them. The maps would provide ways

- To convey the patterns of action of the domain in which the software will be used, in terms of its basic distinctions, repetitive processes, standards of assessment, strategies, tools, breakdowns, and driving concerns
- To connect the linguistic structure of the domain to the software structures that will support the patterns, and to guide software engineers in implementing those structures
- To provide a basis for measuring the effectiveness of the implemented system in practice

The domain actors would find the map a useful depiction of how they work; the software producers would find it useful to configure client–server networks, databases, and applications to support the actors' work; and observers would use it to guide measurements.

These maps go beyond the standard elements of computer code or program specifications. They represent the domain of action, rather than just the system being built. These maps should cover a number of basic patterns.

- A set of *linguistic distinctions* (verbs, nouns, jargon, etc.), around which people in the domain organize their actions (in personal finance, these distinctions include checks, ledgers, banks, bank accounts, bank statements, merchants, bills, fund transfers, deposits, credits, and interest)
- A set of *speech acts* by which domain participants declare and report states of affairs, initiate actions, signify completions, and coordi-

nate with other people (in personal finance, these acts include pay, deposit, withdraw, transfer funds, reconciliation successful, prepare tax report, and cancel payment)

- A set of *standard practices* (recurrent actions, organizational processes, roles, standards of assessment) performed by members of the domain (in personal finance, these practices include paying monthly bills, reconciling the ledger, putting money into savings, preparing quarterly tax summaries, maintaining positive balances in accounts, earning good interest, having a minimum liquidity level, having a maximum debt level, and getting a credit rating)

- A set of ready-to-hand *tools and equipment* that people use to perform actions; a tool is ready to hand if the person using it does so with skill and without conscious thought (in personal finance, these tools include pens, calculators, checkbooks, databases, tax forms, and monthly reports)

- A set of *breakdowns*, which are interruptions of standard practices and progress caused by tools breaking, people failing to complete agreements, external circumstances, and so on (in personal finance, these breakdowns include errors in writing or coding checks, missing payments, discrepancies between ledger and bank statement, lost deposits, errors in credit reports, lost checks, inability to compile tax data, unresponsive customer-service departments, and broken modems)

- A set of *ongoing concerns* of the people in the domain—common missions, interests, and fears (in personal finance, these concerns include a working banking system, good credit rating, liquidity, low debt, steady income, accurate tax data, good return on investment, and fear of tax audit)

This overall framework is sometimes called the *ontology* of the domain (see Winograd and Flores, 1987). Put simply, an ontology is a conceptual framework for interpreting the world in terms of recurrent actions. Building an ontology of the domain in which software will be used, representing it as a pattern language in a standard notation, and coordinating the work of builders are the central activities of a software architect. These skills are analogous to the architect's skills in creating sketches and blueprints, in using them to coordinate builders, and in using them to help clients assess the results. We call the practice of these skills *action-centered design*.

Business-Process Maps

The important aspects of action-centered design are its emphases on speech acts, on the use of language, and on repetitive actions. This perspective is a distinct departure from the traditional functional analysis of a domain, which describes the domain as a process network—a network of interconnected input–output functions that operate on physical or information objects. Speech acts such as "I request," "I promise," "I have completed the task," and "I am satisfied" are important because they are the motivating force for action. Without them, no task would be declared, initiated, or completed, and no one would know whether anyone else was satisfied.

Human beings engage in repetitive processes in which they coordinate action by standard speech acts. Repetitive processes that become mindless routines are ripe for automation. The skilled designer knows how to observe the repetitive processes by watching what people say to one another (verbally, in writing, electronically, via body language, or through other communications media), and then to offer tools that allow people to complete their repetitive processes faster or more reliably.

The notation of business-process maps (see Profile 6) appears to be well suited as a starting point for maps of repetitive coordination processes (Medina-Mora et al, 1993; Denning, 1992b). This notation needs to be extended to show how a process network is triggered by people acting in their coordination processes. The software system would implement the clients, servers, networks, operating systems, and applications needed to perform the tasks and to transfer data and signals among them. It would also detect people's speech acts, and would use them to trigger functions in the software system.

We propose an interpretation of design that is

- Focused primarily on satisfying the customer, rather than on satisfying the system's specifications
- Grounded in a *language–action perspective* (Winograd, 1987), rather than in a system–dataflow–network perspective

- Based on observations of concerns, breakdowns, standard practices, institutions, and recurring actions, and on production of means to connect those observations with software structures

Action-centered design consists of observing the ontology of a domain, then constructing a workflow map, a process map, and the connections between them. The maps can be used by the software architect to review with the client how the system will satisfy each concern, and to coordinate the implementation of the system with the software engineers. The rudiments of this process can be seen in the examples of the successful software packages and systems that we studied, and in the statements of their designers.

Note that we are *not* advocating that anyone abandon process-network diagrams and other formalisms of software engineering. We *are* advocating that designers learn to look much more broadly, rigorously observing the domain of action and then coupling software tools with actions that people perform and assessments that people make.

We propose this interpretation not as a final answer, but as a preliminary step—an opening for a new direction in software design.

Suggested Readings

Christopher Alexander. *A Pattern Language*. New York: Oxford University Press, 1977.

Christopher Alexander. *The Timeless Way of Building*. New York: Oxford University Press, 1979.

James Coplien and Douglas Schmidt. *Pattern Languages of Program Design*. Reading, MA: Addison-Wesley, 1995.

Peter DeGrace and Leslie Hulet-Stahl. *Wicked Problems, Righteous Solutions: A Catalogue of Modern Software Engineering Paradigms*. New York: Yourdon/Prentice-Hall, 1990.

Peter Denning and Pamela Dargan. A discipline of software architecture. *interactions* 1:1 (January, 1994), 55–65.

About the Authors

Peter Denning is Chair of the Computer Science Department and Associate Dean for Computing in the School of Information Technology and Engineering at George Mason University. As chair of the publications board of the Association for Computing Machinery, he led the development of a far-reaching electronic publishing plan and of new copyright policies for cyberspace.

Pamela A. Dargan is a Senior Software Engineer for a nonprofit company in Washington, D.C. that provides consulting services to the government. She has been involved in all aspects of software development for nearly two decades, and currently designs open system architectures for large government software acquisitions.

Profile

6. BUSINESS-PROCESS MAPPING

When new technologies are introduced into a workplace, the work is not just facilitated: The work is reorganized, whether deliberately or unconsciously. Automation changes the nature of what gets done, and triggers shifts in the work practices. Therefore, technological innovation offers an opportunity for organizational innovation, as has been recognized in the literature on *business-process redesign* (see, for example, Hammer, 1993). Business-process designers lead people in an organization to rethink the overall work process, as a prerequisite to deciding where and how to employ computer support effectively.

The designer in the business-process domain needs to go beyond tools for designing software components and dataflows, to identify the structures of *workflow* and to organize information systems around those structures. The analysis of workflow requires a language for mapping what is done in the work currently, and what could be done in the future. This language is the means to express the *blueprints* that Denning and Dargan (Chapter 6) discuss in their description of action-oriented design.

Levels of Work Process

Work can be understood as a network of commitments and actions, supported by information devices. We can analyze work in an organization at three fundamentally different levels.

Profile Authors: Peter Denning and Terry Winograd

1. *Material processes.* Human activities are rooted in the physical world. Nothing happens without physical objects (including people) moving and changing state. If we ask "What is happening?" the obvious answer at the material-process level is a description of physical activity. In traditional factory automation, material processes—in which physical components are transformed and assembled into product units—are the most salient level. Material-process redesign has been used to move and process objects more efficiently, from the early analyses of Frederick Taylor and the production innovations of Henry Ford, through the sophisticated techniques of modern industrial engineering.

2. *Information processes.* With the twentieth-century shift to a white-collar economy dominated by *information work*, the material-process domain fails to capture what is important about everyday activity. The physical activity of a person sitting at a computer workstation is mundane—talking to people, or moving a mouse and tapping keys in front of display screens. More relevant than the physical activity is the nature of what the talk and tapping are about. Theorists and information-technology providers have developed sophisticated methods to analyze and facilitate the flow of information. Current techniques in areas such as dataflow analysis, database storage and retrieval, transaction processing, and network communication have provided a structure for effective information processing. The information-process level is the focus of most applications offered by the computer industry today.

3. *Business processes.* The information perspective is limited because, in the end, information in itself is uninteresting, just as the tapping of fingers on a keyboard is uninteresting. Information is useful only when someone can do something with it, and doing something implies more than just the handling of further information. What do people do that matters? Here we find the level of business processes, in which people enter into language actions that have consequences for their future activities. When a customer hands a supplier an order form, there is a physical activity (transferring a piece of paper) and an information activity (communicating a form with information about a particular set of goods, delivery instructions, and so forth). But the true significance lies in the business-process activity: It is a request for the

supplier to perform particular actions, in return for which the customer is committed to perform other actions (for example, to make a payment).

The goal of business-process redesign is to identify and design the basic structure of work in the business-process dimension: workflows, roles, acts, and incompletions, all of which create expectations for further behavior by the participants. Business processes are implemented in information processes, just as information processes are implemented in material processes. By moving to a focus on the language–action structure of workflow, rather than on the forms or database transactions, we can develop tools that make use of a higher level of organization.

Many current approaches to workflow management are structured around the analysis of information processes. They begin with a class of information objects—such as forms or stored images—and define workflow as a sequence of actions to be done to and with those objects. The primary organizing structures are the routing of information objects among users and the specification of automatic actions to be taken in that routing. This approach is analogous to material-process automation, in which parts are passed along from one station to another in a factory for processing, with certain of the component tasks taken over by automated machinery.

Traditional workflow management is well suited to highly structured heads-down paper processing, but is not adequate for support of newer modes of organizing work, with middle management reduced and more responsibility given to more highly educated workers, who combine structured work with opportunity-based initiative and who take individual responsibility for quality and customer satisfaction. For mapping this kind of work, a more useful blueprint employs a description based on a language–action model.

Workflow Structures

The building block of work is the person-to-person transaction, in which one person fulfills a request to the satisfaction of the other. This transaction has been called the ActionWorkflow in the products and writings of Action Technologies, Inc. (Medina-Mora et al., 1993), and can be depicted as a sequence of four stages: *request*, *negotiation*, *performance*, and *completion*. It is represented on the maps as a loop (Figure 6.4). Movement from stage to stage occurs when one of the participants produces a *speech act* (see Searle, 1969; Winograd and Flores, 1987). The person making the request is called the *customer* (although the action does not need to involve payment), and the person doing the work is called the *performer*. The purpose of the workflow loop is to reach a conclusion with the customer satisfied.

More often than not, the performer must turn to other people for help. The performer may therefore make a subsidiary request of another person. This action initiates a secondary ActionWorkflow, in which the main loop's performer is now the customer. As each participant turns to others for help, the network expands. The entire network of activities that ultimately participate in the fulfillment of an original request constitutes a business process for that kind of request.

The designer approaches the task of computer facilitation for workflow by first analyzing the workflow structure and finding possibilities for improvement and new functionality. This analysis process, or *work mapping*, uses theory-guided observations and interviews to generate explicit representations of the acts, roles, and incompletions that make up the ongoing flow of work. The designer can use computer-based mapping tools that enable the creation of workflow diagrams in the same way that CAD programs enable the creation of mechanical drawings or circuits (for example, the ActionWorkflow Analyst by Action Technologies). Working with these tools, the anlayst can create and maintain complex representations that cover substantial areas of work.

When an analyst first asks people in an organization, "What is the work here?" their natural response is to start looking at the forms and

FIGURE 6.4   A Workflow Map   This map depicts a business process for reviewing job candidates. It is composed of multiple ActionWorkflow loops, each with the four stages of speech acts. The arrows represent dependencies among the loops, and loops can have multiple instances (e.g., evaluation forms are submitted by several evaluators). (From *The Information Society*, 9:4, October–December 1993, p. 395. Raúl Medina-Mora et al, Taylor & Francis, Inc., Washington, DC. Reproduced with permission. All rights reserved.)

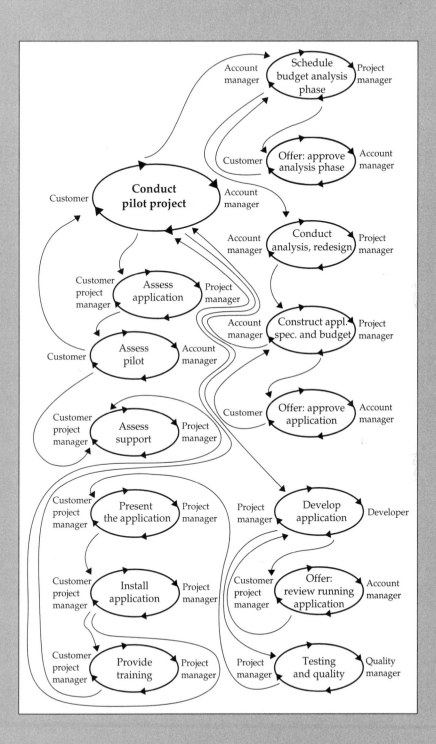

procedures. The designer can move them toward a workflow analysis by pointing out the specific questions raised by the structure: Who are the customers and performers? What are the conditions of satisfaction in each loop? How is each of the four stages carried out? How are the loops related to one another? This questioning leads the people who are familiar with the work to identify the places where gaps and confusions have been causing incomplete workflows, misunderstanding of results, or ineffective information flow. This analysis is then the basis for inventing new forms and procedures, rather than for simply automating the old ones.

New opportunities to improve performance come from the ability to identify, observe, and anticipate potential *breakdowns*, or failures to reach satisfactory completion. From the maps and associated discussions, people can identify places where breakdowns may occur repeatedly, and can see what additional steps or workflows can be put into place to anticipate or cope with the breakdowns. These breakdowns are then the places where new technological support can be valuable. We can apply traditional information-design techniques to provide tools for augmenting people's ability to manage workflow:

- Notifying users about actions that need completion
- Providing users with the specific tools and information to complete a task, in a ready-to-hand way associated with identifying that task
- Managing reminders, alerts, follow-ups, and so on, to keep processes moving
- Giving users an overview of where their tasks fit into the overall processes, both dynamically and through maintaining records of workflow history and providing structured access to those records
- Giving managers an overview of the status of workflow in the organization, both on demand and through generation of regular reports and measures based on workflow structure
- Automating standard procedures and individualized responses, on the basis of the workflow structure

Although the term *business process* connotes a commercial business, workflow mapping and workflow-support systems are applicable in any organization whose size, complexity, and scope make it unrealistic to depend on informal mechanisms of person-to-person coordination.

Software for workflow analysis and support is being used in a wide variety of businesses and organizations (see, for example, Agostini et al., 1993; Schael and Zeller, 1993; Fischer, 1995), integrating computer-based work support with the broader goals and approaches of business-process reengineering (Karagiannis, 1995).

Suggested Readings

Peter Denning. Work is a closed loop process. *American Scientist* 80:4 (July–August, 1992), 314–317.

Layna Fischer (ed.). *New Tools for New Times: The Workflow Paradigm.* Second edition. Alameda, CA: Future Strategies, 1995.

Michael Hammer. *Reengineering the Corporation.* New York: HarperBusiness, 1993.

Peter Keen. *Shaping the Future: Business Design Through Information Technology.* Boston: Harvard Business School, 1991.

nary. The victim was more eloquent. And those crumpled sheets on the bed spoke volumes that those flat white sheets of paper could never match. On those there were only words, words, words.

We are confident that you did not think that this chapter was embarking on a detective story. But why? No doubt our pastiche is not particularly good, but there is enough bad detective fiction around to cover our blushes. So why would no one expect that reading on would reveal "who did it"?

To find that out, we need to shift the question from "who did it?" to "what did it?" What made it clear, before all the pastiche we could muster, that this chapter was never going to be a detective story? The simple answer is the physical book itself. Its heft, its shape, its cover, its paper, and innumerable other things about it tell you, well before you read a word, that the book you are holding is not going to contain a detective novel. Even if a photocopy or a fax has stripped away much of the book's integrity, the remaining page layout, running heads, typography, shape of the chapter heading, indentations, and a tumult of other features implicitly insist that the pages you are holding do not contain a whodunit.

This kind of inference is not just relevant for books. Well-designed media provide peripheral clues that subtly direct users along particular interpretive paths by invoking social and cultural understandings. *Context* and *content* work together efficiently as an ensemble, sharing the burden of communication. If the relationship between the two is honored, their interaction can make potentially complex practices of communication, interpretation, and response much easier for designers and users alike. This relationship is the essence of keeping things simple.

Taking account of context involves more, however, than crafting a well-integrated interface. It also requires taking account of the continually evolving social conventions carried by context. As we suggest in this chapter, it is not enough to design an on-line newspaper that looks like a conventional newspaper or magazine. Designers have to take account of the complex social understanding engaged by the newspaper and underwritten by its physical form. This understanding goes beyond the objects themselves, to the social practices that are—in Gibson's (1979) term—*afforded* by those objects, and that might no longer be afforded if the objects changed. The resources for design are not all in the designer's hands. Many are developed in use. The challenge, then, is not just to design an interface that looks like a book, a newspaper, a magazine, a library catalog, or whatever. It is to engage and develop, in a new medium, the ever-changing social understanding that emerged first around these artifacts and still draws on their material properties.

There are two reasons why it is important to bring the attention of software designers to the interactions between content and context— or between other related divisions, such as center and periphery, content and form, message and medium, or information and noise.

First, the greatest challenge that designers and users face is achieving clarity and simplicity. Yet many discussions of design overlook ways in which peripheral resources can help us to clarify and simplify.

Second, the truly revolutionary impact of the information revolution will be not in the new ways that technology can separate message from medium by making everything digital, but rather in the continually new ways that it finds to recombine message and medium creatively. Software design, in particular, ambiguously straddles divisions of form and content. If we are to go beyond designs that remain heavily dependent on older technologies and forms, designers need to develop a fine sense of the redistribution of resources made possible by software technologies.

This chapter directs attention away from central information and functionality, to the peripheral clues that crucially shape understanding and use. In the future, the role of the designer may lie as much in enabling and seeding new practices and new interpretive strategies as in building new technologies.

Detecting Resources

In opening the chapter with an example drawn from books, typography, and page layout, we may at first appear lost in the Gutenberg revolution rather than concerned with its information successor. The dramatic proliferation of the World Wide Web (Profile 5), however, indicates that both the document metaphor and documents themselves may be as significant to the information galaxy of cyberspace as they were to its Gutenberg equivalent. Furthermore, documents are a powerful example of the way that people use peripheral resources to underwrite the efficient use of all sorts of technologies. We offer document-based examples, then, for two reasons. First, it is still important to understand documents and document use. Second, documents are a specific instance of a more general phenomenon: People read and interconnect artifacts much as they read and interconnect documents, taking into account not just the established text or functionality, but also the clues provided by context.

Consider, for instance, something as simple as a telephone-answering machine. The conventions for its use are not self-evident. A moment's thought reveals that the common message "I'm not here now" is, in the abstract, nonsense. Whomever "I" refers to should be "here," wherever here is, "now," whenever the phrase is uttered. Yet, in practice, despite its formal incoherence, the phrase turns out to be much more efficient than are attempts at formal coherence, such as "If you are hearing this message, then I will not be at home at the time at which you will be calling."

What gives the more pithy phrase its effectiveness? Clearly, the words alone do not clinch the matter. To be understood, they rely on peripheral clues for interpretation. Background clicks and whirs, hisses from the tape, and the recorded quality of the voice itself all help callers to realize that they are hearing a recorded message, and thus prepare them for a message's particular—if in the abstract peculiar—logic. These *peripheral resources* are not usually regarded as part of the information with which information technology is concerned. Yet, appearing unproblematically in the hiss of a recorded message, peripheral contributions can nevertheless be unquestionably informative, allowing the person leaving a message and the person hearing it to communicate with a simple efficiency.

Important though they may be for design, these peripheral resources are not necessarily designed themselves. More usually, they evolve, as people—often unreflectively—enlist the support of contingent properties of a technology to keep things simple. Answering-machine messages once included the clumsy announcement, "This is a recording." As the quality of telephone lines rose relative to the quality of tape recordings, people found that they could drop the introductory phrase. The distinctive tone of the message made the fact that it was a message self-evident. Further changes can render these evolving resources extinct. Now that the quality of the recorded message is again level with that of the live voice, useful peripheral resources have been lost. Callers find themselves addressing a recorded voice as though it were live, so, consequently, clumsy introductory phrases such as "Hi, this is a recorded message . . ." are returning.

Inescapable Evidence

The idea that there is a clear boundary between information and noise, of course, is not a product of new information technologies. Standard accounts of the Gutenberg revolution portray the book as having been a radically new way to liberate information from the con-textual constraints that accompanied spoken language. The informa-tion revolution is portrayed as a continuation of this process, providing more effective ways to free information from restraining material encumbrances.

In attempting to rid communication of peripheral resources, such accounts evoke the old game in which children challenge one another to describe an awkward object, such as a spiral staircase, without using their hands. As a game, this challenge is amusing; in practice, if you have to show someone what a spiral staircase is, it is almost always much more efficient to use your hands—particularly if you can point to an example. The material world is rich with explanatory resources, in part because most of our explanations involve the material world. Abandoning it, therefore, is not only a difficult task, but also a step that is unlikely to make things simpler.

As an example, consider the library. At least since Vannevar Bush (1945) described his idea of Memex (a proto-hypertext system), people have sought to distill information out of libraries. Attempts to extract information from its embodiment have been problematic, because Bush and many of his followers see libraries and books themselves as little more than antiquated storage devices. The trans-ferral of the content of books and other publications to hypertext databases has left behind elaborate and important interpretive resources.

For instance, the piece of information that George Washington said, "I cannot tell a lie" would probably be stored in many different contexts in any conventional American library. Among others, it would be stored in later editions of Mason Locke Weems's biography of George Washington; in Mark Twain's works; in books with titles as varied as *History and Ideology, Our Presidents,* and *Every Child's Own Encyclopedia,* (and perhaps in a book about software design). These different locations are not irrelevant. Where it is stored, how it is stored, and even that it is stored provide important resources for assessing what is stored.

On its own, the sentence about Washington cannot tell us how it should be interpreted and valued. The range of possible interpretations goes well beyond a simple assessment that some of the books contain correct information and others contain falsities. Historical fables, after all, whether true or false, may be highly illuminating. But the reader still has to work out whether the statement appears in a fable, and, if it does, in what kind of fable: sincere, ironic, humorous, popular, local, widespread, and so forth.

In practice, readers rarely have to consider all available options. Before they come to the sentence, the particular bound book and unfolding linear narrative will have significantly narrowed the interpretive options. One book will provide reliable indicators of what Washington is likely to have said, another what Twain wrote, yet another of what Weems said Washington said, and so on.

People need to know more than what a piece of information means. They also need to know how the information matters. Evaluation requires more than the information itself, which cannot validate its authority any more than a bad check would be validated by writing "good" on its face.

All books and all the bits of information that they contain are not equal. Different kinds of books efficiently provide different kinds of warrant for the information they offer. With book technology, society has developed conventions that allow both writers and readers to use the material objects themselves to limit interpretation, to warrant information, and to keep communication relatively simple. Designers of digital libraries, or even just designers of other document forms, such as pages for the World Wide Web, will need to find and create alternative resources for the interpretive reliability and simplicity provided by older communicative artifacts.

Picking Up Clues

Schooling may stress abstract information, but students learn a great deal more than schooling explicitly stresses. As they read comics, novels, biographies, mysteries, true crime stories, and textbooks, they learn to distinguish different types of books and the types of information contained within those books. With the help of external clues to interpretation, readers confidently learn to distinguish fiction from nonfiction; to distinguish books of detective fiction from books about detective fiction; and to recognize irony, parody, and pastiche as distinct from the forms on which they are based.

Moreover, people approach more than books in this way. They seek interpretive clues in the periphery of all sorts of communicative interactions. They distinguish different kinds of movies, videos, and TV programs, and can usually flick unerringly from news breaks to soap operas, from docudramas to movies, from advertisements to MTV videos, navigating as much by the context as the content. They learn to distinguish almost on sight consumer products from commercial appliances, personal media from professional media, educational software from entertainment software, and so on.

In learning to recognize and distinguish information, people behave like good detectives, continually working with the clues that they find at the scene, extrapolating from partial evidence to the whole story. To engage these practices, good designers, by contrast, need to be more like bad criminals than good ones, always leaving behind a traceable array of clues.

Of course, designers and users are not always in cahoots. Although some designers and users have corresponding interests, there are other designers who, for a variety of reasons, set out to penetrate users' defenses by scattering misleading clues. We see this approach in junk mail that imitates personal mail, in advertisements that imitate rock videos, and in bogus software that imitates genuine programs. In each case, if the center looks authentic (if it does not, the subterfuge fails immediately), wary users continually look for more and more refined clues in the periphery to distinguish the genuine. The designers, meanwhile, are equally trying to craft a more perfect subterfuge.

Material Witnesses

Attempts to separate the material form from an informational content are highly problematic, both in theory and in practice. To take a practical example, consider the daily newspaper. At first glance, it certainly seems reasonable to think of separating the material form from the information, the paper from the news. Yet, to date, the conventional newspaper survives, despite the arrival over the years of radio, newsreels, television, and news databases, each of which was thought likely to make newspapers irrelevant. Highly visible failures to sell online news—such as Knight-Ridder's Viewtron, which lost $50 million (DeGeorge and Byrd, 1994)—show that this task is far from easy. The material contribution of the medium helps to explain why the newspaper survives.

The newspaper does not just report news; it makes news. The underlying paper has a significant role in that making. First, only certain items can fit within the bounds that paper provides. In general, what gets in is news; what does not is not news. Second, the circulation of unchanging newsprint through a society (ensuring that the same news is available to everyone at roughly the same time) turns those items into *social facts*—common to a broad readership. Politicians are disturbed to find their scandalous behavior splashed under the headline not because the story is news to them, but because it has become front-page news to 100,000 other people. The newspaper has been described as a "1-day best-seller"—and, as with other best-sellers, the point is that everyone is reading it. It is the collective selection, presentation, and circulation of information that turns that information into news.

Consequently, the idea that readers should gather items individually out of a vast database misses the point. Although the resulting copy might look like a conventional newspaper (as in Figure 7.1), the items included would lack the social status and warrants that come from the combination of editorial selection, location on the page, and wide distribution. The personally tailored, genuinely unique newspaper, selected privately from a database, offers neither physical nor social continuity. Each individual output would be no more than that—individual, with little or no indication of its social significance.

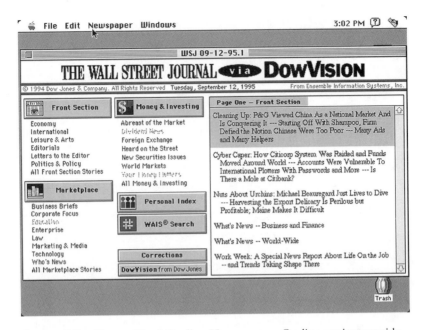

FIGURE 7.1 **Personalized On-line Newspaper** On-line services provide users with personalized information, duplicating the look of a paper newspaper on the computer screen. These custom pages have a superficial appeal, but they miss the underlying social significance of a newspaper, which draws its power from the shared communicative space created by the social traditions of how a newspaper is edited, organized, and distributed. (Reprinted by permission of Ensemble Information Systems.)

In recognition of the newspaper as a maker of news, both broadcast and on-line news services tend to defer to—and often to report—what major papers carry. Furthermore, in acknowledgment of the significance of the newspaper's physical structure, these secondary sources often note whether the story that they report was on the front page or in the business section, and, occasionally, whether it was above or below the fold. In relaying news in this way, broadcast forms indicate that, even though they too make news, they lack the resources to structure news in similarly informative ways. On-line sources, in general, make it clear that they do not even make news. What they carry as news comes from other sources—primarily print media. As yet, however, they have not developed ways to provide and warrant information on their own. Their dependence on the conventional press strikes us as an instance of a significant, more general point. If designers fail to understand how to encode and warrant information within new technologies, they and their new designs will remain unnecessarily dependent on old technologies.

Border Guards

If information is to be socially encoded and decoded, as it is in the newspaper, the peripheral clues must inevitably circulate with the information. The extent to which peripheral objects are shared varies considerably with the type of social interaction and the type of technology. In face-to-face communication, a speaker can use words such as *I*, *you*, *here*, or *that*, knowing that listeners have access to the same periphery.

Similarly, with fixed objects, people can predict with reasonable confidence what clues will be available for future participants. For example, a building remains in a fairly continuous relation to its periphery. As you approach a building, you meet an array of architectural strategies designed to refine these expectations: The landscaping, the relation to neighboring buildings, the massing, and the color all tell you about the building. The ways in which pathways lead you to the building—to the front, around the side, through the middle—further develop your sense of the interior spatial relations and even of the interior social relations. An architect can rely on the presence of these fairly stable objects in the periphery to give a visitor much of the code required to read the building itself.

When interaction is no longer face to face, or when objects no longer have a fixed periphery, use of the periphery is inevitably more complex. When objects travel across space and time, only certain aspects of the original context travel with them. Instead of working in juxtaposition to a relatively unchanging, broad periphery, users have to rely on a far narrower band of unchanging features. We call this area the *border*. Although partial, the border can be helpful. For instance, at the opening of this chapter, we were able to use words such as "we," knowing that the names of the joint authors would be evident, and "this," to refer to the book in your hands. Of course, the border has its limits. We cannot use "now," or "over there," because we have no idea when or where the chapter might be read.

Book covers provide a well-used example of a border resource becoming established. Before the nineteenth century, booksellers bound most books for individual customers, so readers of a book did not all see the same cover. Consequently, a shelf of eighteenth-century books, although it may look beautiful, is usually not informative; it is just a row of large books in calfskin bindings, which tells you more about their owner than about the books' content. By the twentieth century, publishers had taken over the process of bookbinding, and all copies of a particular edition had the same cover. Book covers developed into a highly informative social resource. Look along a shelf of contemporary books, even without reading the titles or cover copy, and it is relatively easy to recognize the types of books—to distinguish the adult encyclopedia from the children's, the political-science treatise from the pot boiler, or whatever.

Admissible Evidence

People learn to interpret the information within buildings or books according to the *type* of building or book in which they find it. Drawing on literary terms, we call these types *genres*. Just as, in literature, deciding whether a piece is a short story or an essay makes a great difference to interpretation, so, more generally, recognizing the genre of a communication or of an object is important. To return to an early example, the genre established by the hiss of the answering machine allows you to leave a simple salutation that a caller can decode despite its problematic logic.

Genres also allow similar information to have different interpretations. The request "Don't miss this event!" on a softball invitation has a meaning distinctly different from the meaning it would have in a memorandum from the boss. Indeed, people are implicitly considering these differences whenever they choose a particular type of communication: the telephone for an informal chat; electronic mail for a reminder; a memorandum for a message with authority; a business letter for a formal bid, and so forth. By choosing a certain border for their message, they are attempting to constrain the interpretation of the message.

Genre is an important concept in software design for three reasons:

First, in any form of communication, genres engage socially shared knowledge. Establishing the genre for a particular communication—whether it be academic essays, collegial electronic-mail notes, film noire, music videos, or computer games—draws on knowledge shared within the groups that use these particular forms. The more that a level of shared expectation can be assumed, the less needs to be said explicitly about how the information should be read. Conversely, the less that is shared, the more that needs to be said, and the harder communication becomes. The borders of genres provide sturdy yet light scaffolding for the simple coproduction of complex structures. In this way, they are central to the task of keeping things simple.

Second, because information is always formed with regard to one genre or another, understanding genres is crucially important to dealing with the demands of the information age. So, for example, one way to make *knowbots* more efficient at navigating through databases is to make them responsive to genre cues. They can then distinguish (as readers do) the different values of the same sentence occurring in the *National Review*, the *Nation*, the *National Inquirer*, or the *National Lampoon*, using broad generic clues rather than specific and particular knowledge of periodicals and magazines.

Third, as we argue in the final two sections, to fulfill their potential, new technologies require new genres. These genres emerge naturally, and can also be the subject of conscious design.

Breaking the Law

So far, the picture of genres that we have painted is inherently conservative. We have primarily noted ways in which it is either important or helpful to stay within the bounds set by genres and their borders. But that is not the whole story. Design evolves and innovates to a significant extent by crossing boundaries, rather than respecting them; by flouting conventions, rather than by heeding them. In breaking through the old, we open new frontiers.

Breaking the bounds is particularly familiar to good artists, who continually push at the constraints of their chosen forms. Their transgressions often involve a two-step process: As unseen boundaries are crossed, they are simultaneously brought to light. In raising the condemnation that "this thing is not art," for instance, artists force people to think about what art is, what its conventions are, and what results from conforming or not conforming to them.

Crossing boundaries is not always beneficial. Staying within the old forms may fail to engage and develop new types of interpretation. But paying no heed to established conventions may fail to engage any coherent interpretation at all. It takes a fine sense of genre to negotiate a path between these two extremes, and the right path is often the subject of much debate over the development of new expressive forms.

In jazz, for instance, Miles Davis claimed that Wynton Marsalis was too respectful of old forms to go anywhere new. Other musicians, however, criticized Davis for moving too far beyond conventional forms to be understood. Almost every time that he moved across musical boundaries, Davis was charged with incoherence. (One reason that Davis disliked the reverence paid to older jazz forms was that he had played them when they were new and judged unintelligible: "Don't tell me the way it was. Hell, I was there . . . no one wanted to hear us when we were playing jazz," he once complained.) Before long, however, it usually became apparent that he had built a new audience for his work, and a new frontier for musicians—often led by Davis himself—to cross.

In a time of changing technologies, it is not surprising to see a profusion of new genres. Through techniques of mixing, dubbing, cutting, and sampling made much easier by the wider availability of recording equipment, hip hop has revolutionized older forms of contemporary music. Hypertext technologies, poaching strategies, and Internet *zines* have innovatively disrupted conventional ways of writing and reading. And cheap editing technology, on the one hand, and the disruption of linear control provided by video players and CD recordings, on the other, have led to creative changes in both video and film. When technology forces the pace, designers—like artists—need to keep an eye not just on emerging technologies, but on the emerging interpretive genres as well. The most responsive will, like

Davis, be capable of developing new forms, and of bringing new audiences into being.

New Forms of Escape

In new media as in old, the general context crafted by designers provides individual producers and consumers with key resources for coproducing the content. Media are clearly no longer neutral carriers. As new genres evolve, old boundaries are erased; what was once the border is absorbed into content, and new borders emerge elsewhere.

Theories of design, however, sometimes shy away from blurred distinctions. Computer design clung too long to an oversimple division between software and hardware. Apple Computer's managers, for example, may have been fatally indecisive in failing to make up their minds whether the company was dealing in hardware or software, and in failing to discover how to avoid the dilemma. Now, new shifts in software are making previously clear distinctions even trickier to maintain. Classic applications—such as spreadsheets and word-processing programs—make software appear as form or content provider. But the software is more intricately a part of the content in media such as computer games, MOOs (a game-based, shared, virtual environment in which on-line participants working on individual computers can communicate and program collectively in real time), HTML pages on the World Wide Web (see Profile 5), and complex documents in SGML (a sophisticated markup language widely used to translate books and other documents into digital form).

As the distinction between program and content is becoming blurred, the distinction between software design and other forms of design is becoming harder to maintain. With games, is it possible to ask where software ends and content begins? In MOOs, are participants building a room engaged in design of content or doing collaborative programming? Is designing a home page for the World Wide Web a matter of document design, multimedia design, or software design? Can the task of design in cases such as these be simply divided between software designers and content designers? If it cannot, does software design teach the skills required for this sort of work?

As the technology shifts, software designers will need to acquire many of the skills and intuitions of other designers. (And, conversely, other designers will need the software designer's skills.) Both will have to develop a sense of the continual evolution of genres and of the way in which people's changing understandings of what is peripheral, what is part of the border, and what is at the heart of a design help to drive that evolution. Given an understanding of these interrelations, designers can influence the direction of evolution by seeding new genres, creating new audiences, and establishing new repertoires, much as artists do.

Design of genres, in our view, is the way to approach design today. New technologies are proliferating, as is the ocean of information with which they have to deal. New forms, genres, and conventions to accommodate technologies and information to human use seem, by comparison, to be lagging behind. The challenge for the future is not to develop new technologies, on the one hand, and new sources of information, on the other. Instead, we need to seed and develop new interpretive conventions to make both the emerging technology and the information more manageable simultaneously.

The future of design in information technologies lies not in developing means of increasingly full re-presentation, but in allowing increasing amounts to be underrepresented; not by increasing what is said, but by helping people to leave more unsaid; not in refining abstractions, but by making use of their inevitable impurity; not by making more explicit, but by leaving as much as possible implicit, and in the process keeping things simple.

Suggested Readings

John Seely Brown and Paul Duguid. Borderline issues: Social and material aspects of design. *Human–Computer Interaction* 9:1 (Winter, 1994), 3–36.

Marshall McLuhan. *The Gutenberg Galaxy: The Making of Typographic Man.* Toronto, Canada: University of Toronto Press, 1962.

Geoffrey Nunberg (ed.). *The Future of the Book.* Berkeley, CA: University of California Press, 1996.

Walter Ong. *Orality and Literacy: The Technologizing of the World.* London: Methuen, 1982.

Adena Rosmarin. *The Power of Genre*. Minneapolis, MN: University of Minnesota Press, 1985.

JoAnne Yates. *Control Through Communication: The Rise of System in American Management*. Baltimore, MD: Johns Hopkins University Press, 1989.

About the Authors

John Seely Brown is Chief Scientist of the Xerox Corporation, and is Director of the Xerox Palo Alto Research Center (PARC). He was a founder of the Institute for Research on Learning, and serves on the advisory boards for a number of design and education programs, including at MIT, Carnegie-Mellon University, the University of Michigan, and the New School for Social Research.

Paul Duguid is a consultant at Xerox PARC and at the the University of California, Berkeley. He has written numerous papers jointly with Brown on situated learning and professional practice, for publications ranging from *Organizational Science* to *Educational Technology*.

Profile

7. MICROSOFT® BOB™

Microsoft released its Bob software in early 1995, promoting Bob as a new class of software for a new population of computer users. Bob's target was the home computer user—not the office computer user who brings work home, but rather the novice who might buy a computer and software primarily for home use. Realizing that the intended audience was widely seen as computer-phobic, Microsoft's designers addressed the intimidation factor head-on. They consciously designed every aspect of the software, the promotional campaign, and the larger periphery, to create an impression of a new *genre*—something dramatically different from previous software applications.

In Chapter 7, John Seely Brown and Paul Duguid point out the contextual information that is conveyed by the binding and physical design of books. We differ in our interpretations, for example, of the Encyclopedia Brittanica and a children's encyclopedia, even though both may contain information about George Washington. In a similar way, Microsoft wanted Bob to be accepted as a computing environment that is fundamentally different from office software, even though both may have a word processor, calendar, electronic mail, and so on.

The Bob interface immediately sets a tone that distinguishes it from Windows, the various *Works* packages, and the other popular operating environments. In place of the familiar desktop metaphor that has dominated user interfaces since the Xerox Star (Profile 2), the user is faced with a cartoon picture of a room in a home (Figure 7.2). A cozy fire burns in a fireplace, surrounded by comfortable furniture. Familiar objects, such as a calendar, a checkbook, and a notebook, are scattered throughout the room. By clicking on these objects, the user

Profile Author: Terry Winograd

FIGURE 7.2 At Home with Bob
(*Source*: Screen shot(s) reprinted with permission from Microsoft Corporation.)

moves into specialized applications for household information tasks, such as scheduling, bill paying, and letter writing.

The room-based metaphor was not original to Bob—it appeared in a number of early Hypercard applications (see Profile 10) and is the basis for the Magic Cap interface for portable communicators. In Magic Cap, as well as in interfaces to several on-line services, (such as Apple's E-World), the metaphor is extended to include multiple rooms, streets, and whole cities. The design assumption behind all these interfaces is that novice users will find it easier and less daunting to operate in a computing environment that mimics the literal look of their physical environment, rather than being focused on a desktop. The message to the user is clear. Bob conveys an immediate impression of "This is not an office—it's not heavy-duty business or technical stuff."

Bob goes further toward pop culture in employing cartoon characters as the primary representation for interactions with the user. Rather than using the abstract *dialog boxes* of most current interfaces, Bob communicates with the user through an animated character, such as a cute little bunny rabbit, or a squawky petulant parrot (the user gets to choose from among a cast of characters with different personalities). The use of characters is based on research done by Clifford Nass and Byron Reeves at Stanford University, on social responses to communication technology (Nass and Reeves, 1996). Nass and Reeves study how computer users project human social traits onto the computers (and other communications devices) with which those users interact. For Bob, they developed ways to take advantage of this natural act of projection, attempting to increase the user's feeling of mastery and connection to the program. Even the wording for each message is tuned to the personality style that the user chooses for her *personal guide*. Hopper the bunny might say "I think you might want to save this file before quitting." Ruby the parrot might squawk "Hey! You forgot to save that."

In more subtle ways as well, Bob's interface attempts to convey a sense of simplicity and absence of difficulty. For example, representing applications with physical objects in a room leads to a feeling that you can easily know everything you need to know. You do not have to cope with a disk full of complex file hierarchies and files. Bob presents a small closed world with only the things you need—a few standard simple-functionality applications for common tasks. This simplicity is carried through in the finer details, such as in the menu of different styles for composing a letter, which offers a few standard formats for different styles of correspondence. Making choices in Bob is more like choosing food at McDonalds than like shopping at the supermarket. Facilities for common tasks come prepackaged with a few standard variants, so the user has little need to remember alternatives, to master skills, or to make complex decisions. Unlike much software on the market, Bob does not entice the user to become an expert—there is no challenge of mastery. The message to the beginner is "You're as good at using the system as anyone else is, so go ahead!"

In addition to "It's simple," the other predominant message is "It's fun." The cartoon characters (referred to as "Bob's friends") are intended to be amusing. They engage in a *social idle* when the user is not doing active work: They perform animated sequences (like the ones in Brøderbund's Living Books for children), make comments, and in general try to keep the user amused. A character's responses to the same inputs may differ from time to time in nonmaterial ways (they convey the same message, but say it differently or perform a different animation). Like Kid Pix (see Profile 3), Bob blurs the boundary between productivity software and entertainment software. You are getting tasks done, but you are also being entertained.

The messages conveyed by the software itself are reinforced by the peripheral elements. The name *Bob*, to start with, sets a tone unlike the one conveyed by *Microsoft Works*, or *OS/2*. No manual comes with Bob, but in the box you find the premier issue of *Bob Magazine*, which is formatted like a magazine, and contains stories such as "Setting up Bob: Simple steps to put Bob on your computer." The packaging and advertising prominently feature a nerdish smiley face, with glasses bearing a resemblance to the ones worn by Microsoft founder, Bill Gates. The slogan under the logo is "Introducing hardworking, easy-going software everyone will use," and the examples on the front of the box include "Write a letter to Mom" and "Get the pet to the vet."

The press releases and extensive advertising campaign for Bob further reinforced a consistent image. Radio advertisements urged "Be the first on your block to meet Bob," against a background of country music and what sounded like a friendly neighborhood get-together. Print and TV advertisements struck a similar note.

Although Bob stands out as a notably large, carefully orchestrated, conscious attempt to design the periphery of a product, it is not the first. Many successful designs have exploited peripheral communication to help lead users to understand and adopt new technologies. Brown and Duguid (1994, p. 13) describe the original Macintosh packaging:

> To make the point that it was not "just another computer," for instance, the Macintosh was not shipped in just another box. Designers produced a skillfully designed portable context that would travel with the computer and help new users cross the distance between their everyday world and the highly circumscribed environment of the device. Opening the box began a carefully structured physical and conceptual induction into Macintosh practice. Objects were oriented to be manipulated, boxes nested within boxes, and icons intriguingly directed the new owner toward a computational world of objects, nested files, and icons. The *Tour of the Macintosh* began long before the user actually ran the program of that name.

When we speak of designing the user's experience, we are speaking of the periphery as well. The experience of a software design does not begin and end with running the program, but encompasses a larger world that includes the box, the product name and promotion, and more. This larger world, as well as the software itself, is a challenge for effective design.

Suggested Reading

Clifford Nass and Byron Reeves. *The Media Equation*. Cambridge: Cambridge University Press, 1996.

An interview with DAVID KELLEY

by BRADLEY HARTFIELD

The Designer's Stance

The designer has a passion for doing something that fits somebody's needs, but that is not just a simple fix. The designer has a dream that goes beyond what exists, rather than fixing what exists.

David Kelley is one of the most visible product designers in the world, especially in the world of high technology. He founded and heads IDEO, a firm that has been widely recognized for quality in design (Profile 8), and teaches product design at Stanford University. Although most of the products that Kelley and his firm have developed over the years are not primarily computer software, the firm has been one of the pioneers in interaction design.

In this interview by Bradley Hartfield, a software designer and teacher in human–computer interaction, Kelley explores the boundary between design and engineering, and describes the place for creativity and openness in design. He emphasizes the degree to which successful design depends on a design mindset: one that is open to possibilities and ready to take risks in a *creative leap* into possibilities that are not yet defined and whose consequences are not yet visible.

Kelley's apparent message is not surprising: Good design takes creativity. His deeper message is that creativity is not a matter of genius or of innate talent. A designer can learn and can be trained to develop openness and a willingness to take the creative leap. The designer's environment also plays a major role—the flow of interactions with other people in that environment can either encourage or stifle creative openness. The challenge to the software-design profession is to foster environments, both in teaching and in industry, that enhance the designer's potential.

— *Terry Winograd*

Bradley Hartfield: David, let's start with a central issue. What is distinctive about design and designers versus other constructive fields and their practitioners?

David Kelley: There is a basic difference between problem solving and actually creating beyond what the problem calls for. It might help to pose two caricatures—two hypothetical extremes. One is engineering as problem solving; the other is design as creating. In this view, engineers are problem solvers. "This device breaks down when you use it for a long time, so we'll beef up the strength of this weak section"—that's problem solving. The designer, on the other hand, has a passion for doing something that fits somebody's needs, but that is not just a simple fix. The designer has a dream that goes beyond what exists, rather than fixing what exists.

You can fix a problem with a creative solution, of course, but I'm saying that that's not *all* the designer wants to do—the designer wants to create a solution that fits in a deeper situational or social sense. It is interesting that people with design experience are able to see the nuances of what makes something appropriate in design. They don't have any trouble coming up with views; they are critical about products. They think beyond the obvious.

BH: Let's explore the differences between engineering and design. My sense is that engineers are taught a particular way of looking at the world—a particular way of assessing situations—and are given a particular set of tools that they can use to address those situations. They are highly trained in mathematics, so they think that they can have a strong degree of certainty—of proof and absolute truth. From my own experience and from talking to other designers, my sense is that design is almost the opposite of mathematics or engineering. Certainty just is not one of the features that you have—none of your tools can lead to it, none of your insights yield it.

DK: I like to say that design is messy. Engineering—as it is taught, if not in practice—is not supposed to be messy. In engineering, you try to assume away the messiness in formulating the problem. You adopt a starting assumption, such as "Assume a spherical cow." That works only when you are solving a well-formulated problem in which, for the relevant practical purposes, cows can be treated as spheres.

I sometimes give my engineering students problems that begin "Assume that this is a linear situation," which is absolutely false. All the interesting design problems show up when stuff is not linear. But, engineering works with a set of rules, so you solve the problem within the context you are given. Because we are trying to make it fit our equation, we assume that a nonlinear phenomenon is linear. But then we aren't solving the greater problem—the kind of problem that I like to give to my design students.

I can't tell analytical engineering students, "The problem is drunk driving."

What is the problem I'm giving them? There's the point of view of the Mothers Against Drunk Driving, there's the point of view of the cops, and there's that of the bartenders (not to mention that of the drivers). What the problem is depends on your point of view. If you say that the problem is drunk driving, engineers quickly get into fixing the car so that you can't start it if you're drunk. That's fine, as far as it goes, but, for the designer, the issues go further, and aren't so easy to formulate.

The designer can handle the messiness and ambiguity, and is willing to trust intuition. Basically, design has to do with intuition. Engineers are prone to assume that intuition does not exist—that you can't make any creative leaps without proving the solution through the use of some equation.

BH: And yet good engineers seem to have a strong underlying engineering intuition about what kinds of solutions should be considered.

DK: That's experience. You feed your intuition by having plenty of experience. Good engineers are really designer–engineers—designers in every sense of the word. I'm just saying that the engineering profession has a self-image that it is based on mathematics and certainty. It justifies its status that way.

BH: You suggest that a designer's approach to a problem situation is dramatically different from that of an engineer. Is that a result of temperament, of training, or of experience after training?

DK: It's certainly a matter of training. I have had good luck taking artists and turning them into designers in the engineering–design sense. They learn the technical base, such as being able to calculate what kind of load a strut can take. Artists, because of their training, have learned to be more open ended, rather than problem oriented. Their training includes "Do something with this clean sheet of paper." They've learned to do something cool. Sculptors, in particular, seem to take well to becoming engineer–designers.

Everyone has the potential to be creative. The proof of that idea for me is the creativity of little kids. Little kids all draw. The refrigerator in a kid's house is full of drawings. Somewhere along the line, some teacher says, "Johnny, that's not a very good picture of a horse. Billy's picture is a good picture of a horse." Then it's all over—Johnny doesn't draw anymore. Kids are inherently creative. Somehow, some designers have been allowed to have experience that allows creativity to show up, to get away with it, to know that their horses are different but are just as good, if not better.

Engineers have been trained to follow a methodology. Whatever comes up, they are supposed to apply the methodology—to analyze and synthesize. At Stanford, we have a program in product design that accepts engineers and tries to move them beyond this methodology. First, we loosen up the students—make them improvise, make them take risks, break cultural sets. People who are willing to loosen up can make great designers, but they have to be willing to take a chance.

When I was a student in the sixties, I took a class where they blind-folded us and had us walk around and feel leaves on trees. Trained engineers have trouble doing that kind of thing—they get upset. "What are we doing? Why are we wasting our time?" They question the value, instead of going with the experience. Attitude is a result of training; but you can cross the line afterward—you can recover.

BH: In developing courses on design, it has struck me at times that the most you can do is to create a situation that allows students to learn for themselves. You can set up semistructured experiences, you can mentor them, you can help them to become reflective about what they're doing. But you cannot tell them what to do and have them know it—that's just not the nature of design.

DK: For me, the important thing is to set up an environment that makes it okay to try things and explore. Every experience that students have in school pushes them in the opposite direction. We want to say that it is okay to fail, it is okay to try something that doesn't work out. We're going to reward a spectacular failure in the same way we reward a success; that's not true in most situations.

Another aspect of training that comes up these days is the importance of hands-on experience. We have classes at Stanford now in the mechanical-engineering department on *mechanical dissection*. Twenty years ago, you didn't have classes in mechanical dissection. All the kids coming through the mechanical-engineering program had already taken apart cars and appliances, and had a toolbox full of tools in the car that they could use to dismantle things and fix things. Today, students in mechanical engineering know the subject from textbooks.

Their hands have never been soiled, so to speak. So, we need to get them back in touch with the physical phenomena. They've built programs on the computer. That gives them a sense of satisfaction of creation, but it's different from mechanical fiddling. They don't get the feel of using a screwdriver to tighten a screw—of having it resist turning, or slip off. The physical experience gives a different feel for what happens with mechanical devices.

BH: What do students learn about design through these experiences?

DK: The term *design* can be misleading. When I say "I'm a designer," people sometimes ask me what I think of the color of their drapes. Their image of a designer is Calvin Klein. Even when you say "product design," the word *design* is a problem.

I like the fact that *design* has such a broad usage—that it is used in so many different contexts and is cross-disciplinary. A narrower definition might be more comfortable, but it would not be accurate. In my opinion, design in companies ought to be like marketing or manufacturing. We now have engineering or product-development departments with their own vice-presidents and official roles in the process, but we don't have design departments. I think we should (see Don Norman's account in Chapter 12). Design defines what it—whether it is drapes or software—ought to be. By contrast, engineering *does* it. Engineering is implementation.

Design has three activities: *understand*, *observe*, and *visualize*. Remember, design is messy; designers try to understand the mess. They observe how their products will be used; design is about users and use. They visualize, which is the act of deciding what *it* is.

BH: What you mean by "deciding what *it* is?"

DK: If I'm trying to design a tape recorder, I can create one that's yellow that you can dunk in water; I can create one that's highly precise; I can create one that has 27 heads or scads of features—that's what I mean by "deciding what *it* is."

When we think of software designers, we picture them in front of the screen. When we think of product designers, we think of them making prototypes. When we think of fashion designers, we picture them cutting out the fabric and making a dress. The key point of design takes place before any of those activities occur, and it requires making an uncomfortable leap—uncomfortable even for the most fluid and flexible people. This leap is the act that needs to come before implementation.

BH: Why is this leap so uncomfortable?

DK: A good problem in design is one for which you aren't sure that there *is* a right answer. In engineering, you might set out to make a tape recorder that meets certain performance or cost specifications. You can feel comfortable about making that tape recorder; you might be able to meet those specs, or you might not, but you're not taking a big risk. The risk is a technical risk, which is not the same as a design risk. When you're doing design, you're making a decision to create a thing, and you don't know who might say "That's the wrong thing." It could be a marketing person, it could be the user. You have to make the leap first, and you can't feel comfortable about the leap because it's too uncertain.

BH: What does it take to leap well?

DK: Who's good at leaping? People who have confidence. It's not that they are *comfortable* with it; they have just somehow been anointed with the ability to make this leap, and nobody is arguing. Look at a Steve Jobs; look at how he started Apple. Somehow, during his life, nobody ever successfully discouraged him from having grandiose ideas about what was possible. I've been with him many times when he made a huge list specifying what a product was going to be, and the list wasn't based on anything that was actually possible. He would say, "Oh, a disk drive, that'll cost about six bucks, so I'll put six down for that." Disk drives don't cost six bucks! But nobody ever discourages him from thinking he can do it.

BH: It's kind of a bravado that to another person could border on lunacy.

DK: Well, think about inventors. All my heroes are inventors, starting with da Vinci. If I had to pick one person who was an extreme, who could make the creative leap to what it ought to be, who could dream up things that didn't exist, he would be my choice. People who are good inventors—good designers—don't mind saying, "How about following this path, which doesn't yet exist?" Most people have trouble doing that; they preface everything they say in a brainstorm with "This idea may be stupid, but here it is." They are afraid that someone else will think that their leap is stupid.

Successful designers just send out their vision to the world; and then, when somebody else builds on it, that's okay. They're not protective of their ideas because they're so used to having ideas. A creative designer has an idea a minute. Publicizing an idea is a way to improve on the idea—someone else can build on it, expand it. If you're fluent with ideas, as most design people are, you don't have to be fearful. You don't protect your one good idea because you're afraid you'll never have another good one.

The other point about making the leap is being able to keep seeing a problem from new perspectives. Anybody who has a strong filter on the world forces everything to fit that filter. In our product-design courses, we assign exercises where you take an object and look at it backward, or you draw it from an ant's point of view, or see it as material. For example, think about a computer monitor. It is just plastic with a piece of glass. Maybe I could do something completely different with it.

BH: So design requires inherent flexibility. We need to let objects and ideas assume new aspects depending on their context—we question an object's already-defined purpose or an idea's previously determined meaning.

DK: A central tenet of design is that you have to avoid stereotyping— the designer has to continue to say, "That's interesting! Look at that!" That skill is hard to teach. All you can do is to give people the experience, and to let them extrapolate from it. A good designer has always had substantial experience. If you ask designers "What's design?" they can't tell you. But a designer who has had experience knows what design is.

BH: How do you organize your company to foster creative design?

DK: Successful design is done by teams. Creative leaps might be taken by individuals, but design thrives on the different points of view found in teams. You want a multidisciplinary team, what we call *x-func* (cross-functional). You want different brains working on the problem. Otherwise, the person with the power, or the person who speaks the loudest, sets the direction for the whole design. You have to keep a broad perspective at the beginning; you have to be comfortable with the fact that you're not moving forward in a straight line toward the goal (and, project managers *do* want to move forward!); you have to feel comfortable with exploring.

It is important to recognize that there are zillions of possible solutions, rather than just one solution. You look at the universe of possible solutions by making use of different brains, considering different functions, different users, and different manufacturers. After you look as broadly as you can, then you can feel more comfortable narrowing.

If you look broadly, your solutions will be completely different from one another. One of them may be based more on the social issues than on the performance and technology; one may be based on focusing on the user more than on the technology. To get all these points of view, you need a huge team with a broad base.

Later, you can use fewer people on the team, because you know where you are heading. As you narrow the focus, you know better what you need and what you don't. The appropriate people remain interested in the problem, and it continually narrows down as you move toward implementation. It's important to have fewer people as you make decisions. A bigger group can't get anything done; the real design still takes a creative leap. A group can't easily take the uncomfortable leap.

BH: How does the narrowing down process get started?

DK: That's a good question. There are two ways of moving a team forward—through a leader, or through user feedback. In the first case, somewhere in the process, a leader naturally emerges out of the group—what I call the *strong, fair leader* with a strong personality who is willing to lead. This leader is not necessarily the person who set up the team in the beginning—the leader has to emerge naturally. That person will be focused on the solution for the right reasons, allowing the design to go wherever it goes, without injecting a personal bias. Such a leader doesn't have a stake in what specific direction the project goes, but just cares about facilitating its progress.

The alternative is what we call *user-chooser.* You build a customer council of users that is strong enough to make significant decisions about the product.

BH: Outside users?

DK: Yes, the potential users of the product. If I'm developing a toaster, I get 25 insightful homemakers, or a cross-section of people who make toast, and I present ideas to them. I give them several choices and ask, "What do you think?"

Using either approach, you can still make mistakes. The learning has to continue all the way to the end. The driving question is how you narrow down the alternatives—that's the uncomfortable part. Coming up with all the wild ideas and possibilities, that's not uncomfortable—that's fun. Asking the question, "How do you narrow?" is the same as asking, "How do you make the leap, given all the choices?"

BH: Again, it sounds like that is the kind of thinking that requires intuition, or experience.

DK: Yes, experience provides a basis, but that isn't the same as a set of methods or rules. When I get a concrete design question, I love to answer in the form, "It's been my experience that...," because no one can argue with that—it's just my experience. I can't offer clients a comprehensive set of rules or a theory from which I can conclude, "Client: You should do this." But that makes them uncomfortable, and they say to me, "Oh, I thought you were good." Or "I thought this was your business." So, I say, "It has been my experience that this is what you should do."

BH: Clearly, experience is central, but can it backfire? Can you have too much experience, such that every situation seems to be a minor variant of a situation you have already seen and understood—so you don't respond creatively to what is, in fact, always a new situation?

DK: That's an interesting phenomenon. Perhaps it's a sort of a laziness in humans. Once you get to a certain point, you say, "I know that subject," so you stop collecting information about the subject. Then, there's another kind of person, the expert. The expert doesn't have that mentality at all. I don't understand such experts, I just love that they exist.

For example, a concert pianist who plays a piece spectacularly well, after taking a year to learn it, still wants to improve the performance to that next level, not being satisfied with near perfection. A virtuoso isn't even satisfied with perfection. Experts don't fall into thinking they know it. Even though someone may be the top expert in optics, or the most accomplished pianist, she hasn't fallen into that trap of thinking that she knows it. Experts are really narrow and really deep. That's different from a designer's mentality.

BH: In some environments, there can be a tension between *my* creativity and *yours.* In other words, there may be a certain group of people who are expected to be creative, effectively precluding other team members from full participation. How do you avoid this situation?

DK: In a company such as IDEO, where you have many creative people, when someone has a great idea, nobody ends up knowing whose idea it was. It's not branded as *George's idea.* Either nobody knows whose idea it was, because of all the discussion that took place, or everyone thinks it was his or her own idea. Either perception is equally good, and both happen frequently.

In our company, the person who owns the solution is the person who posed the question. If I'm the one who says, "Let's create a new toaster," I own everything that happens, because I initiated the discussion. In most cases, the clients are the owners, because they pose the question. You can hold a brainstorm on any subject you want, any time. Just send out a message that says, "I'm holding a brainstorm at 2:00. Will you come?" And everybody comes. You'd think everybody would say, "Oh, I'm too busy." Not true: People know that they are going to need you to come to their brainstorm tomorrow. So the culture requires you to participate in other people's problems.

You eventually get to the point where you look forward to the brainstorm for two reasons. One is that sessions are genuinely interesting. It's like reading a book or reading the encyclopedia—you learn about a new subject. The other reason is that it's not your problem. The guy who's got the toaster problem has the client; he has to get the design done on time; he has to make that leap that makes us so uncomfortable. The other designers come in totally relaxed, totally free to generate ideas in the toaster area, because it's just fun. They're helping, and the only pressure on them is that they want to help their peer.

BH: You say that clients are often the owners of the problems. How much initiative do you take in helping them to define the problem?

DK: Say that a company comes in and says "We want you to design a new toaster." And I say "We're going to study bread crisping in its generic sense." They say, "Look, I told you just to design a toaster. Get going." They think that the world of what a toaster could be is small. But we might say, "Look, our job is to begin by looking at the history of bread." Maybe we want to see whether they had a better way to make toast in Renaissance France or on the Space Shuttle. We don't want just to design the curlicues on the side of the client's next toaster. Maybe what we're going to find from looking at this history is that the best solution is to put more curlicues on the side, but I always say: "Think about how much more comfortable you're going to feel that we are doing the right thing if we do a broad search and then narrow down."

Breadth takes extra effort at the beginning, but that's the best time—right at the outset of the product development process—to take a step back to see the situation. The design part of the product process takes a small portion of time. The next steps after design have 10 times the cost, time, effort, and emotional stress. Then, manufacturing incurs 10 times that. So time invested at the beginning isn't wasted; we make up the cost in later stages easily, by doing the design right.

BH: It seems that there is an implicit tension when you do design in the real world. On the one hand, you've been saying that the design process is inherently unpredictable and you have to be willing to stand naked. You don't know where an idea will go, and you don't know how long it will take to get there. On the other hand, organizations, by their nature, once they reach a certain size and complexity, have a strong need to know—or at least they think they need to know—what the future will be like. How do you balance the uncertainty of design against this need for certainty?

DK: You can't put design in a structure. You can't give a company a methodology manual. If they are unable to accept uncertainty in answers to "When is it going to be finished?" and "What is it going to cost?," I always say to them, "How long does it take you to come up with a good idea?" Of course, that doesn't mean that we should stop trying to be mindful of our process when doing design. Every company should try to extrapolate from what has made a certain design successful—to operate in learning mode.

BH: Can a company learn how to make design projects work?

DK: Let me give you an analogy. Jim Adams, who's a professor in our group at Stanford, writes books on creativity and learning (Adams, 1974; 1986). He uses the example of learning to tie your shoes. When you're a kid and you don't know how to tie your shoes, there's no tension, because you aren't aware that other kids do know. Then, you get to the stage where you know that you don't know how to tie your shoes, so you want to know. The thought of learning how to tie shoes moves into conscious awareness. The prior stage is unconscious.

You've got to be conscious. Companies can't stay unconscious, and say, "We don't know how it happened, so we'll just hire some good people." Once you know that you don't know, that is the opening for all the learning to occur. That's the stage where you're trying to figure out how to tie your shoes, and you're alert when you see other people tie their shoes. You watch.

Then, you get into the next stage, where you have learned recently how to tie your shoes, but you're still mindful when you do it. That's also a conscious state, a good one. Then, you get to the stage where it's automatic: You don't think about it, you just do it. I probably couldn't teach somebody else how to tie shoes, because I don't think about it—I don't remember how I tie my shoes.

You can't quit trying to learn about the process and stop being mindful of it. Companies need to keep striving to understand and improve their design process if they expect better results. But that is not the same as expecting that study will lead to standardizing the process. You think that you've understood a problem, but then it turns out that you cannot solve the next problem in the same way. The typical design situation requires doing something that you don't yet know how to do.

BH: That last phrase echoes what you said at the beginning: that the designer has to dream beyond what exists, as opposed to fixing what exists.

DK: Yes, that is the essence of design. What drives my life as a designer is ultimately the joy of creation, of doing something that works, of working with other people. It's the thrill of hitting that inner need to create, along with that outer need to satisfy other people and to make things go just a bit more smoothly and a bit more elegantly in the world.

Suggested Readings

James Adams. *Conceptual Blockbusting: A Guide to Better Ideas* (3rd edition). Reading MA: Addison-Wesley, 1986. (First edition, 1974.)

James Adams. *The Care and Feeding Of Ideas.* Reading MA: Addison-Wesley, 1986.

Don Koberg. *The Universal Traveler: A Soft-Systems Guide.* Los Altos, CA: Kaufmann, 1974.

Don Koberg and Jim Bagnall. *The All New Universal Traveler.* Los Altos, CA: Kaufmann, 1981.

About the Authors

David Kelley is a Professor in the Design Division of the Mechanical Engineering Department at Stanford University. He is also CEO and founder of IDEO Product Development, America's largest engineering and design consultancy.

Bradley Hartfield is a founder of the Hartfield Design Group, an interdisciplinary interface and strategic design consultancy in San Francisco. Prior to that, he was a vice-president at Fitch, Inc., and a lecturer at Stanford University, where he has played a major role in developing Stanford's program in Human-Computer Interaction Design.

Profile

8. IDEO

IDEO is one of the world's largest and most successful design consultancies, combining industrial design and engineering. Its Palo Alto office has completed projects for many of the high-technology companies of Silicon Valley, and has been responsible for the physical design of many notable computer systems, including early Apple computer enclosures and the colorful Silicon Graphics workstations. IDEO is considered distinctive for its ability to integrate the disparate cultures of engineering and design: It routinely combines creative innovation with pragmatic engineering and manufacturing. IDEO's products (Figure 8.1) include everything from high-tech medical equipment and Apple's first mouse to a lifelike mechanical whale used for special effects in the movie *Free Willy*.

As David Kelley, the founder of IDEO, discusses with Bradley Hartfield in Chapter 8, IDEO's success rests not just on the abilities of individual designers, but even more on an overall approach to design that emphasizes group work and cross-functional development. The IDEO design process calls for an intense focus on understanding the world of the user; on cross-fertilization of disciplines, styles, and personalities; and on the ability to concentrate on functionality, aesthetics, and manufacturability simultaneously.

IDEO was formed as a merger of Kelley's mechanical-design firm (David Kelley Design), and an industrial design firm (ID2) that was created by Bill Moggridge in 1979. In the 1980s, ID2 coined the term *interaction design* to describe its work on graphical user interfaces and smart products. IDEO operates as a federation of small

Profile Authors: Bradley Hartfield and Terry Winograd

165

FIGURE 8.1   IDEO Designs
(*Source:* David Kelley, IDEO. Reprinted with permission.)

design offices with different styles, giving it the diversity to support the breadth of its design interests within a common approach to methodology. That methodology has been explored and articulated over the years through a large number of projects, and can be summarized as a sequence of five interdependent steps:

1. *Understand.* Before attempting to create new designs, the designer needs to understand the context for the product: the relevant technologies, competitive environments, potential market segments, and the current forces for change in the arena in which the product will appear. This step requires doing research on the state of the art, talking with colleagues, and interviewing relevant experts and consumers in the potential market. Through this activity, the designers come to know the problem area intimately and to produce a small set of *key ideas* that will guide the product design. For example, in a project developing portable computers for the Japanese computer company NEC, key ideas centered on the concepts *neutral, essential,* and *creative.* This kind of general orientation gives the design team a common direction, to be interpreted in the light of each specific design area.

2. *Observe.* Once there is a broad direction, it is crucial to focus on the potential users and customers. Observation at IDEO includes conventional methods such as focus groups, and also emphasizes the need not only to observe activities that are tied directly to the intended design, but also to get a broader view of what people do in related areas, what they are used to, and what matters to them. The designers generate concrete representations of the observations that are effective for guiding the work. One technique used by IDEO for communicating observations is the creation of *character maps*: detailed personality and activity descriptions for a small set of envisioned typical users. For example, in developing a product for automobile instrumentation, IDEO developed the characters of Table 8.1. They are fictitious, created to cover a broad range of the different characteristics that the team observed in the potential users of the product. Visualizing these characters helps designers to anchor their thinking about what their designs will mean in practice to the different people who may use them.

TABLE 8.1 **Character Map** This table summarizes the characteristics of four imagined customers of new designs for automobile instrumentation. The personality traits were chosen to be relevant to driving and automobile-purchase behaviors.

	BOB	SARAH	EARL & STELLA	DIMITRI & MELISSA
Location	Los Angeles	Montana	Florida	Greece & Nevada
Age	35	52	70 & 62	24 & 22
Hobby	Work	Riding	Golfing	Hang gliding
Job	Investment banker	Horse ranch owner	Retired from insurance and teacher	Engineer and student
Car (in '92)	Mercedes	Range Rover	Lincoln Continental	Corvette (rent)
Income	High	High	Fixed	Over extended
Personality	A type	Confident	Set in ways	Reckless
Gear	Communication equipment High tech	Dog, rifle	Toys for grandkids	Personal stereo
Misc.	Lives for work	Loves kids and horses	She teases re. his driving	On vacation

(From Bill Verplank et al, "Observation and invention: Use of scenarios in interaction design," Tutorial, INTERCHI'93, Amsterdam, 1993, p. 36. Reprinted with permission of W. Verplank.)

3. *Visualize and predict.* At the third step, the designer's attention finally turns to the object or system being designed. Techniques for brainstorming, sketching, prototyping, simulating, and analyzing designs are intermixed as appropriate for the project. Even in this step, though, attention remains on the user. A central way of fleshing out the details of a design is to develop detailed scenarios or storyboards of a person using the new device (Figure 8.2). Scenarios are fictional stories, with characters, events, products, and environments. They project product ideas and themes into

FIGURE 8.2   Storyboard   A storyboard depicts a sequence of activities in which the object being designed plays a role. By providing a concrete representation for the user, setting, and action sequence, it brings out aspects of the design that are invisible when more abstract specification methods are used. (*Source:* Reprinted with permission of Laurie Vertelney.)

the context of a realistic future. Storyboards are highly visual, using photographs or comic-book sequences of drawings to depict the interactions between people and artifacts. In both scenarios and storyboards, the concreteness helps to reveal aspects of the design that otherwise might not occur to the designer.

4. *Evaluate and refine.*   Once there is a basic structure for the design, the details are filled in, and user testing at a variety of levels is performed to provide feedback. The design team carries out repeated cycles of analysis, observation, sketching, and prototyping, similar to the *spiral* development model discussed by Denning and Dargan in Chapter 6 (see Figure 6.2). At this stage, the cross-functional interdisciplinary aspects are crucial, because

evaluation of each aspect of a design must incorporate disparate evaluation criteria.

5. *Implement.* In the implementation stage, designers focus their attention more on the pragmatic aspects of building the designed object: costs, manufacturability, durability, quality control, maintenance, and so on. The goal of employing cross-functional teams throughout the process is to ensure that these considerations have not been ignored in the previous steps, because in general they cannot be simply patched on at the end. If the design process has gone well, implementation planning should produce no major surprises, but it can require modification of design details.

IDEO designers do not follow this methodology mechanically. In fact, there are several different versions, including ones with three steps, four steps, and seven steps, each rearranging and interrelating the process elements differently. Similar methodologies have guided work at other companies, such as Apple Computer (see Laurel, 1990; Bauersfeld, 1994). The point of a design methodology is not to have a recipe to follow, but rather to have a structure to fall back on—a set of reference points. A designer can use a structured process method as a form of self-reflection, to make the ongoing design process visible and to redesign and improve the process continually, as an integral part of doing design.

Suggested Readings

Bill Moggridge. Design for the information revolution. *Design DK* 4, Copenhagen: Danish Design Centre, 1992.
Penny Bauersfeld. *Software by Design: Creating People-Friendly Software.* New York: M&T Books, 1994.

An interview with DONALD SCHÖN

by JOHN BENNETT

Reflective Conversation
with Materials

There is no direct path between the designer's intention and the

outcome. As you work a problem, you are continually in the process

of developing a path into it, forming new appreciations and

understandings as you make new moves.

Donald Schön has been studying professionals—especially professional designers—for many years. Although his academic home was in a department of urban design, his subjects of interest have ranged from psychiatrists and social workers to architects and jazz musicians. After observing and interviewing practitioners in many domains, Schön was able to characterize the common elements in their practices and their ways of teaching new practitioners. In *The Reflective Practitioner* (1983), Schön drew on examples from these studies to outline the basics of what it means to have and to apply expertise. In a further book, *Educating the Reflective Practitioner* (1987), he delved more deeply into the process of teaching design.

Schön discusses the activity of design in this interview by John Bennett, who has worked extensively with user-interface designers during his 30 years with IBM. Bennett's experience in software design serves as a background for bringing out Schön's broader analysis of design and expertise. Schön describes the different stages through which a designer travels, and notes the interplay of *reflection in action*—the shift that happens when a designer is surprised during the flow of skilled, practiced performance, and shifts to a more conscious mode of analysis while continuing to act. Although software is not Schön's main focus, his observations will be familiar and relevant to practitioners of software design, and complements the discussion of design as a *creative leap* by Kelley and Hartfield in Chapter 8.

—Terry Winograd

John L. Bennett: People working in software design may find it instructive to learn what you have observed in other design communities. One of the key issues that you have written about is the kind of reflection that a designer does while designing. Indeed, the phrase *reflection in action* is identified with your work. Could you say more about it?

Donald A. Schön: We can distinguish reflection in action from everyday action. As we go about everyday life, we all exhibit knowledge in a special way. Although we often cannot say what it is we know, we do know how to take action. We carry out many actions, recognitions, and judgments without thinking about them. In fact, in many cases, we do not even remember how we learned them. Activities as fundamental as walking fall in this category. We could say that our knowing is in our action.

Reflection in action has a different character: It is closely tied to the experience of surprise. Sometimes, we think about what we are doing in the midst of performing an act. When performance leads to surprise—pleasant or unpleasant—the designer may respond by reflection in action: by thinking about what she is doing while doing it, in such a way as to influence further doing. For example, when talented jazz musicians improvise together, they listen to one another and to themselves. Within the structure of the piece and a familiar harmonic scheme, they think—or perhaps feel—what they are doing. While in the process, they evolve their way of doing it. The players keep on playing while, on occasion, noting and responding to the surprises produced by other players.

In architectural design, the "performer" frequently conducts an experiment in the form of a series of drawings, such as those in Figure 9.1. He sketches, for example, how the forms of a building might be butted into the contours of a site. In this process, he may discover—to his surprise—that the contours work against the building's form. In response to this discovery, he may conclude that "the site is screwy," so it requires "imposing a geometry onto the contours." He may then invent such a geometry and overlay it onto his drawing of the contours. He works by drawing, sometimes combined with talking. If he is practiced, he may work smoothly, without stopping. In such an instance, the designer is reflecting in action, both on the phenomena he is representing through his drawing and on his previous way of thinking about the design problem.

In some design situations, on the other hand, the designer responds to surprise by executing what the philosopher Hannah Arendt has called a *stop and think*. Here, the designer exhibits a reflection *on* action, pausing to think back over what she has done in a project, exploring the understanding that she has brought to the handling of the task. She may, for example, construct a new theory of the case, reframing the problematic design situation in such a way as to redefine, interactively, both means and ends.

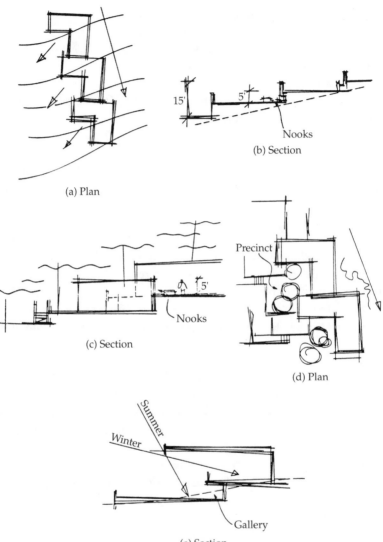

(a) Plan

(b) Section

Nooks

15' 5'

(c) Section

Nooks

5'

(d) Plan

Precinct

Summer

Winter

Gallery

(e) Section

FIGURE 9.1   Reflection in Action   This series of sketches was developed by an architecture student as she tried to fit a building into the contours of a site. The process was an interactive cycle of sketching and then using the sketch to reveal implications for the design. (Adapted from Donald A. Schön, *Educating the Reflective Practitioner*, 1988, San Francisco: Jossey-Bass, p. 51. Reprinted with permission.)

In a third kind of reflection, reflection on *practice*, the designer may surface and may criticize tacit understandings that have grown up around repetitive experiences of designing. For example, he may become aware of having fallen into an unfortunate pattern of design behavior, such as "falling in love with an initial design idea," or "trying to build the diagram."

JLB: Reflection seems to be a critical aspect of design. Are there other aspects that help to define design as a process or an activity?

DAS: If you push the question of "What is design?" one of the key issues that you hit on is a particular sense of complexity. The totality of an artifact, system, or situation includes many elements: materials, a sense of purposes and constraints as the designer sees them, and the designer's sense of the people who will eventually use the artifact resulting from the design process.

A designer makes things. Often, the thing initially is a representation, a plan, a program, or an image to be constructed by other people. Many of the relevant variables cannot be represented in a model; this limitation makes the design process inherently complex. A system is complex in the specific sense that, whenever I make a move, I get results that are not just the ones that I intend. That is, I cannot make a move that has *only* the consequences that I intend. Any move has side effects.

This unpredictability is a central attribute of design—it is not necessarily the defining one, but it is important. It means that there is no direct path between the designer's intention and the outcome.

As you work a problem, you are continually in the process of developing a path into it, forming new appreciations and understandings as you make new moves. The designer evaluates a move by asking a variety of questions, such as "Are the consequences desirable?" "Does the current state of the design conform to implications set up by earlier moves?" "What new problems or potentials have been created?"

Typically, inventions made within a design process to solve present problems produce unanticipated consequences, some of which are perceived as further problems. For example, in the 1950s, product developers at the Gillette Corporation wanted to make their razor blades sharper—perhaps to compete with the newly developed stainless steel blades. They applied a technique of double-honing, which did yield sharper blades. But it had the undesirable side effect of increasing the surface area of the blades, and thereby making them more susceptible to corrosion. The Gillette researchers then found a way of coating the double-honed blades with silicone, which increased corrosion resistance.

Seeing the new problems (and benefits) to which problem-solving moves may lead, the designer may form a deeper understanding of the complex *problem space* in which he is operating. His new understanding of the complexity of the situation may serve as springboard to a new round of problem-solving inventions.

JLB: In your books, you have also used the phrase *a conversation with the materials.* Where does that enter into the picture?

DAS: It is rare that the designer has the design all in her head in advance, and then merely translates it. Most of the time, she is in a kind of progressive relationship: As she goes along, she is making judgments. Sometimes, the designer's judgments have the intimacy of a conversational relationship, where she is getting some response back from the medium, she is seeing what is happening—what it is that she has created—and she is making judgments about it at that level.

One form of judgment in which I'm particularly interested is the kind that I call *backtalk*, where you discover something totally unexpected—"Wow, what was that?" or "I don't understand this," or "This is different from what I thought it would be—but how interesting!" Backtalk can happen when the designer is interacting with the design medium. In this kind of conversation, we see judgments like, "This is clunky; that is not," or "That does not look right to me," or just "This doesn't work." The designer's response may be "This is really puzzling," or "This outcome isn't what I expected—maybe there is something interesting going on here."

JLB: Does a designer ever get this kind of effect from observing how a product of design is used in the field?

DAS: Yes. I once did a study at 3M [Minnesota Mining and Manufacturing], observing how they went about developing new products. Do you know the Scotch Tape story? Scotch Tape was a World War II product, invented by Brandon Cook in the 3M laboratories. He had the idea that you could use transparent cellulose-acetate ribbon, with pressure-sensitive adhesive on it, to mend books. And since you could mend books with it, you wouldn't have to throw the books away, and you could save money; hence, the name *Scotch.*

When 3M put the product out into the marketplace, they discovered that mending books was not the only use that people had in mind. People did bizarre things with Scotch Tape: they wrapped packages, hung posters on the wall, used it to put their hair up in rollers. And then—I guess this would have been in the late forties—3M began to observe what these consumers were doing, and their staff started rethinking the product in light of what they were getting back.

JLB: So, it was a feedback cycle?

DAS: I would say it was a backtalk cycle, because they were not just being told, "You're steering slightly to the left when you should be moving to the right." They were being told, "This product is not what you think it is." Consumers were projecting onto the product meanings different from the intentions of the product designers. As a result, 3M came out with a hair-setting Scotch Tape, a medical Scotch Tape used for binding splints, a reflective Scotch Tape for roads, and so on. I forget how many new uses there were, but they built on the order of 20 or 30 businesses through the differentiation and specialization of the basic product idea. They learned what the meaning of the product was by listening to what people said and by observing what people did.

So, if you were asked the question, "How was the invention made?" you would have to answer, "Through a *conversation* with the users." In this phrase, the term *conversation* does not denote a literal verbal dialog. Rather, it refers to an interactive communication between designer and users in which the messages sent, received, and interpreted may take the form of words, actions, or objects. In the 3M example, Scotch Tape—both the product and its name—conveyed a message to users about the product's intended function. Consumers received that message and transformed it. The designers, in turn, picked up the new messages that users were sending to them through consumer behavior, reframed the meanings of the product that they had designed, and incorporated those meanings in new variations of the product.

JLB: A different aspect of design—one that is commonly observed in software design—has to do with usability. If software is truly well designed, the details of its operation disappear. We sometimes say that well-designed software is obvious or intuitive. People become aware of bad design in its not working.

DAS: Yes, a good designer strives to make the details work so well that they become invisible to the user.

Michael Polanyi was a physical chemist who became a philosopher. His book *The Tacit Dimension* (1966) contains an interesting passage on "What is a machine?" His argument is that a machine is an abstract system whose elements are functions, such as the function of the calculator, the function of the spark plug in the automobile engine, the function of the lever, or the function of the spring. The question of the materials used in the composition of the machine is not pertinent, unless a component fails. Then the issue of what the machine is made of becomes important; until that point, unless the machine fails, its composition is not important at all.

Broadly speaking, we might say that an object's failure or difficulty in use makes visible its insides (how it is made, of what it is made). In a good, smoothly working artifact, materials and mechanisms of operation become, in a sense, invisible—or, as Polanyi would say, *tacit*.

We can illustrate Polanyi's idea of tacitness by considering use of a pen. I'm writing on this pad now with a pen. As I guide the pen along the paper, I am not paying attention to the pressure of my fingertips on the pen. If you numbed my hand, I would have a difficult time writing, although I'm not aware of the pressure at all in the normal course of writing. When I first was learning to write with a pen, I probably was aware of such details.

I'm paying attention to the content of what I am writing, rather than to the process of writing. I manipulate the mark on the paper from a sensory base of which I am systematically unaware. In fact, I have to become unaware of it to become expert in using the pen. The sensory basis on which I use the pen becomes invisible if I know how to use the pen well.

JLB: Then, anything that goes wrong becomes a source of *breakdown*—running out of ink or having to press especially hard because of the surface.

DAS: When my pen begins to run out of ink and I have to press it, then I become aware of the interaction between me and the pen.

JLB: I suppose that this kind of invisibility occurs in other areas of design. I'm thinking of the design of buildings in a city in particular, where we want to be guided by unobtrusive, culturally accepted clues indicating what the building is, where the entrance is. We rely on various cues, indicators, conventional signs—not in the sense of a sign that says "door," but rather of some architectural feature to which a person can relate appropriately—what Brown and Duguid (Chapter 7) call the *border*.

DAS: That's right. In that sense, the city, or the building boundary, or the building is more like interactive software—the software that's made for interaction with human beings on a contingent basis, for a particular purpose. In good design, access to the functionality is more like the visibility of a door, and I suppose is less like the hidden aspects of a pen—at least until the pen fails.

JLB: So far, we have discussed several aspects of the design process. Shahaf Gal (Chapter 11) describes how they showed up in studies that you and he conducted of design students at MIT. Can you say more about that experience?

DAS: Yes, we did a series of case studies of activities in Project Athena—MIT's integrated educational computing environment. Sherry Turkle and I, assisted by several of our graduate students, studied what happened as students were using experimental software that the faculty members were developing in conjunction with their teaching. It was amazing how much difference there was between the intentions that the faculty had for their software and the experiences that people had in using it.

For example, one teacher had developed two programs for students in the mechanical engineering department; they were called McCavity and Growltiger. McCavity was programmed to be an intelligent tutor. It was capable of figuring out your weaknesses in understanding statics and of teaching you what you needed to know, correcting your errors.

The other program, Growltiger, was not conceived as a teaching program at all. The author considered it to be a design tool. It incorporated a finite element algorithm for studying equilibrium forces. You drew on the screen a structure, such as a beam or a truss for a bridge, you specified the materials and the dimensions, then loaded the bridge, and the program would show you deflections (Figure 9.2). It would also show you moment diagrams and shear diagrams for that bridge.

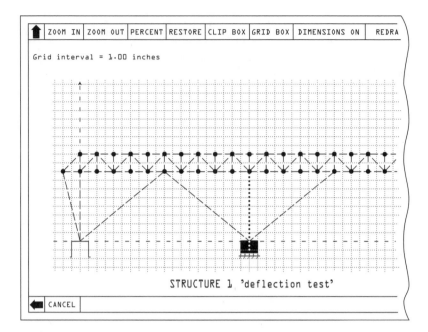

FIGURE 9.2   **Computer Simulation of Structures**   Students could enter a proposed design of a structure into the Growltiger program to simulate the structure's behavior under different load conditions. Growltiger was used by students to explore the space of possible bridge designs, and to find surprises that could lead to major shifts in their understanding of their designs. (From Shahaf Gal, "Building Bridges: Design, Learning, and the Role of Computing," 1991 qualifying paper for Harvard Graduate School of Education. Reprinted with permission of S. Gal.)

We interviewed students about their use of these two programs, and we also observed them working with the programs. It turned out that their dominant response to McCavity—the tutoring program—was boredom. The program was telling them what they already knew. Or, if they didn't know it already, they didn't want to learn it that way. What they did was to turn their intelligence against the program, subverting it so that—instead of tutoring them—it just gave them the answers to their homework problems.

The case of Growltiger was markedly different. Although Growltiger was not intended to be a teaching tool, it functioned as though it were. The students would draw a structure. They would load the structure. They would observe the deflection and say, "My God, how could that possibly happen?" And they would *puzzle* over the surprises. That is a process of reflection in action: interacting with the model, getting surprising results, trying to make sense of the results, and then inventing new strategies of action on the basis of the new interpretation. Students could iterate *very* quickly with this design tool.

JLB: It sounds like the program was genuinely interactive, conversational.

DAS: *Conversational* was exactly the word that was used. Each student was having a conversation with the materials as represented in the computer system. Puzzles came out of the surprising phenomena that the conversation produced—surprising to the students in view of their prior understandings of the way that structures would behave. They had equations available to describe the behavior they were seeing, but didn't think about those equations in relation to the physical phenomena until there was a surprise.

The visual representation was extremely important because it provided something to contrast with the symbolic representation—the formal symbols of the equations. In the conversational interaction with the program, students came to see equations in a different light from what is portrayed in a traditional statics course. A student could consider a question that emerged from experiment, such as "What on earth makes this structure become stiffer as I take material *away*?" and then grasp the formal theory in a new way.

JLB: So what was intended as a design tool was in fact a vehicle for learning, as the students described it?

DAS: That's right. I remember interviewing the graduate student who had helped to develop the program. The graduate student was dogmatic: The program was *not* for teaching. So you could say that the developers of the program did not understand what they had created. What they were designing was not what they thought they were designing. They couldn't discover that until someone was able to observe the program in use and to interview its users.

Here the issue is not only, "How do I make this artifact usable?" but also, "What *is* this artifact?" I don't know what it *is* until I enter into—get access to—the experience that users have with it. That opens up the possibility that, if I learned more about what users did with it, I might think about redesigning it to suit their needs.

JLB: You have also written about the development of taste as one attribute of a good designer.

DAS: I use the term *taste* when I'm talking about the discriminatory appreciation of objects, with respect to, among other things, how well they are designed. A good designer has to have taste. It's clear that having taste isn't sufficient for being a good designer. But you do need to have it, in the sense that you're able to make judgments of quality in many different ways. This discrimination needs to be roughly congruent with the more discriminating of the users for whom you are designing.

JLB: So there needs to be a connection between the taste of the designer and the taste of the people who will be users.

DAS: Unless there is, it is highly unlikely that the designer will produce an object that appeals to those users. In my relationships with doctoral students, I'm trying to help them become designers—designers of research or designers of artifacts. One thing that I watch for is whether they have their own gyroscope—in other words, whether they can tell when they've got something that's good. I look to see whether their sense of what's good meets, at some minimal level, my own sense of what's good. I look to see if there's a big gap that I interpret as a gap in quality, showing that they haven't gotten there yet.

JLB: To say, "They haven't gotten there yet" implies that they could get there, rather than, "Either you have it or you don't."

DAS: Right! It is not at all, "Either you have it or you don't." In fact, it is exciting to see that gyroscope develop over the years—and it does take years.

The reason that the gyroscope is so powerful is that, if students have it, then they can look at their own work—maybe not immediately, but, perhaps a week later—and they can say, "Oh damn, this is terrible!" If they don't have the gyroscope, they can't say that. They keep thinking that their work is good, and when you say it isn't good, they feel terribly let down and also mystified because all they can say is, "What's wrong with it? It looks good to me."

JLB: So taste can't be characterized in terms of specific attributes that you can describe?

DAS: No, it can't. As part of our exploration of taste, every year we have students bring in an object that they consider to be well designed, and then we listen to how they talk about it. We often are surprised by the way that students describe the objects. It is clear that they love these things. One year in particular this point came out in a powerful way with a group of people—one guy brought in his bicycle, another guy brought in his sugar bowl, and another brought in a pen. The way that they talked about these things was profound and moving. Sometimes, we go back and analyze what they say, and we try to discover the attributes that are important to them. We notice that there seems to be a lot of ambiguity, not only with respect to what the relevant properties are, but also with respect to what the relevant dimensions are.

The student who brought in the sugar bowl tried to describe why he liked it—what it was about it that he really liked. He was trying to figure it out, because it wasn't obvious to him—he just knew that he *really* liked that sugar bowl. He talked about the size of it, that he could fit it in his hand. He held it with his two hands on the sides. He liked the sculptural form of it; the ridges on it were helpful. He liked a particular aspect, the place where you could put the spoon in and a depression that allowed you to get a tight fit and closure with the lid. It was a personal statement.

JLB: So he had a personal connection with the attributes of the object?

DAS: Or a personal connection with this particular object was justified by reference to its attributes. The object had an overall appeal for that student. And then, prompted by the situation where he was called on to describe why, he pointed to attributes. But the attributes themselves were not necessarily central—there was something about the design of the object as a whole. The overall impression was distinct from the attributes of the components. As I thought about the students' descriptions, it was clear that the presence of multiple dimensions, multiple attributes of each dimension, and unresolved ambiguity about them, held true across the board for all the objects that the students selected—and about all the objects that we design for people.

When the students are describing an object that they consider to be well designed, I argue that a personal response to the object has a relationship to taste. *Taste* is the familiar term. I suppose *love* is another term—people love certain objects.

Designers need to be able to bridge this gap between the personal and the technical—to be able to work with the medium and to reflect on the surprises, and in the end to produce a design that works both for the designer and for the audience. Not every designer can produce a design that evokes love, but that's not a bad description of what good design is trying to achieve.

Suggested Readings

Michael Polanyi. *The Tacit Dimension.* Garden City, NY: Doubleday, 1966.

Donald Schön. *The Reflective Practitioner: How Professionals Think in Action.* New York: Basic Books, 1983.

Donald Schön. *Educating the Reflective Practitioner: Toward a New Design for Teaching and Learning in the Professions.* San Francisco: Jossey-Bass, 1987.

About the Authors

Donald Schön is Professor Emeritus of Urban Design at MIT. He is best known for his studies of professional practice. He has also written books on other aspects of social organization and technology, including *Technology and Change* (1967), *Beyond the Stable State* (1971), *Frame Reflection* (1994), and, with Chris Argyris, *Organizational Learning* (1978).

John Bennett retired from a long career in IBM research to become an independent consultant, specializing in building partnership and teamwork in multi-disciplinary design teams. He has been active in the ACM Special Interest Group on Computer–Human Interaction (SIGCHI), where he served as conference technical program cochair and on the Advisory Board.

9. THE APPLE COMPUTER
INTERFACE DESIGN PROJECT

In his software design manifesto (Chapter 1), Mitchell Kapor raised the question of teaching software design: What kind of curriculum would foster the breadth of vision and experience that is needed by skilled software designers? In 1990, when Kapor posed this question, there were only a few schools around the world offering instruction in human–computer interaction or in design-related software engineering. These schools provided programs primarily in departments of computer science, with a few in information science or applied psychology. There was little crossover between these technical fields and the traditional design disciplines, and there was little education in the design-studio style of reflection in action, as described by Donald Schön in Chapter 9.

In the few years since the manifesto, new teaching programs have appeared, and older ones have shifted their emphasis in a *design* direction. One of the catalysts promoting this change has been the Apple Computer Interface Design Project, initiated by Joy Mountford in 1991. As a director of research on human–computer interaction at Apple Computer, Mountford was a strong advocate of interdisciplinary work (see Mountford, 1990). She recognized that the students who were graduating from schools into industry did not have the understanding or the skills to do effective design in interdisciplinary teams. To encourage schools to train students for real-world interaction design, Apple set up a competition that called for projects from interdisciplinary student teams. Apple invited selected universities; provided equipment grants to facilitate the introduction of new cours-

Profile Author: Terry Winograd

es centered on the projects; and assigned one of their researchers or designers to serve as a liaison to each site, to critique and facilitate the projects.

In the 5 years that the project has run so far, schools have participated from the United States, Canada, the Netherlands, India, Japan, Sweden, Australia, and the United Kingdom. In addition to technically oriented schools, such as Carnegie Mellon University, the Royal Institute of Technology (Sweden), and the University of Toronto, participants have included art and design schools, such as the Art Center College of Design (Los Angeles), the Royal College of Art (London), and the National Institute for Design (India). Even in those cases where the official connection is with a technical department, the project requires participation from faculty and students in disciplines ranging from art and design to psychology, communication, and anthropology.

The emphasis in the projects is for students to learn how to work in interdisciplinary teams in an iterative, user-centered design process. Students are required to develop prototypes that they test with representative users, and to modify their designs on the basis of the testing results. The deliverables include prototypes of hardware and software, along with documentation (in video as well as writing) of the social, commercial, and educational aspects of the proposed projects. The projects have ranged widely in topics, responding to a broad design brief provided each year by Apple. Figure 9.3 shows one of the projects from 1994.

At most of the participating universities, courses or course sequences have been established around the project. Apple's support has enabled faculty to gain credibility in establishing credited courses across department boundaries, and has provided facilities for student work.

The Apple project was initiated at a time when there was growing interest in teaching software design as a design discipline (see, for example, Winograd, 1990). In addition to the universities that have participated in the Apple project, a wide variety of new and evolving teaching programs are appearing around the world. It is interesting to note both the diversity in their origins and the similarities in the style of teaching that they are developing. Some of the diversity in approaches is illustrated by three teaching programs that have been

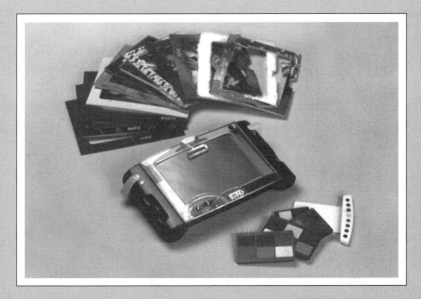

FIGURE 9.3   The PenPal   A student design team from Stanford University developed prototypes of the hardware and software for a portable communications device that enables children to learn by creating images, integrating images with sound and drawing, and sharing the results across the Internet. The design included the physical configuration, the software interface, and a proposed development and business plan for turning the prototype into a project. (Reprinted with permission of Ramon M. Felciano, Jonathan Marsh, Philippe P. Piernot, Roby Stancel & Marc Yvon.)

developed by authors of chapters in this book: the program in Computer-Related Design at the Royal College of Art in London, the program in Human–Computer Interaction Design at Stanford University, and the Program in Media Arts and Sciences at the Massachussetts Institute of Technology (MIT).

The Royal College of Art (Crampton Smith)

This Program in Computer-Related Design at London's Royal College of Art (RCA) was initiated in 1989 by Gillian Crampton Smith. It offers a masters' degree to students from architecture, industrial design, graphic design, furniture design, fashion, software engineering, and psychology. The teaching style draws on the techniques of an art and design school, centered on studio courses that develop the skills of the *artist–designer*, as described by Crampton Smith and Philip Tabor in Chapter 3. RCA student teams have participated both in the Apple project and in a similar University Workshop that Mountford created at Interval Research. RCA projects tend to emphasize the visual aspects of the interface, and the design of the interactions.

Stanford University (Winograd, Hartfield, Kelley, Liddle, Bennett, De Young)

The Program in Human–Computer Interaction Design (HCID) at Stanford evolved as a series of courses within the computer science department, primarily at the masters-degree level. The Apple project has been the focus of an interdisciplinary course combining faculty from computer science and from the product-design program (in mechanical engineering). Students have participated from a variety of departments, including the communications department, which has done innovative research on computer interfaces (see Profile 7 on Microsoft Bob). One of the most prominent elements of the Stanford program has been the extensive use of *mentors* from industry—design and multimedia firms, as well as the computer industry—who work with student-project groups (see Bennett et al., 1992). Stanford's geographic good fortune of being located in an area with a heavy concentration of expertise makes it possible to provide each group with ongoing commentary on their work by experienced practitioners. Work with mentors complements the frequent in-class student presentations of ongoing work, designed to enable students to learn from the ideas and experiences of their peers.

Massachusetts Institute of Technology (Kapor, Kuhn)

The Program in Media Arts and Sciences at MIT is one of the most prominent teaching programs in human–computer interaction, covering a wide range of teaching and research in areas relating to computing and communications media. A multidisciplinary team is developing a course entitled the Software Design Studio, employing the design-studio method that is traditional in architectural and urban design. Students are presented with a rich, multilayered problem to be solved, and have a short time to propose initial concrete solutions to that problem. Successive cycles of criticism and modification of the proposals follow, and creative speculation and innovation are encouraged. At the end of the term, each student presents a working prototype to a jury of eminent software designers. The initial class project was *reinventing the community weekly*, which called for designing an on-line version of a weekly community newspaper. The emphasis is not on the adaptation of existing content to current mechanisms, such as World Wide Web, but rather on encouraging students to use the constraints and affordances of the new medium creatively, to transform the genre itself (as discussed by Brown and Duguid in Chapter 7).

Suggested Readings

Brenda Laurel (ed.). *The Art of Human-Computer Interaction*. Reading MA: Addison-Wesley, 1990.

Gary Strong. New Directions in HCI Education, Research, and Practice. *interactions*, 2:1 (January, 1995), 69–81.

MICHAEL SCHRAGE

Cultures of Prototyping

The great ethnographies of prototyping have yet to be written. However, it is demonstrably clear that fundamental differences in corporate prototyping cultures lead to qualitatively and quantitatively different products. Understanding those fundamental differences is essential for any organization that wants to transform its new-product development.

Software developers have devoted a great deal of attention to the design of software-prototyping tools, with the hope that the use of these tools can greatly increase the software designer's fluidity of iterative design. The use of rapid prototyping to accelerate creativity can also be observed in other design disciplines and is embedded in what Michael Schrage calls a company's *culture of prototyping*.

Schrage approaches the question of design as an observer and journalist—a starting point that is different from those of the practitioners and scholars of design in the previous chapters. As a syndicated columnist writing on computing technology and business for the *Los Angeles Times*, and as a research associate at the Sloan School of Management at MIT, he has studied what succeeds in practice in the commercial world of high technology.

In this chapter, Schrage describes the role and conduct of prototyping in industries such as automobiles and consumer electronics, drawing on material from interviews with design-firm managers. His analysis illustrates how the principles discussed by David Kelley and Donald Schön in Chapters 8 and 9 are put into practice in industry. The reflective conversation that Schön describes takes place in a rapid cycle of building prototypes, testing them, scrutinizing them, and redesigning them. Schrage's portrayal of the culture of the prototype-driven organization, which fosters creativity and innovative design, is based in part on IDEO (Profile 8), which has been built around a prototyping philosophy.

Although the examples in this chapter are drawn from products other than software, the analysis applies directly to software development. Prototypes provide Schön's *backtalk* to the designers, and also can serve as an essential medium for information, interaction, integration, and collaboration.

—Terry Winograd

WHENEVER ORGANIZATIONS INNOVATE, culture matters. The Toyota culture that builds a Lexus projects a design sensibility different from that of the General Motors culture that produces a Cadillac. The technocultural idealism carving Apple's Macintosh (see

Don Norman's account in Chapter 12) is inherently different from the organizational imperatives revealed by Microsoft's Windows development. The values that organizations hold shape the value that they create.

The culture of an organization has a strong influence on the quality of the innovations that the organization can produce. Each enterprise reflects a community of people with characteristic work and thought patterns that show up in the results of their activities. If we truly want to understand and influence how corporate cultures create valuable new products, we need to understand more fully the role that culture plays in creating new prototypes.

The *prototyping culture*—the media, methods, and styles that companies use to manage their multiple models of reality—offers a wealth of critical insights and opportunities into how organizations design and build value. In fact, David Kelley (see Chapter 8) asserts that he can tell almost anything worth knowing about a company's new-product development by simply sampling a few prototypes. "I could tell you absolutely everything, from the care of the models to the quality of the thinking of the designers."

A prototyping culture, like all cultures, is a mixture of the explicit organizational structures and the tacit understanding and practices of the participants. Just as companies have formal organizational charts and informal interpersonal networks, most companies also have formal prototyping processes and informal prototyping activities. In some corporations, formal prototyping processes rule; in others, the informal prototyping culture—like the informal network—is the context in which work actually gets done. At Apple Computer, for example, there is a strong formal prototyping culture. But Apple's invisible colleges of technical and marketing experts ensure that the informal prototyping culture enjoys considerable influence over the ultimate design. Within some innovation environments, prototypes effectively become the *media franca* of the organization: the essential medium for information, interaction, integration, and collaboration.

In this chapter, we first characterize the different aspects that make up a prototyping culture: prototypes and specifications, prototyping media, and the prototyping cycle. Then, we look at what it means to change to a more prototype-driven culture, and how this change can affect the values and the success of a company.

Although the bulk of the observations here are drawn from the world of industrial design, they distinctly resonate with the software-development experience. Software developers have prototyping cultures every bit as strong as those of industrial designers. Much has been written about the difference in corporate cultures among companies such as Apple, IBM, and Microsoft; the differences show up in these companies' approaches to prototyping as well.

Prototypes and Specifications

Virtually all innovative designs emerge in the interplay between two dueling representations: the wish list of specifications that describe and define the new ideas, and the prototypes that attempt to embody them. Prototypes too often confirm that what we wish for is unrealistic or ill conceived. Conversely, prototypes can reveal that the designer's wishes were not sufficiently imaginative. Specifications and prototypes can be mutually reinforcing, or they can prove to be implacable enemies.

The tension between specifications and prototypes is not unlike the historic tensions between theory and experiment in physics. Theory describes what is supposed to happen, and experiment tells what happens. The culture of physics has always been a push and pull between theorists and experimentalists. At times, theory dictates the experimental agenda; at others, experimental discoveries drive the theoreticians. Just as managing the dialog between theory and experiment is essential to the advancement of physics, managing the dialog between specifications and prototypes is essential to the advancement of design innovation.

Simply put, some innovation cultures are specification driven; others are prototype driven. Small, entrepreneurial companies built around a brilliant product concept tend to be prototype driven. Companies that need to coordinate large volumes of information and to manage a large installed base of users—companies such as IBM, AT&T, and Aetna Life & Casualty—tend to be specification driven. Specification-driven cultures also draw heavily from market-research data before they move concepts into the prototyping cycle. In prototyping cultures, prototypes are often used to elicit market feedback before final production.

When the dialog is poorly managed or breaks down, the results can be horrendous. An organization may spend thousands of hours developing detailed specifications, only to have the first prototype invalidate most of the work. This kind of setback has been particularly evident in areas such as software development, medical instrumentation, and airplane-cockpit design.

Similarly, industrial designers can craft absolutely breathtaking prototypes that prove impossible for cost-effective manufacture. The same can happen with software—software designers create a rapid prototype that demonstrates functionality that is impossible to implement with acceptable resource efficiency on the available delivery platforms.

Based on his firm's client experiences, David Kelley argues that organizations intending to be innovative need to move from *specification-driven prototypes* to *prototype-driven specifications*. In any event, it is clear that organizations prizing prototypes over specifications have fundamentally different design perceptions and processes. There are counterpressures, however. Many organizations believe that manageability means predictability. The idea that you can play your way through prototyping to a new product is anathema to managers educated to believe that predictability and control are essential in product development.

The Prototyping Media

Not all prototypes are the same, either in how they are built, or in the role they play in the design process. The medium of prototyping can have a strong influence on the whole design enterprise. Looking at the use of prototypes in the automobile industry, observers such as Michael Barry of GVO (a highly regarded design firm) have speculated that Detroit's competitiveness problems in the 1970s and 1980s can be traced in part to the prototyping media used by American automobile companies. The intricate, elaborate, and expensive clay models sculpted by America's Big Three body designers (Figure 10.1) did not readily lend themselves to easy modification or rapid iteration. The work required to craft them made them more like untouchable works of art than malleable platforms for creative interaction.

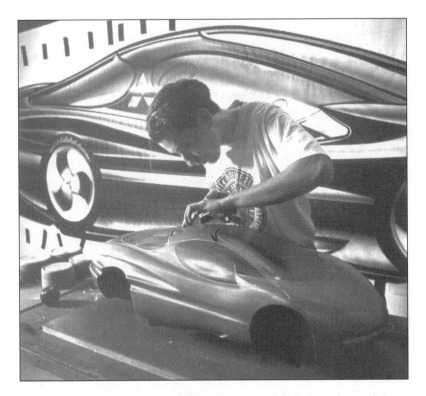

FIGURE 10.1   **Prototypes in Clay**   The automobile industry has traditionally based the design of new models on mockups done in clay that give a highly
polished impression of how the finished product will look, but do not invite
further changes. (Model by Scott Ashry, Photo by Steven A. Heller/Art Center
College of Design. Reprinted with permission.)

Based on a survey of the role of computer-aided design (CAD) tools
in Japan, Daniel Whitney of the Draper Laboratories at MIT observed
that, until recently, American car companies attempted to use the clay
models as input for their CAD systems—a laborious and imprecise
process. By contrast, Toyota did precisely the opposite: It insisted that
its stylists design the car body with CAD tools from the beginning.
The clay model became the output of the CAD system, based on the
computer representations, such as those shown in Figure 10.2.

When a clay model is the design *input*, it becomes a bottleneck to
effective use of the CAD tools. Capturing in digital form the aesthetic
essence of a clay model is difficult. When a clay prototype is the *out-*

196

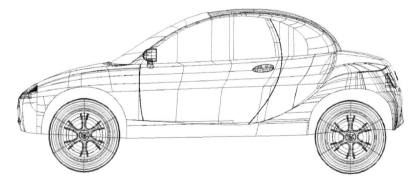

FIGURE 10.2   **Virtual Prototypes**   With modern tools for computer-aided design (CAD), much of the design of an automobile can be completed on-line, and can be visualized through high-quality graphics. The ease of visualizing changes greatly speeds the prototyping cycle and enhances the potential for fluidity in design. (Model and photo by David Hickey/Art Center College of Design. Reprinted with permission.)

put of a computer model, modification and enhancement become comparatively quick and easy. Toyota can go from a new idea to a one-quarter–scale clay model in just 40 days.

The properties of these prototyping media undeniably shape the prototyping process. Although it would be foolish to blame the past decline of General Motors on clay, it would be equally foolish to ignore the role that prototyping media play in determining the speed and quality at which automobiles are built.

The Questions that a Prototype Can Answer

Prototypes are designed to answer questions. The quantity and kind of questions that generate prototypes are at the heart of prototyping culture. Different questions may require different kinds of prototyping media—such as foamware or stereolithography. In software, different questions may lead to the use of different representations or even different languages. Note that sophisticated questions do not necessarily need sophisticated prototypes to answer them. Conversely, seemingly simple questions may defy even the most creative efforts to prototype. The questions that organizations choose not to ask are just as important as the ones that they do ask. This point is particularly relevant in software development, where each bit of functionality demanded may require a prototype.

One benefit that prototyping can offer is to generate new vocabulary for describing product features. When IDEO prototyped a toothpaste tube for a consumer-products company, one of the questions that the prototype identified was what level of *suckback* the tube provided. *Suckback* refers to the way the tube pulls back the toothpaste into the tube after the user stops squeezing it. Prototyping enabled both designer and client to create a vocabulary and to calibrate the desired characteristic.

The Prototyping Cycle

The role of time in prototyping practice offers one of the clearest markers to distinguish among cultural priorities. At a moment when management wisdom insists that speed to market is the key ingredient for competitiveness, the time dimension of prototyping assumes greater significance. An organization that advocates product-development speed will have to attend to the speed at which it designs, builds, and tests prototypes. *Rapid prototyping* has become a buzz phrase of the nineties.

For example, Sony and 3M take great pride in the speed at which they can produce a functional prototype. Companies such as Microsoft and LSI Logic (a custom silicon-chip designer) also have cultures where the *mean time to prototype* is exceptionally short. Other companies—notably IBM, AT&T, General Motors, and Johnson & Johnson—tend to study a concept for weeks before even beginning to turn it into a prototype. The culture of the latter companies treats the prototype as an end product of thought, rather than as a partner with the functional specification in development.

Historically, companies go through several prototyping iterations before moving a product into production. Sometimes, several weeks elapse between prototype iterations; at other points in the development cycle, the delay can be months. As a general rule, companies with short mean times to prototype tend to generate more prototypes and to go through more prototyping cycles than do those with slower ones.

Many companies have evolved a methodology based on a fixed number of prototyping cycles. This number is as much a function of tradition and culture as of economic or competitive necessity. Industrial designers with whom I have spoken report that few companies go through as many as five prototyping iterations over 1 year. As a rule, the more prototypes and prototyping cycles per unit time, the more technically polished the final product (Figure 10.3).

FIGURE 10.3 **Multiple Prototypes** The Microsoft mouse went through many cycles of prototyping before the designers settled on a final version. (*Source:* David Kelley, IDEO. Reprinted with permission.)

The Players in the Prototyping Culture

The key elements of a prototyping culture are who gets to be a part of it and why. Nothing says more about an organization's culture than that organization's networks of power and communities of influence.

Who owns the prototype? Who manages it? Who gets to see it—and when? Who determines which constituencies have a say in the next prototyping cycle? Is there an internal model shop responsible for prototyping on demand? These are the questions that most starkly reveal the corporate prototyping culture.

At one highly regarded Silicon Valley company with a strong engineering culture, people are happy to show peers their bench prototypes, but avoid showing the prototypes to executives. Their edict is "Never show fools unfinished work." Good ideas may be rejected by ill-informed executives based on what is perceived as inadequate execution of the prototype. Top management may find it difficult to see beyond prototype roughness to the ultimate product. As a result, many engineers conceal provocative prototypes from senior managers until the models have been polished appropriately. In addition, a danger can arise from showing a prototype to an executive and finding that there is an order to ship the prototype even though it is not up to industrial strength. Here again, an ill-informed manager can make a wrong decision.

Demonstrations to senior management at times assume the character of theater performances, rather than of interactive dialogs among members of the team. In some cases, showing a prototype assumes all the logistical trappings and investment of a Broadway musical. The prototype becomes a medium for persuasion, rather than a vehicle to evoke discussion. It is used to prove a point, rather than to create a platform for a design dialog.

As a result of managers not having access to a dialog around emerging prototypes, top-manager insights in some organizations tend to come later in the design cycle than they should, thereby losing value. The later the time, the more likely that the top managers are being asked to approve—rather than to review or assist—new-product creation. Any organization that wants to gain a deeper understanding of its prototyping culture would do well to time how long it takes between the initial creation of a prototype and the moment that the prototype is first shown to senior management.

Ownership of the Prototype

If it is to succeed in its purpose, a prototype cannot be seen as the property of the engineers, of the developers, or of the marketer. It has to be community property. Traditionally, prototypes have been a weapon in interdepartmental power struggles. At high-tech companies, for example, engineers and technicians traditionally own the prototype, and bicker with marketing and manufacturing over suggested modifications. At packaged-goods companies, the brand manager typically owns the prototype. In other cultural contexts, prototypes are little more than sales tools and technical stalking horses for the politically adept. The politics of prototypes play a large part in shaping their potential value.

These politics extend beyond company walls. Organizations must ask themselves, "When do customers and suppliers get to see the prototypes?" Indeed, do customers and suppliers participate in the prototyping process at all? At some companies, showing outsiders the prototypes is a widespread practice. At others, only senior management can authorize such displays. Both extremes have their problems. On the one hand, pre-release familiarity may take away the excitement from release (and ideas may even be stolen); on the other hand, developer isolation can lead to developer arrogance and ignorance.

Collaborative prototyping with customers and suppliers can yield competitive benefits. Nike's successful creation of a new product design language (see Chapter 4) stemmed from intense collaboration between athlete and designer. IBM attributes much of the success of its AS/400 minicomputer to participation by key customers. Microsoft's collaboration with applications-software companies was an integral part of the widespread acceptance of Windows. More generally in the software industry, no successful piece of personal-computer software is launched before potential customers interact with alpha- and beta-version prototypes.

As part of an evolution from technology-driven products to customer-centered design, the customer becomes an important member of the prototyping community. The customer must have the opportunity to see and try the prototypes as they evolve. Customer involvement has been the key to the success of companies such as Intuit (see Chapter 13), which solicited extensive customer feedback in developing its home financial product, Quicken (see Profile 13).

Changing a Company's Prototyping Culture

If we take seriously Kelley's claim that organizations intending to be innovative need to move from specification-driven prototypes to prototype-driven specifications, then we need to look at the ways that change can occur, and at the ways that change is already underway.

The great ethnographies of prototyping cultures have yet to be written. However, it is demonstrably clear that fundamental differences in corporate prototyping cultures lead to qualitatively and quantitatively different products. Understanding those fundamental differences is essential for any organization that wants to transform its new-product development. A shift in the prototyping practices is a necessary part of a shift in the culture of the enterprise, and, in the end, a shift in that enterprise's role and values in the market. Companies that want to build better products must learn how to build better prototypes. Change initiatives that do not deal explicitly with the culture of prototyping are initiatives that ignore organizational reality.

I see two strong cultural shifts gradually taking hold in both the industrial-design and software communities:

1. The implicit belief that a structured innovation process drives prototype development is yielding to the belief that emerging sequences of prototypes drive the innovation process.
2. The notion that innovative teams generate innovative prototypes is giving way to a recognition that innovative prototypes are the focus for generating innovative teams.

The innovation process

The move toward a prototype-driven innovation process is most evident in those companies that have instituted repeated quick prototyping. The increased emphasis on speed to market has produced a practice that is radically redefining prototyping culture, called *periodic prototyping*. Instead of producing prototypes when design teams think that doing so is appropriate, many time-sensitive organizations are now institutionalizing the prototyping process around explicit schedules. The result is that developers are now forced to double or even triple the number of prototyping cycles per unit time. Quantitative changes inevitably lead to qualitative changes. At Honda, for example, an automobile might go through 10 or 12 trial builds, with a new prototype being built every 2 weeks. Motorola required a similar periodic prototyping schedule for its popular Bandit pagers.

By comparing the prototype changes per cycle, management now has a rigorous vehicle for measuring progress. Designers who are held to periodic prototyping schedules are likely to become more prototype driven than specification driven.

The innovating team

As companies push toward cross-functional development teams, the role of the prototype can change. When the community of stakeholders in the development of new products and processes broadens, physical objects that help to bridge disciplinary and functional boundaries become more important.

In essence, prototyping becomes not only a medium for interdepartmental integration, but also a medium for organizational redesign. Prototype-driven innovation ends up promoting a radical deconstruction of the existing organizational charts. It becomes increasingly important to avoid the departmental turf wars that cripple prototypes, which in turn demands a fundamental change in the prototyping culture.

Indeed, mapping the flow of prototypes through the enterprise is one of the most significant exercises that an organization can undertake. Who—insider and outsider—gets to see what when? When are modifications made? Who requests them? Which requested modifications are ignored? This map—rather than an organizational chart—can be the best starting point to evaluate core process redesign. Such a map reveals how essential—or how marginal—the formal prototyping process truly is.

Precisely because a prototype is a manipulable artifact, it can be meaningfully tracked and measured. An organization can quickly discover the power points and political bottlenecks that govern the value-creation process.

Conclusions

Organizations can seek to revise the dialog between specifications and prototypes; they can pick prototyping media with desirable properties ranging from flexibility to cost; they can reset the sense of time for prototype management; they can create prototyping communities; and they can change their prototyping culture.

There is no one right answer to "How should we prototype?" Prototyping strategies are varied, and a company needs to develop a mix that serves its markets and its products. Prototypes are as much a medium for managing risks as they are a medium for exploring opportunities. They can be treated as an insurance policy or as an option on the future.

Ultimately, one of management's greatest challenges is to integrate its portfolio of prototypes effectively into an integrated product or family of products. That is the arena where politics, economics, and organizational culture are often in sharpest conflict. Effectively answering that challenge will not only display the organization's cultural priorities, but also will define the organization's ability to innovate effectively in an increasingly competitive marketplace.

Suggested Readings

Michael Schrage. *No More Teams.* New York: Doubleday Currency, 1995.
Steven Wheelwright and Kim Clark. *Leading Product Development: The Senior Manager's Guide to Creating and Shaping the Enterprise.* New York: Free Press, 1995.

About the Author

Michael Schrage both writes and consults on the ways technology reshapes how people interact. He is a research associate at MIT's Sloan School of Management and at The Media Lab. He is the author of *No More Teams* (1995), a book about collaboration and collaborative media.

10. HYPERCARD, DIRECTOR,
AND VISUAL BASIC

When Donald Schön (Chapter 9) speaks of an artist, such as a sculptor, who is engaged in a *conversation with the medium*, we can imagine the picture clearly. The sculptor molds clay or chips stone, and then she looks at and feels the sculpture to see what it has become. Creative designing lies in the interplay between intention and the surprise at what emerges.

Everyone who has written interactive software has experienced the same interplay. The programmer writes some code, runs it, and sees how it behaves and feels. The results are partially expected, partially surprising, and they feed into the next cycle of design. The ability to shape and reshape software requires a capacity for rapid prototyping—for turning an unarticulated idea into a working prototype quickly enough to be able to change it, to listen to it, even to throw it out and to go on to another. In this activity, the nature of the programming language and environment can make a large difference—perhaps as large as the difference between modeling in clay and sculpting in stone.

The goals and possibilities are varied, and they are reflected in prototyping tools that are suitable for different *prototyping cultures*, as described by Michael Schrage (Chapter 10). In the organizational process of design, it matters whether the prototypes are done as a program or as cardboard or video mockups. Some prototyping purposes are effectively achieved with highly refined pixel graphics; others are better served by scanned-in pencil sketches. Sometimes, functionality

Profile Author: Terry Winograd

is a key issue in the prototype; at other times, the prototype needs only to be a facade that demonstrates a look and feel.

Current software-design practice relies heavily on software systems that were created to enable rapid prototyping. Hundreds of such systems are available on dozens of platforms, each with its own features and problems. Some are called *authoring tools*, others *prototyping languages*, and others *development platforms*. What they share in common is a focus on making it easy for designers to build, and then to experience, interfaces and the programs that lie behind them. Three of these systems are profiled here, to illustrate Schrage's points about how prototyping tools affect both the activity and results of prototyping.

HyperCard

Bill Atkinson and his team developed HyperCard at Apple Computer in 1987, as the next step in the path that Apple had proclaimed in the slogan for the Macintosh: *the computer for the rest of us*. HyperCard ushered in a new capacity of *programming for the rest of us*, promising to enable every Macintosh user to become an application designer. Since HyperCard was given away free with every Macintosh system, it quickly became a widespread standard (an example followed by later products, such as Mosaic, as described in Profile 5). HyperCard's *card-stack* metaphor was appropriate for many new applications, and led to a proliferation of creative programs that exploited its novel interface techniques. HyperCard's primary place in software design, however, is due to its utility as a general scriptable interface builder, providing direct-manipulation creation of interfaces that are based on standard graphical user-interface elements, such as icons, buttons, text fields, and scrolling windows.

The writers of HyperCard applications range from sophisticated interaction designers to schoolchildren. In fact, HyperCard is now one of the most popular and widespread programming environments for students from elementary school through college. HyperCard's programming language, HyperTalk, differs from conventional programming languages in using Englishlike constructions, such as "put the number of this card into card field XYZ." This format makes

HyperTalk more approachable for novices, but is awkward for experienced programmers.

The *stacks* (as programs are called) that have been built in HyperCard range from juvenile exercises to sophisticated exploration games, such as Spelunx (Cyan, 1991) and Earthquest (Earthquest, 1991). It is impossible to show a *typical* HyperCard screen, because HyperCard's facilities to draw artwork onto cards have been used to produce every look imaginable. Figure 10.4 shows a demonstration stack that comes with the HyperCard application, and is typical of one widespread style of HyperCard use.

The HyperCard culture emphasizes ease of use, and encourages simple, playful designs. Although some HyperCard prototypes have a high degree of sophistication and polish, many are immediately recognizable as HyperCard by their use of common icons, buttons,

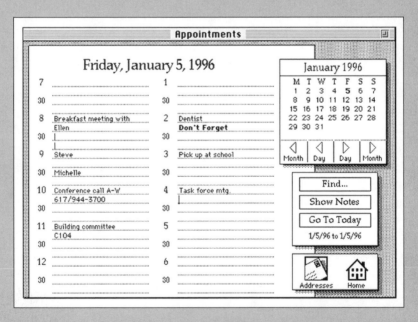

FIGURE 10.4 HyperCard Appointment Book This simple application demonstrates several of HyperCard's commonly used facilities for prototyping, such as text fields, buttons, icons, and the ability to create cards with a graphic look that mimics print conventions. (*Source:* Reprinted with permission of Apple Computer, Inc.)

clip art, and other standard visual elements. HyperCard's limitations, such as slow execution and limited support for use of color, have been ameliorated in later versions and successors, such as SuperCard, but the overall niche remains the same. For applications requiring complex computation, portability to different environments, or efficient performance, the HyperCard prototype is discarded after testing, and the final code is written in another programming environment.

Director

Macromedia's Director represents a point at the opposite end of the user spectrum from HyperCard. Director was designed for use by sophisticated multimedia developers, and rather than being bundled free, it costs several hundred dollars. Its appeal lies not in its ease of use, but rather in the sophisticated results that can be produced by users who are willing to learn complex mechanisms. In particular, it can be used for animations that are well beyond the capabilities of most other software-development languages.

The metaphor of Director (as its name suggests) is that of the stage or of an animated film. A Director application is built around a *score*, which represents a carefully coordinated and timed sequence of activities by a *cast of characters*. The basic programming structure offers frame-by-frame animation of the kind used in producing movie cartoons. By using Director's scripting language, Lingo, the designer can synchronize sound and motion in sophisticated ways. In contrast to HyperCard's aim to be usable on even the smallest Macintosh, Director emphasizes high-quality graphics, animation, sound, and video, and hence requires relatively high-end hardware. Although Director does provide support for standard Macintosh interface elements, such as buttons and text fields, it encourages designers to produce more open-ended and graphically original interfaces, making use of high resolution graphics, video, and animation (Figure 10.5).

For specialized applications, such as a multimedia information kiosk, Director is suitable for a final product. In many other cases designers use it to give a polished demonstration of what an applica-

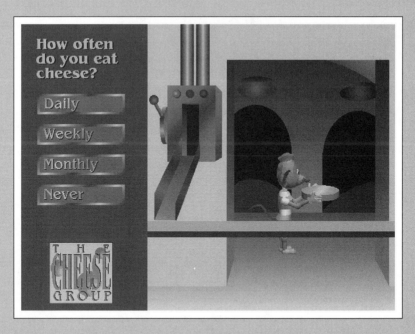

FIGURE 10.5 **Director Prototype** Director is well suited to kiosk applications, which require high visual appeal and relatively simple interaction. In this fanciful example, which is included on the installation disks for Director, the animated mouse takes wheels of cheese from the conveyor until the user selects a button. (From Macromedia Director 3.1. Reprinted with permission.)

tion might look like, concentrating on the interface without trying to implement all of the functionality. Since Lingo was developed as a supporting language for animation, rather than as a regular programming language, it is not well suited to performing sophisticated computation behind the interface.

Visual Basic

Visual Basic was developed for Microsoft's Windows operating system, which positioned it for a market different from the HyperCard users on the Macintosh. Instead of aiming for every schoolchild and home-recipe-book creator, Visual Basic was designed for professional system developers, who are competent programmers but are not user-interface wizards. Visual Basic is designed to enable a programmer to create interfaces using the facilities of the Windows environment with relative ease. Visual Basic is built around a simple, conventional programming language (a variant of Basic), in conjunction with a direct-manipulation interface builder. The designer can create and place standard interface elements, set and modify their properties, and associate them with programs that operate when they are invoked by a user of the interface.

A typical Visual Basic application does not have the flash and originality of many HyperCard stacks or Director prototypes, but instead operates within the normal interface conventions for Windows applications (Figure 10.6). The programming environment makes it easy for the designer to convert a Visual Basic project into an executable file that can be distributed and run by users who do not have the Visual Basic system, on any computer that runs Windows.

The Visual Basic culture emphasizes software engineering and programming values: efficiency of execution, straightforward logical design, and minimal use of machine resources, such as memory. The focus is not on making it beautiful, but rather on making it work. The integration of Visual Basic into the Windows system makes it possible to deliver end-applications that use Visual Basic interfaces and perform sophisticated computation, without incurring high computational costs. In this sense, we might think of Visual Basic as less of a prototyping language and more of a development language—many of the interfaces built with it are intended directly as products, rather than as footholds in the software design process (see Chapter 11).

Choosing a Prototyping Medium

In setting out to build an interactive software prototype, the choice of prototyping language and system can have a major effect on the outcome, just as the choice of CAD or clay models will shape the design of automobiles. The characterizations in this profile of the three languages and their emphases (HyperCard for amateurs, Director for artist–designers, Visual Basic for software engineers) are suggestive but simplistic. Many factors determine which will be the best choice, and often the determining issues are contextual: the hardware and software readily accessible to the design team, the availability of prior examples

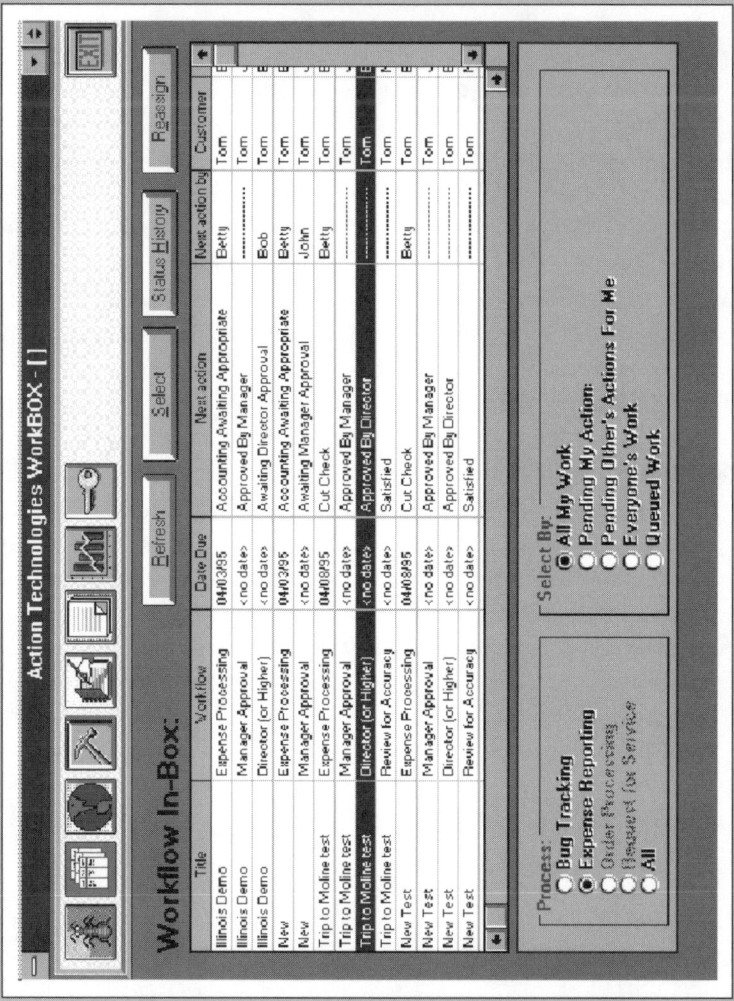

FIGURE 10.6   Application Built in Visual Basic
(Reprinted with permission of Action Technologies.)

on which to build, and the fit with the overall prototyping culture of the organization. As Kelley, Schön, Schrage, and others in the previous chapters have pointed out, the first step is awareness—seeing prototyping as a significant part of the design, recognizing the tradeoffs among alternative ways to prototype, understanding the constraints of the setting, and making choices with the aim of enhancing the overall design process.

Suggested Readings

Robert Arnson, Daniel Rosen, Mitchell Waite, and Jonathan Zuck. *Visual Basic How-To* (Second edition). Waite Group Press, 1993.

Danny Goodman. *The Complete HyperCard 2.2 Handbook* (Fourth edition). New York: Random House, 1993.

Jason Roberts. *Director Demystified*. Berkeley, CA: Peach Pit Press, 1995.

Terry Winograd. Environments for software design. *Communications of the ACM*, 38:6 (June 1995), 65–74.

S H A H A F   G A L

11

Footholds for Design

In a design environment, knowledge is generated, enacted, and reflected on in an ongoing process between the materials and the participants' intentions and attached meanings. Learning occurs when users create concrete things, such as drawings and models, based on their knowledge, and then reevaluate that knowledge based on what they have just learned.

In conjunction with Donald Schön (see Chapter 9), Shahaf Gal conducted a series of studies of engineering students completing design projects. The story of Ray's bridge, recounted in this chapter, was one of four cases that Gal analyzed in detail. Ray's experience in a 3-week student design competition offers us a distilled and visible version of what happens in more sophisticated and hidden ways in every design project. The problems that Ray grapples with have direct mappings onto software-design contexts: top-down versus bottom-up approaches; the practice of basing new designs on standard examples; the temptation to use materials because they are available; and the struggle between adding features and simplifying.

Ray goes through a directed but winding search, adding and dropping concerns that constrain his design, being surprised by the results of explorations, and making messy decisions that change over the course of the project. He is a student, not an expert, and his lack of sophistication helps to reveal the process more clearly, since the breakdowns are more visible without the facade of expert polished performance. We can clearly see the tradeoffs between different concerns, the abandonment of a path when it seems to have reached a dead end, and the pain of getting stuck. As David Kelley points out in Chapter 8, these phenomena happen to every designer, and are not to be avoided.

—Terry Winograd

COMPUTERS CAN PLAY AN IMPORTANT ROLE in the design process, as *image footholds*. In a design environment, knowledge is generated, enacted, and reflected on in an ongoing process between the materials and the participants' intentions and attached meanings. Learning occurs when users create concrete things, such as drawings and models, based on their knowledge, and then reevaluate that knowledge based on what they have just learned. If we are to respond

Author's acknowledgment: I thank Vanessa DiMauro for bringing the rock-climbing analogy to my attention.

effectively to design situations, our tools—including those based on computers—need to be aligned with the process of the design inquiry.

An analogy for the role of computers in a design environment is that of rock climbing. A rock climber knows that she wants to get to the top of the mountain. She chooses a route for the climb based on her knowledge when she is at the bottom of the hill. As she climbs, she constantly faces new situations where she needs to choose a new footing to proceed. She seeks footholds that are safe and stable on which to pause momentarily to catch her breath and to plan her next step. Each foothold is both an endpoint that sums all the steps she has taken so far, and a point of departure from which to plan the next one. Her choice of a new foothold is determined by the steps that she has taken to get to her current position on the mountain in relation to her goal. She is also guided by her past climbing experience, and she uses her rock-climbing tools as an anchor. At each step, she needs to plan her next step considering what is in her reach; each step presents her with new and different conditions. Thus, a rock climber continuously faces a challenge of making future decisions based on the here and now of her foothold.

Like the rock climber, designers face similar challenges in design settings. Situations of design evolve constantly as a designer secures a point in the design on which he feels safe relying, then moves on again. The following story of a student designing a bridge illustrates the use and value of a computer program that serves as a design foothold. The general principles discussed at the end of the chapter show how the lessons go beyond this case.

The Riddle of *Die Brücke*

Ray was a senior in mechanical engineering at the Massachusetts Institute of Technology (MIT). As a high-school student, he gained experience working with wood, especially with balsa wood. Ray designed and constructed a bridge as part of the fourth annual bridge-design contest at MIT in the winter of 1988. This bridge contest was his first; he worked by himself, in competition with 16 other students from different departments within the School of Engineering. Their task was to build models of bridges that could best withstand a test load. Participants were given a kit of materials containing strings, wire, glue, and a variety of wood blocks—basswood, balsa, and pine. They had 3 weeks to complete the project.

Students were encouraged to use the engineering laboratory and Growltiger—an expert-system engineering program—to build their models. Growltiger's purpose was to serve students as a design tool and as a virtual laboratory for experimentation in structural engineering. As a virtual laboratory, Growltiger is programmed as a channel of guided discovery, where the system guides designers to enter the necessary data for structural analysis, to manipulate the appropriate computational components, and to evaluate the results against known parameters of structural engineering. The program also assists the designer by providing a default setting that offers standard-sized beams, properties of standard construction materials, and four types of indeterminate structures. Thus, students can test how their designs behave in accordance with a range of standardized degrees of tolerance. The test can serve as a starting point from which students try to optimize the structure. They can then change the shape of the structure, the loading, and the stiffness. Within seconds, the new structure can be analyzed and tested.

Students can also use Growltiger as an open-ended design tool, building their own structures. With the exception of curved supports, students can design the structure, and decide on the kind of material and the loading system; the program will display the deflection. (See Figure 9.2).

Top-Down Design

Ray chose a strategy for building his bridge that attempted to address a range of issues. He strove to manage effectively the time and manufacturing constraints (gluing, amount of work), while creating a strong bridge that was beautiful and original. He aimed to build with a clear design concept. As a partial response to the tradeoff, Ray searched for a bridge with simple structure that would be easy to manufacture. In a design notebook that he kept throughout the contest, Ray wrote at this early stage:

- Main problem: TIME! TIME! TIME!
- Main constraint: Bridge must be finished in time!
- Main tradeoff: Aesthetics and partial stability versus speed of construction

Ray believed that he could build the bridge in a classical top-down approach: arrive at a concept, prepare a few alternative designs, narrow down to one design, work out its details, check the materials available, and move on to manufacture the bridge.

> What I originally proposed was a clear top-down approach. You start off with comparison of main frames, which means main ideas for designing a bridge, as I did here with several design sketches. For example, take those six ideas of bridges, then take the two best ones, and then elaborate on those to get a good idea of how the geometry looks. Then, go back to the material. From there on, it's a circle among material, manufacturing, and the design; they are all factors from then on, but only from then on. That is a classical top-down approach.

Following this top-down scheme, Ray started by collecting ideas about bridges, and searching for a bridge-design concept. He watched a video of the previous year's bridge contest, looking especially for the mistakes participants made in their design, and he leafed through a book on bridge designs. The Roman arc bridges caught his attention first—they last long, which is proof that they work, he reasoned. Following more reading, he contemplated two other kinds of basic designs—the bow bridge and cable-stayed bridge—and leaned toward the latter in which he had more trust.

After his search, he decided to stick with one general structural idea: to use twin towers—a two-legged bridge—in his design. The concern about settlement of such a bridge introduced the idea of a hinged center span so that each tower would act as an independent element in carrying the load. Given these three considerations, he drew his first design: a two-towered, cable-stayed bridge with a hinged center span (Figure 11.1).

Ray soon realized, however, that the hinge mechanism would destabilize the bridge, and would require much construction work. Still worried about the uneven settlement of the towers, he considered

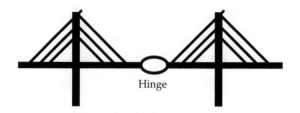

Hinge

FIGURE 11.1 **Fan Cable-Stayed Bridge with a Center Hinge** Working with sketches, Ray could explore both the visual and mechanical properties of his proposed designs. This bridge had a certain elegance, but the hinge could destabilize it.

a bridge with a freely suspended span that would rotate and compensate for the settlement. The bridge would be like an arc, and would swing back and forth to compensate automatically for the settlements (Figure 11.2).

Time constraints and concern about the strength of the strings caused Ray to drop this idea altogether. He decided to tolerate the settlement problem as a constraint, and remained with cable-stayed bridges.

He then tried another angle on bridges, seeking *beautiful* bridges. Hyperbolic bridges and classical cable bridges—such as the Golden Gate Bridge in San Francisco—attracted him the most. In his design notebook, he experimented with cable-stayed bridges arranged in hyperbolic patterns. Ultimately, however, he found this pattern impractical because the nearly horizontal members could carry only small loads.

Feeling the pressure of time, Ray dropped the search for aesthetic bridges and focused on function: cable-stayed bridges with vertical

FIGURE 11.2 **Arc Bridge** Each half of the arc could swing back and forth to compensate for settlement. This rough sketch was an attempt to solve a specific technical problem, as a prelude to a more comprehensive design.

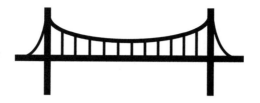

FIGURE 11.3 **Suspension Cable-Stayed Bridge** The classical suspension bridge was aesthetically pleasing and made use of the string as a tensile member. In looking for the best overall design, Ray was balancing constraints in several different dimensions, including beauty, strength, and feasibility of construction.

tension members. Ray then placed an additional constraint on his bridge: to use as much as wood and strings as possible, for maximum strength. The kit had plenty of materials, and he liked to include horizontal tension members:

> I am trying to make the maximum with the material that I have been given. The string is the longest piece of material I've been given, and it's a tensile member, so I want to take advantage of it. You could design it without strings, of course: I just believe in using all the material.

The bridge design was then changed into a suspension bridge, as in Figure 11.3.

Ray eliminated this design soon after its inception, because a top cable would weaken the bridge—the bridge needed to be very large and the vertical strings to be very long, and the forces acting on them would be very strong. A few days into the contest, Ray was stuck. Time was becoming a critical factor, and his brainstorm sessions had resulted in neither a clear design nor any elaborate specific structural constraints. Ray decided to change his general approach.

Simulation as a Design Tool

Ray now turned to Growltiger to help him choose from the various designs. His decision to use Growltiger for that purpose did not come easily. After seeing a demonstration of the system, he felt a general mistrust of its capabilities and usefulness. Growltiger, he reasoned, did not design; it simply helped the user to evaluate design parameters. In addition, he surmised that the system would not be useful for constructing the bridge, because its design model was too simplistic to match an actual bridge in its environmental context.

At this point, however, Growltiger proved useful. Ray prepared six preliminary models of the main bridge types, each reflecting main modes of handling load, and had Growltiger predict their success using default material properties. During the comparison of the designs' general structural behavior, he noticed that two designs showed the greatest strength. He therefore narrowed the possible bridge candidates to two designs: the cable-stayed bridge and the girder bridge.

He then ran a comparative analysis of the two bridges, elaborating and changing their design, and testing various structural options. The bridges, he found, were both strong, but they behaved differently:

> These two performed well. The girder bridge was decent, too, to my surprise. It's the simplicity that gives it a rigidity that's amazing. Looking at how it bends and how it behaves, I could see how stable, it would be— what the overall performance would be.

Ray was using the computer as a medium for reflection, in which to explore the kind of surprises that Schön describes in Chapter 9. His *conversation with the materials* (even in this simulated medium) led to new insights and provided a way to test his specific design ideas.

Conversation with the Materials

After using Growltiger, Ray realized that bridge construction must begin from small components of the bridge. Most important, he realized how critical it was to link the overall design approach with the process of constructing the pieces of the bridge. This realization was the catalyst for another shift in Ray's approach. He changed the direction of his work from top-down to bottom-up, as he became concerned with construction issues, which he had thought he could leave for later. He also began to have second thoughts about building a cable-stayed bridge that relied solely on strings as the main system to transfer the load. The strings, he realized, had limited reliability as tensile members, especially because the strength of the bridge largely depended on the string attachment to the wood, where the stress will be concentrated. This shift in approach brought about a change in Ray's activities. Ray now needed to test the various components of the bridge. He decided to use the physical laboratory to test the performance of the deck and the supports, which he believed were important to any bridge. He started testing generic examples made of wood.

> When you do experiments, you get an idea of the material. That's something Growltiger doesn't give you at all. You build the box, touch the materials, glue them. I got a lot out of it.

The laboratory tests provided him with a deeper understanding of the structural behavior of the beams and ribs for his deck, which could not be provided by Growltiger's simulation. For a structure of the deck, he compared three alternative approaches. Based on the results, he eliminated two options and decided to go with the box girder, which had unexpectedly proved to be the strongest.

Ray's concern about the weight of the bridge and the use of strings as the main material for the tensiles caused him to recheck the literature on cable-stayed bridges for the kinds of tensiles and cable arrangements used. He learned that the most effective cable arrangement for carrying load keeps the tensiles vertical to the deck. By this point, his bridge design had become detailed and definite: the overall design would be a cable-stayed bridge, with a box-girder deck, two towers, H-supports, and many tensile members made of strings (Figure 11.4).

FIGURE 11.4   Cable-Stayed Bridge with H-Supports and Strings
Ray's experiments with the physical materials led him to consider this design, in place of the earlier suspension design. Working in the laboratory gave Ray insights about practical construction feasibility that were not provided by the computer simulation.

Following his experiments in the laboratory, Ray remained concerned about the use of strings to support the towers. At first, he tried to calculate the load that the strings would carry. He returned to the problem of how to attach the strings, and could not find a solution. At that time, he considered dropping the idea of a cable-stayed bridge. But he could not tolerate the thought of omitting the strings.

> I could not let go 100 feet of worthwhile material! So, I looked for a different solution, and that was the first time that I came up with the idea, "Why not use an additional bar across, and use vertical strings?"

Ray then planned one deck on top of the load-carrying deck, and another below, from which 30 to 40 strings would link the load-carrying deck with the bridge's deck. That design would use the strings and the remaining basswood. This idea also linked and resolved many of his earlier concerns about structural forces, use of strings, and use of as many vertical tensiles as possible.

> I didn't come up with the idea of vertical strings. It came from constraints propagation—from the top and from the bottom. It just suddenly popped up. I stuck with it because I felt good about it. All the problems I was worried about before—the materials, strings that I had, vertical alignment, vertical force performance—were solved by this design.

Ray's bridge design, which he called *Die Brücke* (the Bridge), now looked like Figure 11.5.

FIGURE 11.5 **Triple-Deck Bridge with Strings as Vertical Tensiles**
Ray was led to this design in a creative leap (see Kelley's discussion in Chapter 8) that grew out of his persistent focus on how to make use of a single design element—the strings.

FIGURE 11.6 **Ray's Final Design** Structural analysis, construction concerns, and a desire to use all of the available materials all played a role in producing the final bridge design.

In the final moments before the contest, Ray decided to add trusses, which he had considered previously, to strengthen the support of the towers. His final bridge is shown in Figure 11.6.

At the testing session that culminated the bridge-design competition, Ray's bridge drew much attention from other participants and from the audience. It passed the first loading test, but failed in the second round, when both ends of the deck were crushed. In the overall contest, the bridge came in fourth place.

Growltiger as an Image Foothold

This detailed case illuminates the many and messy decisions that take place over time in a design situation. The process of design evolves as a process of identifying emerging new questions to address. Through the task, a personal design world is created within which answers are sought out with the use of tools (Figure 11.7).

The personal design world is bounded by the designer's tools and design knowledge. The challenge of the situation is to create a way to test a proposed design solution—which in turn generates new questions. Each point of testing requires the designer to pause on the question, while considering future design questions. She uses design tools, drawings, and models to create design pauses that momentarily freeze the knowledge, and that represent a culmination of the knowledge gathered thus far. Engineering drawings, geometric displays, and algebraic computations assist engineers in maintaining an image, a

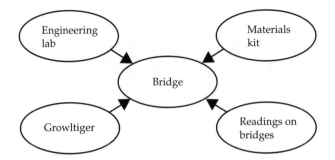

FIGURE 11.7 **Ray's Personal Design World** Ray's design world is composed of the tools and design knowledge that he applied to the bridge problem. Each component can lead to new questions and new solutions.

map for orientation, and a language for explaining the design in the process of work.

Reflecting on Ray's experience, it is interesting to observe his use of the computer. Ray used Growltiger to hold images of his design ideas, to test their quality, and to set constraints on his work. And—unintended but perhaps more important—his use of Growltiger shifted his design process. Ray first attempted to work top down. Time constraints and his inability to yield enough concrete constraints on his bridge design caused him to rethink his design approach. When he got stuck, Ray used Growltiger to come up with basic bridge-design ideas that guided his work. From the bridges' simulated performance, he learned about their load mechanisms: the cable-stayed bridge using cables to transfer the load, and the girder bridge using its rigid beam. This knowledge led him to try alterations on each bridge.

The session with Growltiger turned out to be important to his work in another way: It placed the first concrete design reins over his work—from there, he worked within the conceptual frame of these two bridge designs.

Growltiger also served as a preliminary trigger to a moment when—not by intention—all Ray's bridge design theories and work strategies amalgamated into one cohesive image of a bridge. Growltiger provided the critical piece: It was an *image foothold* in the jigsaw puzzle that he was putting together. He used the computer to trigger, *unintentionally,* a critical reflective moment that allowed him to focus on a bridge design. It also provided him with a reflection of his design strategy. The design strategy and image foothold are part of the same design initiative. They are not easily separated, because it is the strategy that gave birth to the image, and it is the image that informed the strategy.

A significant challenge exists here for software designers. They need to create tools that assist designers to reflect on past steps, and to inform plans for the next foothold—while allowing for the designers' creativity to emerge and to be tested in an *intentional* way.

Suggested Readings

Ken Baynes and Francis Pugh. *The Art of the Engineer*. London: Lund Humphries, 1981.

Shahaf Gal. Building bridges: Design, learning, and the role of computers. *Journal of Machine-Mediated Learning*, 4:4, 1991, 335–375.

Chris Jones. *Essays in Design*. London: Wiley, 1984.

Donald Schön. The design process. In V. Howard (ed.), *Varieties of Thinking*. New York: Routledge, 1990.

About the Author

Shahaf Gal directs the Computers for Instruction Department of the Centre for Educational Technology in Tel Aviv, the largest educational computer research and development company in Israel.

Profile

11. THE SPREADSHEET

One of the major developments that changed the face of computing was Dan Bricklin's introduction in VisiCalc of the conceptual model of the spreadsheet. Neither VisiCalc's command interface nor its information display (limited by the capacity of the machines that were available, and by how much space VisiCalc required) was remarkable. However, the conceptual model was exceptionally durable. With the additional design work of Mitch Kapor and an implementation on the IBM PC, the successor program, Lotus 1-2-3, quickly surpassed VisiCalc, and was the killer app that moved the microcomputer from the hobbyist's and student's desks into the mainstream of the business world. In its time, it was a radically new idea; it led to the PC revolution that populated millions of offices all around the world with desktop computers.

In hindsight, the idea of a computer spreadsheet seems obvious. The accountant's ledger sheet, with its two-dimensional grid of rows and columns, has long been a fundamental tool in professional accounting practice. When an accountant prepares a budget or financial statement, typically each row represents a different line item, and each column presents the amount of that item in a given time period. There were many programs on mainframe computers, before VisiCalc, that produced outputs that looked like ledger sheets. But a dramatic (and largely unexpected) change came from the spreadsheet's interactivity, and from the role that interactive use played in the activity of financial modeling.

Forecasting is a basic business activity, which calls for projecting alternative financial results based on choices and assumptions, such as the expected sales, cost of goods, possibilities for investment, and so on. Results, such as the amount of profit or loss, are calculated for

Profile Author: Terry Winograd

each of the alternatives, often for a sequence of time periods (month by month, or quarter by quarter for several years). In practice, preparing a projection or a budget is an iterative design process. Different sets of assumptions lead to different results. On the basis of seeing these results, the financial analyst often wants to see what would happen if assumptions or strategies were changed. Doing multiple revisions on paper requires laborious reentry and recalculation. Programmable calculators sped up the calculation aspect, but still left users with much furious button punching and number scribbling.

Bricklin's insight was that the financial-projection process could done interactively on a microcomputer. He created a computer screen that mimicked the structure of the paper ledger sheet (Figure 11.8) so that it would be familiar and easily adopted. He extended the possibil-

```
B31: (,3) [W11] +B20-B29                                        READY
Line  Bar  XY   Stacked-Bar   Pie
Bar Graph
         A            B         C         D         E         F
15  Profit and Loss Statement
16
17  (in Millions)        ---------Actual--------    - Projected -
18                        1984      1985      1986     1987      1988
19                     ----------------------------------------------
20  Revenues             3.865     4.992     5.803    6.022     6.481
21
22  Expenses
23    Salaries           0.285     0.337     0.506    0.617     0.705
24    Utilities          0.178     0.303     0.384    0.419     0.551
25    Materials          1.004     1.782     2.046    2.273     2.119
26    Administration     0.281     0.288     0.315    0.368     0.415
27    Other              0.455     0.541     0.674    0.772     0.783
28
29    Total Expenses     2.203     3.251     3.925    4.449     4.573
30                     ----------------------------------------------
31  Profit (Loss)        1.662     1.741     1.878    1.573     1.908
32                     ----------------------------------------------
33
16-May-87  1:15 PM
```

FIGURE 11.8   The Spreadsheet   The now-familiar format of a spreadsheet was developed for VisiCalc and refined in Lotus 1-2-3, shown here. The traditional arrangement of rows and columns in an accountant's ledger was the base for a new kind of affordance—the ability to calculate changes in an entry automatically, based on a formula that defined the entry's value in terms of other entries. Although the idea seems simple, it revolutionized the way that financial work is done. (*Source:* Courtesy of Lotus Development Corp.)

ities for the contents of an individual cell, to include not just text or a number, but also a formula for calculation, which can be based on results from other cells. With this structure, all the logic necessary to recalculate the spreadsheet is stored in the spreadsheet. When the contents of a cell are changed in a spreadsheet, all the cells whose values depend on that one are automatically, almost magically, changed. All the complexities of intermediate calculations are invisible, unless the user chooses to examine them.

The spreadsheet was fundamentally different from earlier programs for financial calculation, with their unbridgeable separation between program and data—corresponding to a nearly unbridgeable separation between programmer and accountant. The key innovation was not in the interface elements or the software structure, but rather in the *virtuality* provided to the user—the underlying world of objects and their behaviors. The spreadsheet virtuality combines the regular structure of the familiar ledger sheet with an underlying structure of interlinked formulas. The nontechnical user can build a complex financial model incrementally, and can explore the model through successive iterations of inputs. This quantitative change in ease meant a qualitative change in how people worked with the data.

The interactivity of the spreadsheet made it possible to create what Shahaf Gal (Chapter 11) calls *design footholds*. The person designing a financial plan can quickly represent alternatives and explore the consequences of specific decisions. The power of the spreadsheet lies in the interaction between calculating results and inventing new possibilities.

An additional dimension that appeared in the next generation of spreadsheets, initiated by Lotus 1-2-3, was the ability to write short macros that could reproduce the action of a series of key strokes. Further, by the inclusion of simple control constructs (if–then, go to, etc.) and interfaces to the user interface (to display and process menus and prompts), the macro capability provided a general capability for user programming. In a way, user-created macros were the solution to the tension between direct manipulation, with its direct mapping of action to result, and programming, with its use of abstractions to create patterns of activity that do not depend on the specific data. The initial spreadsheet moved away from the programming-based models of mainframe financial software, making it highly usable but limited in power. The addition of macros brought back a good deal of that programming power to the ordinary user, or at least to the *superuser* (or local expert) whose background was in the financial world, but who could produce macros for use by other users (see Nardi, 1993).

Now that the spreadsheet is widely available, it has come to be used for many tasks that have nothing to do with finances. A spreadsheet can be used for any activity that calls for calculating regular arrays of values that are interrelated by regular formulas—especially for those activities that call for exploring alternatives. Professors use spreadsheets for grading courses, scientists use spreadsheets for interpreting data from experiments, and builders use spreadsheets for keeping track of materials. New kinds of spreadsheets have been developed that fill the cells with visual images, sounds, and other data representations, inter-linked by formulas that perform calculations in the appropriate domain.

The lessons to be learned from this history are not about the specifics of the spreadsheet; they are about the underlying reasons for its power.

The power of representations. Although the underlying calculations for financial modeling were not new, the representation of an active array of formula-based values created a new virtuality—a world in which to work.

The power of interactive modification. Because the recalculation of a spreadsheet could be done interactively as part of the flow of a modeling process, it could be used as a design foothold—as a way of making concretely visible a set of assumptions and relations, see-ing what they produced, and using the results to guide the next round of modifications.

The power of incremental programmability. The macro language for spreadsheets created a vast army of superusers, who did not see themselves as programmers, but who could produce spreadsheet templates that carried out complex and useful work for themselves and for colleagues in their workplaces. Giving end users control of their tools was a major theme of the PC revolution. When users became less dependent on a priestly caste of programmers to accomplish their tasks, their productivity flourished.

Suggested Reading

Bonnie Nardi. *A Small Matter of Programming: Perspectives on End User Computing.* Cambridge, MA: MIT Press, 1993.

Design as Practiced

When you are asked to solve a problem, look beyond it. Ask why that particular problem arose in the first place. Search beyond the technical: Question the business model, the organizational structure, and the culture. The path to a solution seldom lies in the question as posed: the path appears only when we are able to pose the right question.

Donald Norman is one of the founders and professional leaders of the discipline of cognitive science, and of its predecessor field, cognitive psychology. He is well known for his pioneering experiments on memory and attention in humans, and he created one of the first departments of cognitive science, at the University of California, San Diego.

Norman was not satisfied, however, with the rules of the game in academia. As he said in one of his recent books, *Things That Make Us Smart* (1993, p. xii), "University-based research can be clever, profound, and deep, but surprisingly often it has little or no impact either upon scientific knowledge or upon society at large. What matters is precision, rigor, and reproducibility, even if the result bears little relevance to the phenomena under study." Over the years, Norman moved away from the rigorous irrelevance of the academic journals, shifting his attention to the things that we encounter every day in our lives—the doors, faucets, and computers—and to complex systems, such as airline cockpits and nuclear power plants (see Profile 12). For each of these objects, design succeeds or fails, depending on how well it works for people.

At Apple Computer, Norman is now Vice President for Advanced Technology, heading Apple's research program. When he first arrived at Apple as an Apple Fellow, Norman established a small, high-level group, called the *User Experience Architect's Office*, which worked across the company to make Apple products easier to use. A key goal in instituting this office was to get *user-experience professionals* involved at product conception, and to have them be part of the design team throughout the development process. Norman chose the phrase *user experience* to emphasize that his office's concern was not just the interface. It was more than menus and icons; it was everything related to the user's experience of the product.

In this chapter, Norman reflects on his experience in trying to accomplish his goals at Apple. He tells the story of the Macintosh power switch: of how he tried to simplify its placement and function, but was thwarted on all sides by sensible, reasonable technical problems. His central point is that design as practiced is very different from

Author's acknowledgment: My thanks to Sue Bartalo, who co-led the power-switch committee, and struggled through all the issues and draft reports, and to Laura De Young and Julie Norman for valuable editorial comments.

design as taught. In the actual situation, cultural, social, and organizational issues can dominate the user-oriented aspects of design.

—Terry Winograd

◠◡◠

DESIGN AS PRACTICED IS CONSIDERABLY DIFFERENT from design as idealized in academic discussions of "good design." A few years ago, I made the transition from the university to industry—a deliberate decision on my part to practice what I had long been preaching, and to try to understand the constraints and pressures from the business point of view. How nice it would be, I thought, to be able to see products in the marketplace that reflected my design philosophy. This chapter recounts one stage of my learning process: Issues that seem simple from the vantage point of academia are often extremely complex when seen from inside the industry. Indeed, the two sides seem hardly to be speaking the same language. In the course of my experiences, I have come to recognize that industry faces numerous problems that are outside of the scope of the traditional analyses of design. In particular, there are management and organizational issues, business concerns, and even corporate culture.

Management and organizational issues reflect that humans work well in small groups of five to 10 individuals, and work less well as the group size increases. As a result, over the past few millennia, various organizational structures have arisen to allow people by the hundreds, thousands, hundreds of thousands, and even millions (in the case of armies) to work effectively. Each organizational solution, however, has its tradeoffs, emphasizing one aspect of control to the detriment of others. University laboratories, with their emphasis on small, innovative groups, where individual work is highly rated and group activities often are deemphasized, do not face these pressures.

Business concerns deal with profit and loss. Innovative products do not necessarily succeed in the marketplace, and no company can afford to bring out unsuccessful products. The list of companies with the right product at the wrong time is long, and their names long forgotten. Had you bought stock in the first American manufacturers of automobiles, typewriters, or personal computers, you would have lost your money. Even successful companies have difficulty in making the transition to a new product generation: Tell your customers that you have an entirely new and superior approach, and they will stop buying the old, but will postpone buying the new until it is "proven," by which time you are apt to be bankrupt. The problems of maintaining the *installed base*, and what have been come to be known as *legacy systems*, can throttle an otherwise innovative industry.

Cultural issues are perhaps the hardest to identify and deal with. Once people are acculturated, their thoughts, beliefs, and actions are biased, without their conscious awareness. Of all the problems that beset the design industry, cultural issues are probably the most insidious.

The Problem of the Macintosh Power Switch

To illustrate the depth of the design problem, I will tell you the story of the Macintosh power switch—of how a dedicated committee tried to simplify the placement and function of the switch, but succeeded only through multiple compromises in the face of many reasonable technical problems. The power switch is a relatively trivial matter, and that is why it is such a good example. Even the most trivial problems are constrained by so many issues that their solution becomes complex or even impossible.

Apple produces numerous models of its Macintosh computer. They all run the same basic software, with technical modifications in the underlying drivers and core operating system to reflect different hardware structures. All current Macintosh computers come with a number of standard physical controls and connectors. A good deal of attention has gone into the development of a consistent design language for hardware features (see the discussion by Rheinfrank and Evenson in Chapter 4). In this context, the lack of standardization of the power switch seems bizarre. Some machines have it in the front, others on the back. Some have toggle switches, others have pushbuttons. Some machines do not appear to have any power switch at all. Users continually have trouble finding the switches.

The design that finally called for remedial action was the one in which the power switch was a button underneath the slot for the floppy disk, as shown in Figure 12.1. Some customers, unaware that a

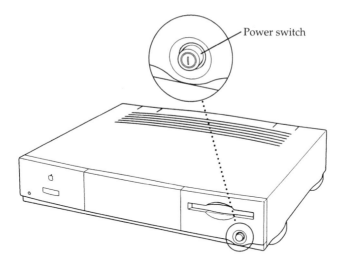

FIGURE 12.1   A Misleading Power Switch   The power switch on the Macintosh 610 (and later related models) is a button underneath the slot for the floppy disk. Users confused it with the disk-eject button that is located similarly on other brands of computers, leading them to shut off the Macintosh's power accidentally. (From *Getting Started With Your Macintosh Quadra 610* (Eng.P/N 030-4621-A). Reprinted with permission of Apple Computer, Inc.)

Macintosh floppy disk is ejected automatically under program control (and a few who were not paying attention), would push the button, expecting it to eject the floppy, only to discover that they had turned off their machine, possibly losing their work.

Eventually, a customer complaint to one of the Internet's news groups got bounced around the internal networks at Apple. The director of the industrial-design department and I contacted the vice-president who supervised three of the divisions that produced Macintoshes. We all agreed that the problem was detrimental to our customers and completely unnecessary. We were asked to devise a solution, and were assured that it would be followed. "Aha," I said to myself, "the power switch can be a test case of my desire to restructure the design process at Apple. I don't care much about power switches, but perhaps this case will not only solve the power-switch problem but also make a small improvement in usability—one that is easy to implement and that would indeed make a difference." Was I mistaken!

Design in a Large Organization

Remember, people work well in small groups, so as soon as the size of the organization gets large, communication problems arise. Organizations are in a continual struggle against this problem, with repeated attempts to "reorganize," as though there were a perfect structure that would somehow solve all difficulties. There isn't. So the story as told here reflects the organization that existed then—not the one that exists now. Then, I was an Apple Fellow; now, I am a vice-president. Does that make any difference? No, not really. Then, the hardware and software divisions were separated; now, they are merged. Does that make a difference? Yes, a little. Today, there is more cohesion in the organizational structure, but, as a result, there are larger organizations, which pose their own communication difficulties. Does that really make a difference? No, because although the top of the organization has been restructured, as far as the lowest-level engineers—that is, the people who do the work—are concerned, nothing has changed except the names of the bosses of their boss's boss.

The first problem was to discover who was in charge. Answer: No one. Apple did not have a single design center. Design was done across the company. Moreover, the Macintosh was produced by four different divisions of the company: Macintosh Entry Systems, Desktop Systems, Portables, and Apple Business Systems.

Entry Systems built the least expensive line of machines. Entry Systems staff were cost conscious, for they were in an incredibly competitive marketplace, where a few dollars in selling price makes a difference. Desktop Systems was responsible for the high-end machines, where cost is still important, but not nearly as much so as for the entry-level machines. For Portables, weight, size, and power consumption dominate the design issues. Size limitations meant that there was no physical room to implement some of our proposals. Apple Business Systems produced servers—machines meant to be tucked away somewhere out of sight, and to deliver files, printing, or communication services unattended, with great reliability. In this case, the power switch sometimes has to be hidden, locked, or otherwise protected against accidental use or access by unauthorized people.

In addition to the product-design centers, a number of other groups were involved in design, including the central industrial-design

238

group and the human-interface group, which serviced the software division and all the hardware divisions except for the two that had their own human-interface groups: Business Systems and the Personal Interactive Electronics Division (where the Newton was produced). Several groups were concerned about *localization*—the process of adjusting designs to the languages, customs, and regulations around the world. In addition, there were safety issues, especially relevant to power switches, and another office dealt with equal access by the handicapped. My own contribution was in the User Experience Architect's Office, which worked with all Apple divisions.

When I thought that Apple had numerous people qualified to solve this problem, I was correct. The trouble was that each of them chose a different solution, appropriate to their product division. Still, this obstacle did not appear to be insurmountable. All we needed to do, I thought, was to get together all the relevant people in one room to discuss the issues, to reach agreement, and to write a draft report. The draft would be circulated and discussed, and then perhaps a second meeting would resolve any disagreements. End of story, right?

The Search for a Solution in a Complex Design Space

We quickly gathered a small team: One person from product design, one from human interface, and one from hardware. Then, we sent notices across all of Apple, soliciting interested parties. We gathered names of about 30 people representing a wide variety of interests and groups, appearing to cover all relevant constituencies.

The committee was extremely cooperative and constructive. Everyone agreed that the current problems with the power switch were unwarranted and ought to be solved. Everyone shared numerous concerns and issues. But each person also came with a set of constraints dictated by the concerns of a particular organization. Each person explained those constraints in logical, rational form, and, after each explanation, the entire group would nod in sympathy, and say, yes, those are all valid points. Alas, the constraints were mutually incompatible. Three months later, after numerous meetings and roughly 10 draft proposals, and further meetings, we were still working on a solution.

First, there was the incredible variety of machines: from those used as high-power workstations, to servers (which need protected power switches), to office, home, and educational machines, as well as portables. Some machines were placed on the desk, often with the monitor on top. Some were placed on the floor. Some were rotated to stand on their side. Some required clearly marked, easily accessible switches. Some needed switches out of reach.

Several otherwise-simple solutions were ruled out by cost considerations. In the low-end market, where cost dominates, even a slight extra cost can disrupt product sales. If we wanted a uniform policy for all machines, it had to be acceptable to the most cost-conscious product—50 cents of added cost could be prohibitive.

Other solutions were ruled out by data from our customer-service centers, which are treated seriously in the user-oriented culture at Apple. Nontechnical users of computers—the vast majority of our customers—were confused by the existence of the power switch. If they saw one, they used it to turn off the machine—instead of using the shutdown software—with the potential to cause massive software problems.

Other companies put the burden of safety on the users; if users destroy files, it is their fault for failing to use the proper procedure. On a machine running Unix, only the system operator is supposed to turn off the machine, and then only after following a set of procedures, including running a special program (*sync*) to ensure the integrity of files on the hard disk. On DOS and Windows® 3.1 machines, the power is supposed to be turned off only when the machine is in the DOS mode with no open files (Windows 3.1 users must leave Windows first—Windows® 95 has adopted the Macintosh design). If the user of any operating system turns off the machine while it is running an application, or when files are open, there may be damage to the system or loss of data. Putting the burden on the user to do a task properly goes against the culture of the Macintosh community.

An elegant solution emerged in the early days of the Macintosh: Shutdown was done by the computer, rather than by the person. When you were finished working, you evoked the *Shut Down* procedure from a menu, and let the machine turn itself off in a graceful, safe way, as illustrated in Figure 12.2.

A switch on the keyboard, the *keyboard power key*, was used only to turn on the computer. Today's Macintosh models—like many

Choose Shut Down
from the Special menu

Some models of the Macintosh
turn off automatically when you
choose Shut Down. Others
display a message on screen
telling you that it's all right to
turn off the computer.

FIGURE 12.2   A Safe Shutdown   The shutdown procedure designed for
the original Macintosh is initiated by the user via a menu action. Each application provides a procedure for cleaning up properly before exiting, so the system can put itself into an appropriate state before shutting down the power
under program control. This design was later adopted by other operating systems, such as Windows 95. (From *Getting Started With Your Macintosh
Quadra 610* (Eng.P/N 030-4621-A). Reprinted with permission of Apple
Computer, Inc.)

consumer-electronic devices—use *soft power control*: They never have
all power removed. Just as the power button on the TV remote does
not cause a hard shutdown of the TV set, neither does the *Shut
Down* menu entry on the Mac. After all, if these selections really
shut down all power, the TV remote would not be able to turn the
power back on, and the Mac's keyboard would not turn on the
machine. *Hard power switches* do disconnect full power; they physically break the circuit from the power mains. But these solutions are
being phased out and, in any event, lead to severe software problems
if they are used at inopportune times.

   With soft power control, it is not necessary to have a power switch
at all: You can put a switch on the keyboard to turn on the machine,
and use menu control to turn off the machine. For this reason, our
machines made for the home and school markets took away the power
switch and added an extra *Shut Down* command to the *Apple* menu
that was visible in almost every Macintosh application (in addition to
its traditional location in the menu labeled *Special* in the Finder). On
certain machines, we experimented with adding a shutdown dialog
with the user, to be triggered whenever the power key on the keyboard was hit. Experience indicated that we should hide the power

switch, while making software shutdown as readily available and visible as possible.

Occasionally, it is necessary to disconnect power fully, such as when you are installing parts, or moving the machine from one place to another. Certain safety regulations require that it be possible to disconnect all power. Also, when the operating system crashes, a soft, graceful shutdown under software control is not possible. Here is the beginning of the technical problem: How can you provide for software control of shutdown, yet allow an emergency means of shutting down when the software has failed? The emergency method has to be available when needed, but must be sufficiently inconspicuous that it is not invoked under normal conditions, because then it might do more harm than good.

So, what we wanted was a simple and effective way for people to turn on their machine and to shut down or close safely all files, applications, queues, and caches, and to turn off all power except for that required to monitor essential machine states. But then we had to worry about abnormal situations, where the software was corrupted such that the software-controlled shutdown process would not work. In this case, there had to be some easy way of forcing either a shutdown or a reboot. We also needed to provide a method of putting the machine into an energy-saving, or sleep, state, and of awakening it. Programmers wanted a way of forcing entry into the debug state. And, of course, the scheme had to be protected against accidental initiation.

The proposals therefore were variations of the following:

> Use the keyboard power key to power on the machine when the machine is off, and to initiate a shutdown dialog when the machine is on. In addition, provide a means of entering the debug state and of triggering a forced shutdown in case of emergency. Finally, include a real power switch on the main box housing the computer, where it will be inexpensive, not be too easily accessible, but easy to find in an emergency. The functioning of the switch has to be readily understood by people who have never used a Mac before, but must not annoy our skilled, power users. Moreover, the solution has to work both for the normal shut-down situation and when the system software is no longer responding.

The problem was further complicated by the need to satisfy international safety requirements, to work across the world with a variety of languages and cultural expectations, and to be usable by people with a variety of disabilities.

For example, one problem that we encountered was totally unexpected: You would not believe how much time we spent on the problem of labeling the keyboard power key. In our current models, the keyboard power-on keys are labeled with a left-facing triangle. Why? Because that symbol does not mean anything! The symbol used earlier (a vertical line inside a circle) was not permitted because the European standards authorities insisted that it was reserved for hard power switches. The triangle has no meaning, so it does not violate any standards. Few people—European or American—are confident about the meaning of the vertical bar and circle (on and off, respectively), let alone a bar inside of circle (a toggled on–off), or a vertical bar inside a broken circle (toggled soft power), but the European standards committee is strict. There are safety risks associated with thinking that a shutdown switch removes all power from the machine when it does not.

So, what seemed to be a simple task—one that would remove all the confusions of our power-switch locations—turned out to be incredibly complex. The final proposal had a soft power key on the keyboard, labeled "on/off," (translated into whatever was appropriate for the language of the keyboard). The real power switch was on the rear of the CPU box. The user could initiate an emergency shutdown by holding down the power key for greater than 5 seconds, or by depressing the rear power switch twice (the first attempt tries a normal soft shutdown). We recommended a separate reset button, but, in deference to the cost considerations of the entry-level systems and the space considerations for portables, we did not require one. A policy of indicator lights was established, so that a user could tell whether the machine was on, off, or in energy-saving mode.

I hear people saying, "What if someone accidentally hit the power key, or what if a book fell on it, or a cat walked across the keyboard— would you lose all your work? And how would anyone ever discover that holding down the power key for 5 seconds caused a forced shutdown? Doesn't that violate all sorts of design rules, including ones that you (Don Norman) have been advocating?" Yes, these are valid points. We obviously considered these problems. I am not happy with the solution that we reached, but given the technical and business constraints that we faced, I could think of no better answer.

The Macintosh Culture and Design Constraints

Why were there so many technical problems? Macintosh designers had made early decisions about the appropriate way to simplify tasks for the user, which launched the power-control system along a particular technical path. This path got ever more complex as the variety of computers increased. Meanwhile, part of the culture forced on every computer company with an installed base is the emphasis on *backward compatibility*: Once a concept is introduced, maintain it.

Our committee started with a number of assumptions, many of them unstated. We took for granted that there would be soft control of power under normal circumstances, that the machine would be started through the power key on the keyboard, and that the hard power switch should be used only under exceptional circumstances. In addition, we wanted to keep the ability for programmers to get to the debug state, and to make possible emergency solutions. The possibilities of removing the keyboard power key or of moving away from soft power were never even discussed.

The cultural values associated with simplicity and compatibility were seldom stated, and some may not even have been conscious. In fact, it was only after all the power-switch meetings were finished that we were able to reflect on the incidents and to realize that many of the so-called technical issues were really a result of the underlying Macintosh culture, and that, if we now went back and changed certain of those cultural assumptions, the technical problems would change. Changing the culture of the keyboard power key and the *Shut Down* menu item is exceedingly difficult. In fact, we didn't even consider it until late in the power-switch deliberations—not because we knew that it was difficult, but because the assumptions were so embedded in our culture that we didn't even realize that we had the option.

Apple Computer culture emphasizes *ease of use* to the extreme. Ease of use is part of the *core competency* of the corporation. It causes many programmers and engineers to feel empowered to design the user side of the product just as readily as the technical side. That is not necessarily good, when it leads to incompatibility as seen by the users.

Moreover, because of the corporate organizational structure, there is no single design center. Even if a design is put to user test, with human-interface professionals, the solution for a problem for the product produced by one group might differ from the solution to the same problem in a product produced by a different group. The many different power-switch options produced confusion for users because they violated the principle of creating a consistent design language across an entire product line, as discussed by Rheinfrank and Evenson in Chapter 4.

Another problem is organizational. As a result of corporate history, Apple had a particular organizational structure, with separate profit centers, each making one kind of product. This organizational structure was ideal for certain aspects of corporate business, but was inefficient for others. In particular, it did not lend itself to coherent, consistent design decisions. Centralized groups are ideal for that purpose. Centralized groups, on the other hand, tend to lead to bloated bureaucracies, with long decision chains and inefficient and slow processes. These organizational issues end up dictating just how design is done.

Why did Apple have four different divisions: Personal Interactive Electronics, AppleSoft (operating systems), Apple Business Systems, and Apple PC (hardware)? Why were there three different divisions within Apple PC that produced three different types of Macintoshes? Why was industrial design centralized, although human interface was not? Why was industrial design separate from human interface? Why was industrial design high in status, and human interface low (although the concept is regarded highly—a core competency after all)? And why was there no human-interface group in the hardware division? (Answer: Because hardware is thought to be relevant to industrial design—software is where human-interface issues arise. This attitude prevails despite its obvious fallacies, even though the hardware division writes software, such as control panels and drivers.) These issues would require another chapter to cover; they result from historical accident, cultural attitudes, and difficult trade-offs in the organization of large corporations. In fact, the product-division organization described above was changed after the power-switch committee published its report. As of 1995, all Macintoshes are produced in the same division and some of the problems described in this chapter have gone away. Most still remain.

Epilogue

Just as we were about to call the final meeting and to issue the proclamation, a new problem arose. IBM and Apple Computer, after months of deliberation, determined to issue a new, common hardware platform (CHRP, pronounced "chirp") for computers powered by the PowerPC chip. IBM and Apple agreed to manufacture machines that all met the CHRP standards, thereby ensuring that machines made by either manufacturer would run the same software. Oops! What about the special circuits that implement the keyboard power key and the emergency shutdown procedures? Would there even be a power key? In fact, would all computers have the Apple Desktop Bus that connects the keyboard and mouse to the CPU, and through which the power key works? Did the new reference standard even discuss the power switch? As of the publication of this book, we still do not know the answers: Some of these details were not decided in the original announcement; they were left for further committees to resolve. One thing we did learn: the special power-management circuit on which we had counted to monitor the state of the operating system and to control the power operation of the machine would no longer be used. It would be replaced by a new system, as yet not specified.

What will we do? We will schedule more meetings. We will add representatives for the common reference platform to the list of contacts. That may be a blessing in disguise: With the advent of the common reference platform, we have an excuse to change the culture. We could decide to get rid of the keyboard switch, or to change the power-management circuits, or to eliminate or greatly modify the *Shut Down* menu item. Cultures are easier to change during periods of galactic upset. On the other hand, is the power switch really worth all this effort?

There is no easy solution. There is no way to prevent problems such as this one from arising—no matter how cleverly we redesign the machines or redesign the organization. But the lessons of this story do lead to a positive prescription for design—one that I have long taught my students and have followed myself. When you are asked to solve a problem, look beyond it. Ask why that particular problem arose in the first place. Search beyond the technical: Question the business model, the organizational structure, and the culture. The path to a solution seldom lies in the question as posed: the path appears only when we are able to pose the right question.

Suggested Readings

Donald Norman and Stephen Draper (eds.). *User Centered System Design: New Perspectives on Human–Computer Interaction.* Hillsdale, NJ: Lawrence Erlbaum Associates, 1986.

Thomas Landauer. *The Trouble with Computers: Usefulness, Usability, and Productivity.* Cambridge, MA: MIT Press, 1995.

About the Author

Donald Norman is Vice President of the Advanced Technology Group, responsible for managing advanced technology and research for Apple Computer, and Professor Emeritus of Cognitive Science at the University of California, San Diego.

12. The Design of Everyday Things

You have probably had the experience of entering a bathroom that contains a modern stylish sink—so stylish that you can't figure out how to turn the water on or off. Or you may have encountered a door that person after person tried to push open, even though it was designed to be pulled, and even though it exhibited a large label saying *Pull*. The form of every object that we encounter suggests the *affordances* of what can be done with and to that object. Our everyday world is filled with objects whose design communicates possibilities that are inadequate, or are downright misleading.

In a series of popular books, Donald Norman has applied theories of cognitive psychology to the study of these everyday things, and to the psychology of how we approach them, interpret them, and use them. In *The Design of Everyday Things* (1990; original edition, 1988, titled *The Psychology of Everyday Things*) Norman points out why computers and other everyday devices are often so difficult to use. He shows how we can learn the design principles that apply to complex systems—such as commercial aircraft, nuclear-power plants, and computer interfaces—by observing people's interactions with mundane objects such as doors, water faucets, and light switches.

As a simple example, he points out the difference between the *arbitrary mapping* of controls for a cooktop, as shown in Figure 12.3(a), and a *natural mapping*, as shown in Figure 12.3(b). The natural design does not require labeling to make clear which knob controls which burner, and it is much less likely to lead to errors. In fact, Norman points out that the need for a label such as *On* or *Pull* is often a clue that the affordances have not been designed well.

Profile Authors: Laura De Young and Terry Winograd

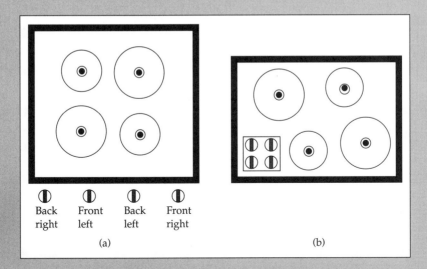

Back   Front   Back   Front
right   left   left   right

(a)   (b)

FIGURE 12.3   **Mapping of Controls**   In the arrangement of controls for a cooktop, the use of a natural mapping makes labeling unnecessary and saves the user from having to learn or remember how to use the controls properly. (From *The Design of Everyday Things* by Donald Norman. Copyright ©1990 by HarperCollins Publishers, Inc. Reprinted by permission of HarperCollins Publishers, Inc.)

Software design is filled with examples of arbitrary mappings that create problems for users.

In two further books, *Turn Signals Are the Facial Expressions of Automobiles* (1992), and *Things That Make Us Smart* (1993), Norman looks more deeply into the social impact of modern technologies. He decries a trend that he sees toward a *machine-centered* view, which produces an estrangement between humans and machines—people's continuing and growing frustration with technology and with the pace and stress of a technologically centered life.

If you lock your keys inside your car, you are likely to feel stupid or to be angry at yourself for failing to pay attention to such a simple detail. You have probably just caused yourself, and perhaps other people, significant inconvenience, all because you weren't paying attention. Norman asks us to take a different perspective. He distinguishes what people are good at from what—by nature—is difficult for them. He points out that human cognition is extraordinarily good at complex reasoning, but often is not so good at keeping track of details.

TABLE 12.1   Machine- and People-Centered Views

	PEOPLE ARE	MACHINES ARE
The machine-centered view	Vague	Precise
	Disorganized	Orderly
	Distractible	Undistractible
	Emotional	Unemotional
	Illogical	Logical
The people-centered view	Creative	Dumb
	Compliant	Rigid
	Attentive to change	Insensitive to change
	Resourceful	Unimaginative
	Able to make flexible decisions based on context	Constrained to make consistent decisions

(From D.A. Norman, *Things That Make Us Smart,* © 1993 Donald A. Norman. Reprinted by permission of Addison-Wesley Publishing Co., Inc.)

Apparently, you were not thinking about where your car keys were at the moment that you closed the car door. Your absence of attention was not necessarily bad—you might have been thinking about something much deeper or more important to your life and current activities: something that takes substantially more brain power than remembering the whereabouts of car keys.

We can look at the contrasting qualities of people and machines from two different viewpoints, as described in Table 12.1.

Norman asks designers to appreciate these uniquely human abilities, and to design things to help us with those skills that are less natural—to populate our world with *things that make us smart.* If we blame ourselves in a situation such as the locked-in car keys, we are falling prey to a machine-centered way of thinking. In contrast, a human-centered view would put the blame where it belongs: on the faulty design of the car. After all, why are we expected to keep track of a certain uniquely shaped, flat metal object at a moment when we are doing a physically unrelated action, such as closing a door? At the very least, the technical apparatus—the car—could remind us where the object is. In fact, most newer cars draw our awareness to keys left in the ignition by making a distinctive noise. The driver's door on many cars can be locked only from the outside—with the key—ensuring that the key is not inside the car when the door is locked. It may take innovative design to create an environment in which key keeping is natural and does not require special attention. But that is the kind of human-centered design that we should pursue.

In the frontispiece to *Things That Make Us Smart*, Norman presents the motto of the 1933 Chicago World's Fair: *Science Finds, Industry Applies, Man Conforms*. He ends the book (p. 253) with a response:

> That was a machine-centered view of the world—unabashedly, proudly machine-centered. It is time to revolt. We can't conform. Moreover, we shouldn't have to. It is science and technology—and thereby industry—that should do the conforming. The slogan of the 1930s has been with us long enough. Now, as we enter the twenty-first century, it is time for a person-centered motto, one that puts the emphasis right: People Propose, Science Studies, Technology Conforms.

Suggested Readings

Donald Norman. *The Design of Everyday Things*. New York: Doubleday, 1990.

Donald Norman. *Turn Signals Are the Facial Expressions of Automobiles*. Reading, MA: Addison-Wesley, 1992.

Donald Norman. *Things That Make Us Smart*. Reading, MA: Addison-Wesley, 1993.

LAURA DE YOUNG

Organizational Support for Software Design

Software design is an art as well as a science. Designing products

that meet the needs of customers requires insight, creativity,

knowledge, skill, and discipline....An organization can do

much to support the process and to help ensure success. By the

same token, the organization can impede the design process, stifle

creativity, and damn a project to the software hell of producing

a product that is unfit for customer use.

In this chapter, Laura De Young examines the world in which software designers work: both the organizational setting and the larger world of markets and customers that together provide the context, motivation, and ultimate evaluation for design.

In her discussion, she draws on her years of experience as a software designer and consultant, pointing out the pitfalls that can lead to software hell. In contrast, she highlights what she learned in a series of interviews with employees and customers of Intuit, an upstart startup company that captured a major applications market from Microsoft (which eventually attempted to buy Intuit at a remarkably high price). Within a few years from its beginning, Intuit's personal finance program Quicken rose to become the leading software of its kind (see Profile 13). Quicken's acceptance grew primarily through word of mouth by satisfied customers. This satisfaction wasn't accidental: It was the result of a carefully considered and religiously followed strategy of watching and listening to what users did in practice, and of considering how the software worked for them.

—Terry Winograd

S OFTWARE DESIGN IS AN ART as well as a science. Designing products that meet the needs of customers requires insight, creativity, knowledge, skill, and discipline. It is a complex process that is almost always done in the context of organizations. An organization can do much to support the process and to help ensure success. By the same token, the organization can impede the design process, stifle creativity, and damn a project to the software hell of producing a product that is unfit for customer use.

This chapter describes how an organization shapes the environment for software design, and offers practical steps that organizations can take to produce better software products. Our focus is on the three most important objectives in organizational support of software design: setting and maintaining clear goals; focusing on customers; and empowering designers. Effectively meeting these objectives increases both the potential for a successful software product and the satisfaction derived by the software designers who work on the project.

Although these objectives may sound like simple common sense, every experienced software designer has participated in—or knows someone who has participated in—software projects that started with common sense, but that failed. This chapter gives examples of how such failures can result from inadequate attention to the three basic objectives—how projects can lose their common sense. It also includes examples of how successful software companies can maintain adequate focus on these objectives and thereby foster good software design.

Clarity of Goals

One of the most difficult tasks for a designer is to create a successful design in the context of an organization or a project in which the participants do not know what they are trying to achieve. Most managers will tell you that it is critical to have clear, realistic goals, and yet software projects fail every day because of problems with goals. Why is it so difficult to set and maintain effective goals? There are two reasons. First, since the purpose of having a goal is to get everyone moving in the same direction and to determine when success has been achieved, the goal must be shared by everyone. For everyone to have the same definition of the goal, that goal must have limited ambiguity. Second, goals change. They can continue to be shared only if these changes are articulated and addressed realistically.

The potential problems in setting and maintaining goals showed up in a case that I encountered in my consulting (names and details have been modified to protect confidentiality).

ManuSoft produced software for manufacturing. Its primary product was an inventory-control application that was rated number 1 in the market. But it was losing market share because Factorex, which had the number 2 inventory-control application, offered in addition a reasonably good financial package, and many customers preferred dealing with a single vendor. ManuSoft also provided a financial product, but that product was outdated and no longer met customer needs. ManuSoft hired Jane, a highly motivated and committed software designer, to design a new financial product.

Jane set out to produce the biggest and best financial product that could be imagined. She assembled a substantial team of analysts and engineers; and after 18 months, she proudly presented the first proto-type to ManuSoft's executives. They were gravely disappointed—the project was a failure. The managers were appalled by the resource burn rate, and they were not prepared to apply the resources necessary to make Jane's grand vision a reality.

What went wrong? Basically, the project goals were ambiguous, allowing for different definitions. Management's definition of the goal, albeit unvoiced, was to produce a financial product that was merely sufficient to support the sales of their bread-and-butter applica-tion. Jane, in her desire to make a striking new product, was aiming at a different target. Why did it take so long for everyone to recognize this discrepancy? First, it took a full $1\frac{1}{2}$ years to produce the first con-crete representation of the product concept. It is easy to believe that everyone is working toward the same results, as long as all they are doing is talking.

Concrete representations push us to clarify our goals and help us to see ambiguities in those goals, as Michael Schrage describes in his analysis of prototyping cultures (Chapter 10). ManuSoft did not have a prototyping culture that served effectively for communication within the organization. Even without the prototype, however, if people had stated and restated the project goals, and had discussed their views of those goals explicitly, they would have noticed that they did not have a universally shared goal.

In addition, Jane's goal did not fit neatly under the umbrella of the company's mission. Not that the company's mission was clear. It is unlikely that anyone in ManuSoft at that time could have articulated the mission, and certainly they could not have done so with consen-sus. But even given that state of confusion, the main focus of the com-pany was the domain-specific application, rather than the financial product.

Last, but most important, the project goal (regardless of the ver-sion) was not tied closely enough to customer needs. The question of how this product would make the customer's life better was never addressed. Goals are slippery and ephemeral, and are effective only when they are grounded in the reality of how they meet customer needs.

Another example shows how difficult it is to hold onto a goal, for even a short time. A small team of software designers at FinanceCo, a producer of banking software, was given the task of creating a proof-of-concept prototype for a loan-processing application. This prototype was scheduled to be shown to upper management in 3 weeks. During a status check after the initial storyboard was created, the manager responsible for the prototype asked how many screens would be produced. The answer, according to the initial design, was 28. By the end of the second week, it became clear to the team that they would have to modify their design to meet the deadline. At the next status meeting, the manager asked how many screens would be finished for the demo. The answer "20" caused considerable upset. This manager had lost sight of the original goal, which had been to create an impressive and realistic prototype that communicated the design concept. Instead, the manager's goal had become "produce 28 screens." In the manager's mind, to produce fewer than 28 screens meant failure and humiliation.

Everyone involved in a software project is susceptible to goal transmutation. Keeping aligned requires communicating in a way that restates the project goals continuously, with each of the participants attempting to be honest about what his goals are for the project, as he sees those goals each day.

It is difficult enough to specify clear goals that are grounded in customer needs, shared by everyone on the project, and held in focus. To add to the challenge, goals change continuously: The process of design leads to continuous goal refinement, as every design decision may lead to the recognition that goals need to be modified. Each change should provoke basic questions: Does what we are about to do align with the goal? If not, should we modify the goal or our decision? If the goal is modified, how can the change be made explicit and communicated to everyone involved with the project? *Everyone* means more than the immediate team. It includes engineering, marketing, sales, and support: Literally everyone whose work touches a project needs to be continually apprised of the project goals, to operate from a consistent vision.

Goals also change as the result of people obtaining new external information. Market needs change. Competitors' actions require responses. Additional research refines ideas of what should be done. The rapid pace of the software industry wreaks havoc with project goals—even with corporate missions. It *is* possible for software designers to cope with this reality, but only if change is acknowledged, and realistic steps are taken to address its effects.

If marketing decides, for example, that a particular product will be used to reach an audience for which the product was not initially intended, this change must be considered seriously in light of the current design. Time and resources must be allocated accordingly. Often, however, such decisions are made without anyone even acknowledging their consequences. Design failure is imminent if either designers are required to hold to their original design, without considering the design's appropriateness for the new audience, or are held to original schedules, while being given the responsibility for updating to fit the new audience.

In an attempt to avoid this path to failure, continuous goal setting is an explicit activity at Intuit. John Monson, the company's Vice President and General Manager for Business Products, describes a product-definition process in which two fundamental questions are asked: What benefits is the customer seeking? How are we going to deliver those benefits? Major objectives are defined, based on the answers to these questions. Monson says that "These objectives get associated with every thought process during the project, from beginning to end. We're rigorous about stating the objectives at the beginning of every document created for the project. From the high-level objectives, we form a strategy for how to achieve them. When you can give that kind of direction to people who do creative work, you make it far easier for them to get the messages right."

Customer Focus

Everywhere we turn, we hear how important it is for businesses to be customer focused. Still, the quality of most software tells us that many products are not being designed based on an understanding of the needs of the customer. Customer focus is not just an attitude. It requires work. It requires a structure that supports staff interacting with customers, and a commitment to gathering data from users at every step: in the market research that lays the groundwork for knowing what to design, in the day-to-day programming decisions, in usability testing that helps to determine whether or not you have succeeded, in verification through quality assurance that the product meets the customer's needs, and in customer support.

In almost every organization for which I have consulted, the people who do software design (and their managers) demonstrate an extreme reluctance to talk with customers. They consistently make decisions in a customer-awareness vacuum, basing their reasoning on assumptions, rather than on data. They offer any number of excuses for not talking with customers. "We know what they want." "We don't have time." "It's too hard." "It's too expensive." "We can't let our people talk to customers—important information will leak out." "Customers don't know what they want, anyway."

DataSoft produces database applications for the insurance industry. The company wanted to develop a rich and consistent corporate image through the visual appeal of its software. When the designers found that they could not reach this goal effectively with the 16 colors available on a VGA display, they were concerned that their customers might not be willing or able to use 256-color displays. At first, they decided to limit the visual design. I encouraged them to talk to their customers about equipment in use and plans for upgrades, to see whether their initial decision was appropriate. Instead, without further data on their customers' needs, they reversed the decision and kept the original visual design, changing their requirements for running the software to include a 256-color display. They never asked their customers what would be most suitable from the customer's point of view. For all DataSoft knew, their customers might not be willing to move to the more expensive displays, or they might have wanted thousands of colors and full-motion video, to provide more effective training and communication. Perhaps DataSoft missed a great opportunity to strengthen their relationships with their customers. Talking with their customers might have uncovered information that would have led them in new and profitable directions.

Unfortunately, this scenario is extremely common. Software designers often do not know enough about the situations and circumstances under which their products will be used: the customers' hardware and other software applications; the customers' technology visions; or the customers' needs for speed, simplicity, clarity, ease of use, consistency, and so on. They do not know the turnover rate of employees using their software; employers' attitudes toward training;

users' education levels, backgrounds, or language preferences; or a host of other user characteristics. Many people who design software products have never seen the environment in which those products will be used, and have little, if any, first-hand knowledge about the people who work in those environments.

In some companies, upper-level managers visit customers occasionally, or marketing gathers information. By the time that this information reaches the people doing software design, however, it is often diluted and is possibly outdated. In the software industry, what you heard from your customers 6 months ago may not be relevant today.

Once, in my consulting, I questioned a design assumption and asked for data backing it up, the Director of Engineering told me, "I've been in this business for 20 years and I know what the customers want." But his contact with customers was limited. He talked only with people at his own level of management. He did not gather information that was sufficiently specific to support design decisions, and he was unable to communicate effectively what he did know to the people who were doing design.

Customer Focus in Action

If gathering data from customers is so important, why don't software designers gather data more often?

First, they don't know which people they should consult. Without support from the organization, they do not have access to the people who can give them the information that they need. The company needs to take explicit actions to facilitate communication. At Intuit, for example, virtually everyone in the company talks with customers. Intuit employees are encouraged to create relationships with customers and to interact with customers on a regular basis. Monson advocates a simple but effective method to get customer input regarding questions that don't warrant expensive and time-consuming analysis. He advises his employees that, when there is a question about what customers want, they can start by calling 10 customer contacts. A brief talk with just 10 people might answer the question. If it does not provide a definitive answer, at least the caller will have learned more about what questions to ask. This technique does not provide a scientific sample, and it succeeds only when accompanied by judgment about whether the information is representative or misleading. But it can offer a significant gain with a relatively low investment.

Intuit takes steps to reduce the risk of divulging sensitive information in conversations with customers. In addition to using standard nondisclosure agreements, Intuit employees screen participants for broad programs, such as beta tests, to ensure that they are not sending their beta releases to competitors. Beyond these standard procedures, there is continuous support for staff as they interact with customers. The work is done as a team, so designers can talk with other designers and product managers about what should or should not be disclosed.

Designers also need support in learning how to gather useful information. It does not work well to ask customers what great invention they would like to have. It is more useful to pose specific questions about needs or features. The key is to ask customers questions that they can answer. It is often necessary to provide them with a vision—an image of how a new product might look or behave. What designers provide depends on what kind of information they are seeking. For example, if the goal is to find out how users can enter checkbook information easily, designers can learn much by watching users enter data from their own checkbooks into a prototype, or even into a real system. But if a designer is developing a new paradigm or an innovative new feature, she can get more useful responses by suggesting general ideas, such as "financial planning for your retirement using the computer"—ideas that are rich enough to create a vision, but are not so concrete as to limit the user's creative thinking.

In one example, Intuit designers were exploring different conceptual models for a user interface (see Liddle's discussion of conceptual models in Chapter 2). They devised the idea of a financial calendar, and then in focus groups with customers—in particular with women who manage family finances—they learned that women often think about their finances in terms of the calendar: they know when their paydays are, and they have a mental idea of when expenses will occur through the rest of the month, and how much cash they are going to need. When the potential users were presented with the calendar idea, they sparked to it—it fit their model.

Support for Customer Focus

Even the most customer-oriented companies can find it difficult to maintain customer-focus momentum. Engineers and designers are not naturally inclined to seek interaction with customers, and they need to be repeatedly encouraged to do so. Monson finds that "You have to push people to do it. Once they do, they get fired up again, but it is cyclical. This dynamic has to be managed carefully."

It is particularly difficult to maintain customer focus with products that are far from the designers' personal experience. Since Intuit's Quicken product is for personal finance, everyone at Intuit is a potential Quicken user and has friends and associates outside of Intuit who use it as well. It is easy to talk with people at any time about how Quicken can be improved. On the other hand, the people who would be likely to use QuickBooks, an application for small-business accounting, are not as readily available. It takes more encouragement to ensure that designers have ongoing interaction with them.

In addition, there is a natural tendency for a company to lose customer focus as it grows. Startup companies tend to be intensely customer focused. The market defines them. They are driven to fill a niche, because their success depends on their doing so. After the startup phase is complete and the company is producing a product, the focus of energy and attention shifts from the external needs of the customer to the internal processes of getting the product into the customers' hands. The organization is now dealing primarily with the problems of production and growth: Resources are concentrated on providing an infrastructure to support the organization, and the focus turns from looking out to looking in.

George Land and Beth Jarman describe this phenomenon in detail in their book *Breakpoint and Beyond* (1992). They demonstrate that the more successful a company is in producing a product or providing a service, the more difficult it is for that company to move on to a new idea, to renew the organization by inventing new products and methods of production, and, particularly, to reconnect with the customers. Many companies get stuck, and eventually die, at this point in their evolution.

There are many ways in which a company can foster user involvement. Structured interactions with users—such as focus groups, consumer advisory panels, usability laboratories, and scheduled site visits—can contribute to practices in which contact with customers becomes expected and accepted. In addition, creative designers find innovative ways to gather data from customers.

Intuit's *Follow-Me-Home* program was started when software designers realized that testing in the usability laboratory could not reflect accurately the experiences of users who tried to install and use products in their own environments. Customer surveys were not timely enough or detailed enough to expose potential problems. So, staff from Intuit went to local stores and asked people buying Quicken for permission to observe them as they first tried to use the product. Watching people in their own homes with their own machines revealed subtle problems, such as the user who was confused by the *Register* item on the main menu, thinking that it had something to do with the product-registration card.

The most important skill for interacting effectively with customers is that of careful listening—a surprisingly difficult art to master. In *The Seven Habits of Highly Effective People*, Stephen Covey writes (p. 37), "Listening involves patience, openness, and the desire to understand—highly developed qualities of character." Covey describes listening techniques and the importance of moving beyond technique to *empathic listening*, where a person listens with the intent to understand.

One of my clients asked me to evaluate the user interface for a business application that was scheduled to go to market in a couple of months. As I began to use the product and discovered problems with its organization of features and with misleading labels, I got the distinct feeling that nothing I was saying would have any influence on the design. The two people running the usability test were not recording what was happening; their responses were blank; they did not ask follow-on questions that would allow them to understand the difficulties that I was having. They became defensive about their design. They plainly did not want to know what was wrong with their product, or what could be improved.

It is pointless—perhaps even damaging—to conduct usability tests merely because testing is fashionable or required by management. There is nothing to be gained by going through the motions without listening. If designers do not have the time, energy, or authority to make changes, or if they are too deeply attached to their design to be willing to change it, there is no point in asking customers what they want. On the other hand, if they listen, software designers may find what they hear valuable and surprising.

Customers frequently find ways to use products that designers never intended (see, for example, Schön's account of Scotch Tape in Chapter 9). Only a company with customer focus will have insight into how its products are actually being used. For example, through close contact with customers, Intuit learned that Quicken, which had been designed for personal accounting, was being used for small businesses. That came as a complete surprise. According to Monson, "We had to rerun the market research to be sure. We didn't believe it." Many people in small businesses could not use the accounting software that was on the market, since it required an understanding of double-entry bookkeeping. They had no formal accounting training; furthermore, they did not want, or need, to learn. This insight led Intuit to the design of the highly successful QuickBooks product.

Designer Empowerment

Throughout this chapter, I have talked about what software designers and their organizations need to do: to have clear goals, and to be in touch with customers. What further do organizations need to do so that designers can perform their jobs well? In a way, the answer is again just common sense—but common sense that all too often is missing.

Often, the people who make design decisions do not have access to the tools and materials that they need to do their work effectively. DinoCom, an applications-development company that was moving from mainframe systems to personal computers, wanted its new software to adhere to the industry user-interface standards. When I suggested that each designer be supplied with the book describing those standards, their manager refused, saying, "There are two copies in the library. They can walk down there and get them." Two dozen people across the company were making design decisions, and none of them were familiar with the new delivery environment. But how often could they afford to make the trek to the library? The failure to spend a few hundred dollars on books can lead to costly errors and the need for interface changes in the future.

Could we imagine anything more penny wise and pound foolish? Yes. People doing software design often do not have access to competitors' products, to current state-of-the-art machines, or to the latest off-the-shelf software on the market. Designers need an environment that is rich with ideas and examples if their creativity is to thrive.

Decision-making power is also central to designer empowerment. Popular management literature indicates that we should put greater decision-making power in the hands of the people who are closest to the work, regardless of the positions that those people hold in the company. The people doing software design should have the authority to make design decisions. In contrast, at one company that produced accounting software, the software designers were required to get sign-off from two levels of management before they could make any design changes. This procedure was imposed while the design was still vague. Creativity died, and productivity ground to a snail's pace.

Having the power to make design decisions does not mean operating without constraints. In Chapter 12, Don Norman shows how difficult it can be to arrive at acceptable design solutions in a complex environment that has distributed decision making. Empowering designers requires finding an appropriate balance of framework and freedom. Creativity in design is also aided by rich brainstorming—as described by David Kelley in Chapter 8—in which everyone is encouraged to contribute ideas to all the projects of the company, and nobody owns ideas for individual gain. The reward structure at Intuit, for example, supports this philosophy. Designers are encouraged to pursue the most promising ideas, regardless of the ideas' origins, and to use the customer as the final judge of success. There are no special bonuses. Employees share profits equally. Even the salespeople do not work on commission. So, in effect, it does not matter whether a particular idea makes it into the final product. What matters is that the most effective ideas drive the products.

Creativity and Engagement

Empowerment goes beyond policies and process. I began this chapter by saying that software design is an art as well as a science. Because design is an act of creativity—of social interaction and understanding—it is imperative not to overlook the power of commitment, drive, determination, and spirit; or the importance of dedication to making the software work for people, and of caring about the people who are engaged in the process. These soft and fuzzy emotional aspects might make us feel uncomfortable, but their fundamental power requires that we do not ignore them.

Jim, a software designer, described to me his feelings of disempowerment. He talked about how, during his first few years with his company, he had been seriously dedicated, happily working long hours. Now, however, he no longer had such inspiration or dedication. Instead, he lived for weekends, just going through the motions at work. What had happened?

Jim had previously worked on a team that had produced a successful product. He had demonstrated his skill and creativity. The product, however, although it drew rave reviews from customers, was not valued highly by his company. It was a training product, so it was not part of the mainstream business. Still, the organization might have recognized that Jim and his team had made an important contribution. Beyond designing an excellent product, they had evolved a successful design process and had learned a great deal from the experience. Instead of rewarding the team, shortly after the product was released, the team was disbanded, and one-half of its members were laid off as part of a reduction in force. The layoff affected only about 10 percent of the company at large. The message was clear: What this team had done did not matter to the organization. Jim moved to another product, but it and two others that followed were eventually cut. The work that Jim had done, although it was interesting and creative, was not recognized as useful or important.

Projects are canceled for many reasons—often for reasons outside the control of the project team. Doing software design inherently requires taking risks, and the risk is that design ideas do not always work out. Yet the designers' work and creativity must be acknowledged, and their taking of further risks must be supported if their creativity is to thrive. People need to feel a sufficient level of safety and support in the organization. They need to know that they are making a difference.

In *Artful Work* (1995), Dick Richards describes the importance of bringing artistry to work, regardless of what that work is. He invites us to express ourselves through work; to engage in our work; to employ not just our physical and mental energies, but also our emotional and spiritual energies. Exceptional software design requires this kind of engagement. Not every company can create an environment that inspires intense commitment, but every organization can work to foster people's engagement, and can let people know that they make a difference.

In writing about effectiveness at work, Covey says, "Always treat your employees exactly as you want them to treat your best customers. You can buy a person's hand, but you can't buy his heart. His heart is where his enthusiasm, his loyalty, is. You can buy his back, but you can't buy his brain. That's where his creativity is, his ingenuity, his resourcefulness." (p. 58)

Ultimately, the care with which we treat one another within our organization is the source of empowerment, and provides the foundation for good design.

Suggested Readings

Stephen Covey. *The Seven Habits of Highly Effective People*. New York: Simon & Schuster, 1989.

George Land and Beth Jarman. *Breakpoint and Beyond*. New York: HarperBusiness, 1992.

Dick Richards. *Artful Work*. San Francisco: Berrett-Koehler, 1995.

About the Author

Laura De Young is a cofounder of Windrose Consulting in Palo Alto, California. She has done software design in a wide variety of organizational settings, has observed and advised software-producing companies on their development processes, and conducts workshops on creativity in software design.

Profile

13. QUICKEN

Quicken was the founding product of Intuit, Inc., started in 1984. In addition to helping people with typical home-accounting tasks, such as balancing the checkbook and paying bills, Quicken is used to manage investments, to track loans, to produce reports, to maintain budgets, and to do financial planning. Quicken's popularity, however, is more notable than is its feature list. Quicken was first released in 1986, and rapidly became the market leader against a dozen existing products. After nearly 10 years on the market, it has maintained that lead, having gone through many updates and revisions; it now has more than 7 million users.

It is not accidental that Intuit's founder, Scott Cook, had a background in marketing, rather than in computing. He received his MBA from Harvard Business School, and joined Proctor & Gamble as an assistant brand manager; his first assignment was Crisco. After 3 years with Proctor & Gamble, Cook looked for opportunities to reach a mass market in the software domain. He recognized that more and more consumers were buying PCs, and that all these home-computer users were writing checks and keeping financial records.

To find out what consumers would want in financial software, Cook and an assistant made hundreds of telephone calls to middle- and upper-middle-income households. Most of the people who responded to these calls reported that they did financial work every month, that they did not want to spend so much time on it, and that they would consider using a computer to do it. They wanted more control over their home finances, but worried that it would be

Profile Authors: Laura De Young and Terry Winograd

too complicated and time consuming to use a computer for their financial tasks.

Cook created a panel of computer users and had them compare the way that they had been keeping records by hand with the job of managing their finances using existing computer financial products. In every case, the job took them longer using the computer than it did by hand. Cook recognized that a successful personal-finance program would have to excel in being fast and easy to use.

To make the software easy to use, Cook proposed a design that would mimic the way people did financial tasks by hand: They could fill out a check just as they would with their checkbook, or enter a deposit as they would in their check register. The resulting Quicken interface drew heavily from the graphics of traditional printed banking materials, as shown in Figure 13.1. Even when people used new capabilities, such as making electronic payments, the format was familiar.

As De Young describes in Chapter 13, the development of Quicken was customer centered. From the beginning, the software designers brought in a wide variety of potential customers to test what they were producing. Throughout the design and development process, they engaged users in many ways and in many aspects of the project, to find out what would work. They even had a *Follow-Me-Home* program, to observe the problems that came up in a home context, that might not be visible in a usability laboratory. This kind of participatory design (see Profile 14) revealed many aspects of the product that were not anticipated by the designers, and produced revelations that led to changes in the program.

A user of Quicken immediately recognizes that a tremendous amount of care has gone into the details of the user interaction. A simple integer (e.g., 14) typed in the date field produces a date in the current month (e.g., May 14, 1996). The QuickFill feature makes it easy for a user to create a new check that duplicates all the details of a previous one (such as the category of expenditure, and an address typed on the check) by just typing the first few letters of the name of the payee. For regular payments, the program can enter the full check information, ready for printing, on the basis of a user-defined schedule. Numerous detailed features provide ready-to-hand help in a specific activity, such as the mini-calculator tape (Figure 13.2), used for calculating an amount to be entered in a field.

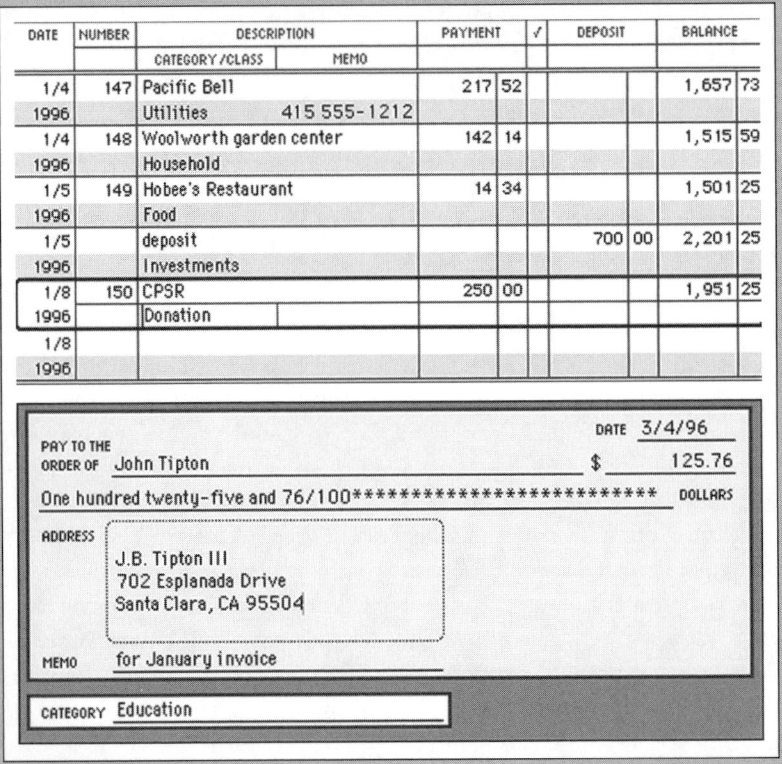

DATE	NUMBER	DESCRIPTION		PAYMENT		√	DEPOSIT		BALANCE	
		CATEGORY /CLASS	MEMO							
1/4	147	Pacific Bell		217	52				1,657	73
1996		Utilities	415 555-1212							
1/4	148	Woolworth garden center		142	14				1,515	59
1996		Household								
1/5	149	Hobee's Restaurant		14	34				1,501	25
1996		Food								
1/5		deposit					700	00	2,201	25
1996		Investments								
1/8	150	CPSR		250	00				1,951	25
1996		Donation								
1/8										
1996										

PAY TO THE
ORDER OF John Tipton

DATE 3/4/96

$ 125.76

One hundred twenty-five and 76/100************************** DOLLARS

ADDRESS
J.B. Tipton III
702 Esplanada Drive
Santa Clara, CA 95504

MEMO for January invoice

CATEGORY Education

FIGURE 13.1   **Interface Borrowed from Paper**   The user interface for Quicken mimicked the familiar look of paper checks and registers, so new users could understand what was being displayed and would have good initial ideas about how to do standard operations, such as filling out checks and entering deposit information. (*Source:* Quicken Version 5.0 for Macintosh.)

Overall, the impression that you get when using Quicken is that, over time, thousands of users have asked "Why can't I just...?" or "What would happen if I...?" and that thoughtful responses to those questions have found their way into the software and its interface. The result is a product that has succeeded in spite of direct competition from the most formidable competitor in the software market. In late 1990, Cook learned that Microsoft was about to enter Intuit's market, with Microsoft Money. Intuit put together a Windows version of Quicken in 10 months, and launched it only 3 weeks after Microsoft

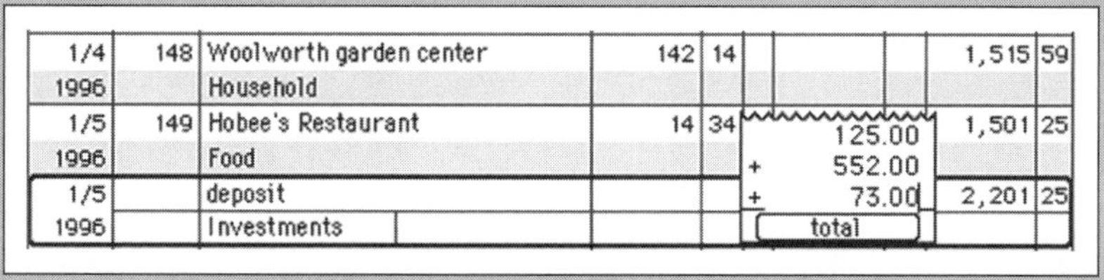

1/4	148	Woolworth garden center		142	14				1,515	59
1996		Household								
1/5	149	Hobee's Restaurant		14	34		125.00		1,501	25
1996		Food				+	552.00			
1/5		deposit				+	73.00		2,201	25
1996		Investments					total			

FIGURE 13.2 **Care with the Details** Quicken has been developed through extensive user testing, leading to a great many details that add to its ease of use. For example, when a user needs to calculate an amount to be entered in a field, she can hit a key that brings up a mini-calculator tape, which accepts calculator commands and then enters the result into the field. (*Source:* Quicken Version 5.0 for Macintosh.)

introduced Money. Microsoft slashed prices, eventually going down to $15—below Quicken, and well below normal software prices—but Intuit was able to hold on to its 60-percent market share, and has continued to excel. The result was an offer by Microsoft in 1995 to buy Intuit for $1.5 billion. The sale was eventually blocked by concerns over potential antitrust violations that could result from Microsoft's complete dominance in the personal financial software market. The offer stands, however, as a monument to the kind of success that a company can enjoy as a result of understanding how to design software that truly serves consumers.

Suggested Reading

Nielsen, Jakob. *Usability Engineering*. Boston: Academic Press, 1993.

SARAH KUHN

Design for People at Work

In the excitement over the seductive world of personal computing, it is easy to forget that the experience that most people have of computers in the workplace may not be liberating....Most people who encounter computer-based automation at work do not choose the software with which they work, and have comparatively little control over when and how they do what they do. For them, the use of computers can be an oppressive experience, rather than a liberating one.

Those of us who work in the computing profession—especially in design and development—see the computer as a wonderful resource. It is an opportunity for creativity, a tool for productivity, and a medium in which to create new worlds. But for much of the rest of the world, *computerization* is a derogatory term. People see computers threatening to change their lives in ways that are stifling, disempowering, and dehumanizing. This difference in perception often leads to suspicion and scorn on both sides: scorn of the "Luddites" who are stubbornly resisting progress, and scorn of the "technonerds" who love machines, but ignore human values.

Sarah Kuhn and her colleagues at the University of Massachusetts at Lowell address these problems in their studies of the implementation and use of computers in industrial settings. They collaborate extensively with the workers who encounter computer systems in their daily work, and who daily experience both satisfaction and frustration. In this chapter, Kuhn outlines an approach to systems design that takes into account the complex social and political factors that are at play in the development, deployment, and ultimate success or failure of the systems.

In the course of designing for the workplace, a software designer inevitably faces situations in which design choices are constrained by the conflicting goals and values held by the different parties who have a stake in the changes that new technologies will bring to the work. Workers and managers have many common interests, and they also have different stakes in how computers in the workplace change productivity, working conditions, and job satisfaction. In advocating an orientation toward *human-centered design*, using the techniques of *participatory design* (see Profile 14), Kuhn suggests how the software designer can serve the interests of workplace democracy by creating systems that give workers greater control over their work.

—Terry Winograd

IN THE EXCITEMENT over the seductive world of personal computing, it is easy to forget that the experience that most people have of computers in the workplace may not be liberating. The independent professional—who chooses her own software, experiments with new electronic tools, and sets her own schedule—lives in a different occupational world from that of the fast-food clerk, the bank teller, the machinist, or the airline customer-service representative. Most people who encounter computer-based automation at work do not choose the software with which they work, and have comparatively little control over when and how they do what they do. For them, the use of computers can be an oppressive experience, rather than a liberating one.

The effect of new computer software and systems on people at work depends on what assumptions about work are designed into the system, and on how well those assumptions correspond to the reality of what people do on the job. Well-designed systems can boost productivity, enhance job satisfaction, and give both workers and managers a clearer sense of what is going on in the organization. But a system that interferes with crucial work practices—either deliberately or through oversight—can result in reduced effectiveness and efficiency, reduced satisfaction and autonomy, and increased stress and health problems for the people who use the system.

Systems and Assumptions

First, let us look at some cases of systems that embodied assumptions about work, which were in conflict with the activities required to get the job done.

Case 1: The Trouble Ticketing System

The Trouble Ticketing System (TTS) was a mainframe-based system, developed in the early 1980s for use by telephone-company repair personnel, for scheduling, work routing, and record keeping. When trouble was reported, a job ticket was generated, and was sent to the appropriate telephone company office. There, a worker picked up the ticket and began work on the job. When the repair was completed, or when the worker had done all that she could do from that location, the ticket was sent back to the central TTS.

Before TTS, job tickets were generated, but work was more collaborative. Testers called one another, consulting with someone at the other end of a problematic line, or someone who knew a particular part of the system especially well, for help with troubleshooting. One of the motivations for the development of the TTS was to ensure that workers spent more time on repair tasks by eliminating conversations between workers, which were thought to be inefficient and "off task." With the TTS, each tester worked alone. If she could not complete a repair job, the tester recorded what had been done and sent the ticket back to the TTS for someone else to pick up and work on.

The need for conversation was eliminated, but the benefits of conversation (more information available to diagnose problems, and the chance to learn more about the system) were lost too. Because TTS also monitored the number of hours that each worker spent doing jobs, testers who spent time consulting with one another or training new workers (neither of which activities were accounted for in the system) were penalized. As reported by Patricia Sachs (1995, p. 27):

> While TTS was designed to make job performance more efficient, it has created the opposite effect: discouraging the training of new hands, breaking up the community of practice by eliminating troubleshooting conversations, and extending the time spent on a single job by segmenting coherent troubleshooting efforts into unconnected ticket-based tasks.

Case 2: Big Bank

At a large urban bank, teller operations were supported by a computer-based system, which was designed and modified over time by the bank's systems department. The system had to meet the bank's needs for accuracy, efficiency, security, and customer service, although, as this case illustrates, not all of these goals can maximized simultaneously. The Big Bank system embodied in a rigid form the rules and procedures of the bank, which before automation would have been enforced by people—generally supervisors—who were relatively close to the action and who exercised professional judgment based on experience with the day-to-day work of bank tellers. One of the security features built into the system was that, "under a specified set of exceptional situations (defined by management at the bank through the setting of software parameter settings), the teller's terminal will freeze with a message about the account on the screen." (Salzman and Rosenthal, 1994, p. 94). The transaction could be completed only after a bank officer's authorization card was passed through a card reader on the teller's terminal. The purpose of the freeze was to ensure supervisory oversight in circumstances that were deemed exceptional, such as more than three transactions on a single account on a single day.

It turned out, however, that at a large downtown branch of the bank, the exceptional happened every 5 or 10 minutes. To keep lines flowing and to avoid costly inefficiencies, the manager gave a bank officer's card to the tellers, which they passed among themselves to unfreeze their terminals. Only once or twice an hour did the tellers judge that a supervisor was needed—when a customer was unknown, or when an unusual situation arose. Of course, overcoming this one feature undermined *all* security provisions in the system, because the officer card was now freely available to the tellers. As Salzman and Rosenthal (p. 97) reported, "This implementation of the system increases the responsibility of the teller although, at the same time, the design of the system is reminding the teller that, formally, the bank management does not trust him or her to make even routine decisions. The result of the system's design is the worst of both worlds."

Case 3: HELP system

In a large machining area in a production plant, a major U.S. aircraft manufacturer installed a new computer-based system known as the HELP (Help Employees Locate People) system. The system had two principal functions. The first—which was the source of its official name—was to enable machinists to signal for assistance when they needed replacement tooling, wanted consultation, or were due for a break. At the push of a button, a machinist could indicate his location and the nature of the request. This aspect of the system got good reviews from both machinists and shop management, because it enabled operations to run more smoothly.

The second function of the system, not acknowledged in the official name, was the monitoring of 66 machines in the shop. A panel in a control room above the shop floor displayed the status of each machine with colored lights. A supervisor could check these lights, and could gain further information by glancing out at the floor below. Daily reports told supervisors not only about production levels, but also about how each worker spent his time. Upper management received weekly and monthly reports.

The purpose of the monitoring system was to gain greater managerial control over how machinists spent their time, as an aid to increasing productivity. The problem was that the information captured by the system and reported to the managers provided only a partial view of the work of machinists—a view so one-sided as to be nearly useless. The very concreteness of the statistics, however, invited unwarranted conclusions. For example, managers wanted to discourage machinists from slowing down production unnecessarily, so the system was designed to report all the time that a computer-controlled machine tool spent halted or operating at less than 80 percent of the programmed feed rate (the rate at which the cutting tool moves across the surface of the metal). What the system did not report, however, was whether the programmer who wrote the program for that particular part had set the feed rate correctly. It is common for feed rates to be set incorrectly, and one of the skills of the machinist is to judge whether conditions require slowing down or allow speeding up. Information about the appropriate feed rate is crucial to the proper interpretation of the data generated by the monitoring system.

The data generated by the HELP system could mislead managers into thinking that any machine status other than "running" was an indication of unproductive activity. "One machinist...had to work long and furiously to set up a particularly intricate part to be cut. As a result, his machine sat idle most of the day. While he felt that he had never worked harder, his supervisor reprimanded him because the system reported that his machine was idle." (Shaiken, 1989, p. 295).

The sense of a hostile, intrusive presence in machinists' work life gave the system its unofficial shopfloor name: The Spy in the Sky. The system was tolerated by the machinists because of its benefits as a signaling device, and because their union was able to negotiate an agreement with the company that data from the system would not be used for disciplinary purposes. Still, the system could be used for informal discipline, and it served as a constant reminder of managers' mistrust of the workforce. Productive work relies on the skills of machinists, yet the monitoring system embodies the assumption that, if machines are running at less than 80 percent of the programmed rate, the fault lies with the machinist, rather than with the engineer who wrote the parts program.

Representations and Misrepresentations of Work

We have touched on many themes in these cases. One principal theme is that misunderstandings of the true context of work become embodied in computer-based systems, with negative consequences not only for the people who do the work, but also for the productivity and efficiency that the system is intended to enhance. The system, and the data collected by it, become themselves a representation of work. They define, at least within a limited context, what counts in the organization. At the telephone company, time "on task" counts, but training new workers to work more effectively does not. In the machine shop, time spent cutting metal counts, but time spent setting up, so that problems are avoided, does not. Of course, managerial discretion plays a significant role, too, but data from the computer carry the weight of seeming objectivity, and can be difficult to refute. (For interesting discussions of representations of work, see Suchman, 1995.)

Sachs contrasts what she calls the *organizational* or *explicit* view of work with the *activity-oriented* or *tacit* view. An *explicit* view of work assumes that jobs are made up of a set of tasks or operations that could be defined, say, in a company handbook of methods and procedures. A *tacit*, or activity-oriented, view of work suggests that the range of activities, communication practices, relationships, and coordination that it takes to accomplish business functions is complex, and is continually mediated by workers and managers alike. An activity-oriented analysis of work centers on everyday work practices—on how employees actually make the business function effectively.

Sachs notes that all work contains both explicit and tacit elements, and argues that the efficiency of work is determined not so much by the logic and sequencing of taskflow as by the capabilities of people for troubleshooting vexing problems in complicated situations, which inevitably arise. She points out that most work-reorganization projects, such as workflow analysis and business-process reengineering, take only the explicit view, ignoring the tacit. The result is systems that ignore—or deliberately try to eliminate—tacit elements of work, sometimes making it more difficult (or even impossible) for workers to do their jobs effectively and efficiently. In these situations, workers often invent workarounds, to bypass the problematic limitations imposed by the system and to allow them to do their jobs more effectively. In the case of Big Bank, tellers and managers colluded in the workaround involving the shared officer card. In the Trouble Ticketing System, testers started to contact coworkers informally, using the TTS only to provide a formal record of the work. Although these workarounds correct some of the problems with the systems, they are a symptom of an inefficiencies that have been introduced unintentionally in the design process.

The High Cost of Bad Design

Computer-based systems that are poorly suited to how people actually work impose costs not only on the organization (in terms of low productivity) but also on the people who work with them. Studies of work in computer-intensive workplaces have pointed to a host of serious problems that can be caused by job design that is insensitive to the nature of the work being performed, or to the needs of human beings in an automated workplace:

- *Displacement.* Although fears of massive unemployment in the United States—predicted during the automation scares of the 1960s and 1980s—have proved overblown, there are countless specific situations in which far more work can be done by far fewer people than before automation (Richardson, 1996). Furthermore, the spread of computers in the workplace has coincided with a dramatic rise in employment insecurity—a rise in involuntary part-time work and temporary employment, a fall in real average weekly earnings, and an overall reduction in health benefits (Kuhn and Wooding, 1994a). Although many factors seem to be responsible for this rise in insecurity, the use of computers in the workplace is one of the factors credited with facilitating the change.

- *Intensification.* For people who are employed, competitive pressures often mean an intensification of work—working harder and working longer during the work week. The average worker works 163 hours more per year today than he would have worked two decades ago (Schor, 1991). For companies, it is generally less expensive to pay overtime to existing employees than to hire new ones, particularly in the face of uncertain future demand. Computer use and the electronic pacing of work can further intensify work. Airline-reservations agents, who answer numerous calls every hour, can have the length of their rest breaks between calls controlled to the split second, and managers can—and do—reduce breaks to nothing, simply by resetting the system parameters (Bravo, 1993; Garson, 1989).

- *Heightened visibility through electronic monitoring.* Integrated electronic office systems allow detailed monitoring of certain aspects of an employee's work day: keystrokes, "unplugged" or machine idle time, bathroom breaks, number of calls (for reservations and customer-service agents), time between calls, and so forth. Many employers collect and post these statistics on a weekly or monthly basis. Supervisors often listen to conversations with customers, without the consent or knowledge of either employee or customer. According to a survey on workplace stress conducted in 1984 by 9to5, the organization of women office workers, workplace monitoring is the biggest single contributor to stress at work (Bravo, 1993).

- *Reduction or redefinition of skill.* There is nothing intrinsic to the automation of work that guarantees that the introduction of computers will either raise or lower aggregate skill requirements. Sure, someone needs to know how the system works, but the people who use it daily may or may not need to use more skill and judgment than before automation. In the insurance industry, for example, specialized data-entry jobs are slowly being eliminated, and the data are being entered by a variety of personnel directly at the point where the data are generated. Also, there are cases in which computers make it possible to push decision-making functions down the occupational hierarchy to lower-level workers; for example, loan clerks and automated loan-rating systems bypass the need for professional risk assessment (Baran and Gold, 1988). Elimination of jobs and loss of job challenge—or increase in job demands without an increase in authority or pay—can lead to negative outcomes for employees.

- *Loss of work autonomy and control.* Electronic pacing or monitoring, standardization of work, rigidification of policies and procedures, and reduction in skill requirements can all contribute to a loss of autonomy and control that can accompany the implementation of software or systems. If the teller system at Big Bank had been implemented as designed, the autonomy and control exercised by tellers would have been even more circumscribed than usual—with dismal consequences for customer service. Some of the newer computer-based systems today are designed to give front line workers more, rather than less, authority—for example, allowing customer-service representatives to access all relevant information needed to resolve a problem on the spot, rather than referring the customer to another employee. But the drive to routinize, standardize, and automate the work of hourly employees still remains strong, and guides the development and implementation of many systems.

Even those systems that avoid causing inefficiencies and workarounds still impose a heavy cost on the people who must perform stressful, routinized, exacting work. Health effects include stress, boredom, headaches, repetitive-strain injuries, neck and back strain, and other serious problems. Studies have confirmed the connection between job design and health outcomes; in particular, workers who face high job demands and who have low job control (inadequate power, authority, and autonomy to meet the demands their jobs place on them) are at significantly greater risk for serious health problems, such as cardiovascular disease (Karasek and Theorell, 1990).

Work-Oriented Approaches to System Design

In Chapter 13, Laura De Young describes how Intuit has thrived due to its strong focus on learning what customers want, on observing the customer's context of use, and on anticipating new features even before customers themselves have identified new needs. What happens if we try to translate Intuit's approach into a corporate setting? Two differences immediately become apparent. First, software in the workplace is situated in a context that is far more complex than that of software in the home—even in the home office. Second, in contrast to Intuit's customer base of individual users purchasing for home use, in corporate settings, the purchaser and the user are generally not the same. Whom is the developer trying to satisfy? To the extent that the end user and the person making the purchasing decision have different needs and objectives, whose should prevail? The traditional answer is that, to the extent that the customer's needs or objectives are considered at all, priority goes to the explicit needs and objectives of managers. This answer is true both for packaged software and for custom or tailored systems. If end users are considered, it is usually only to test whether they are able to use the system as intended. The two following sections describe two alternative approaches, focused on the end user and the work context: *human-centered design* and *participatory design*.

Human-centered design

Martin Corbett contrasts the usual approach to the design of manufacturing technology, which he calls the *technology-centered approach*, with a *human-centered approach* to design. The technology-centered approach is characterized by *hard-systems thinking*:

> Hard systems thinking involves the imposition of a clear-cut problem definition on a relatively unstable organizational reality and a "fuzzy" system. It also means the adoption of linear, top-down design procedures that handicap design in a very complex organizational reality. The overriding concern in a hard design approach is technical design; little attention is accorded either the organizational context in which the system is to operate or the social implications of the system. The technology-centered approach leaves the engineering and computer professionals to decide the extent to which user participation is useful and permissible. (Corbett, 1992, 140–141).

By contrast, human-centered design (which is discussed from a different perspective by Denning and Dargan in Chapter 6) puts human, social, and organizational considerations on at least an equal footing with technical considerations in the design process, seeing operators (end users) as central to an effective manufacturing system. Well-designed technology should make use of human strengths—such as skill, judgment, capacity for learning—to create a robust and flexible production system, rather than seek to minimize and strictly control human intervention.

Participatory design

Advocates of participatory design (see Profile 14) emphasize the importance of meaningful end-user participation and influence in all phases of the design process. This approach was developed initially in northern Europe among academics and practitioners concerned with the design of computer-based systems. In recent years it has spread among North American developers and researchers. Although projects differ in their precise definitions of what constitutes participation, this formulation of the basic requirements is typical: "The employees must have access to relevant information; they must have the possibility for taking an independent position on the problems; and they must in some way participate in the process of decision making." (Kensing, quoted in Clement and Van den Besselaar, 1993.)

In Sweden, beginning in the 1970s, the *collective resource approach* to participatory design stressed equality and collaboration between designers and users in the design of systems (see Ehn, 1992). One of the important motivations for this approach was a commitment to what the researchers and designers called *industrial democracy*. Concerned about the consequences that computer systems were having for job design and working conditions, they consciously sought to design systems that would help workers to retain (or regain) control over the planning, methods, and pacing of work. They did so in the context of asserting the broader rights of workers to have a voice over the design of technology, the control of company resources, and other decisions affecting the workplace.

In emphasizing industrial democracy, the proponents of the collective-resource approach were responding to what they saw as the failed promise of the *sociotechnical systems* approach, then highly influential in job design and industrial-democracy initiatives (see, e.g., Pava, 1983). Sociotechnical projects often lost their grounding in industrial democracy when conflicting interests between labor and management led to the adoption of management priorities over union priorities. Advocates of the collective-resource approach took a deliberately worker-centered, pro-union approach to technology design. They worked with trade unions in Scandinavia in projects focused on allowing the unions and their members to influence the design and implementation of the computer-based systems that were then being introduced. The UTOPIA project, for example, used mockups and

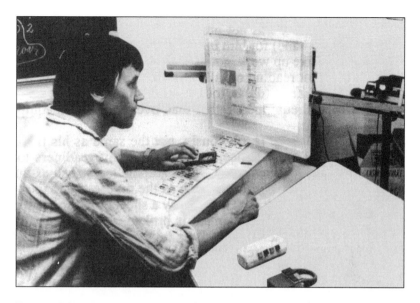

FIGURE 14.1 **Prototyping UTOPIA**   Mockups, such as the one depicted here, were used as a medium for communication between computer-system designers and members of the typographers' union with whom they worked. Prototypes—even rough ones—can play a key role when designers cross boundaries between groups that have different domains of expertise (see Chapter 10). (From Joan Greenbaum and Morten Kyng, *Design at Work*, 1991, NJ: Lawrence Erlbaum Associates, Inc., p. 180. Reprinted with permission.)

prototypes, such as the one shown in Figure 14.1 to facilitate communication between designers and members of the typographers union, with whom they worked on new designs for newspaper-layout systems (Ehn and Kyng, 1991).

The Designer and Democracy

Designers of workplace computer systems often experience a tension between designing for efficiency and designing to support the autonomy and skill of workers.

First, let us look at the easy cases of inadequate attention to the work setting—those in which the tension is absent. In these cases, the designer's failure to understand the context and the tacit aspects of work lead to system features that make work less, rather than more, efficient and effective. The cases described in the opening section of this chapter fall into this category. In Salzman's words, these systems achieve "the worst of both worlds." Despite the challenges in diagnosing and remedying problems of this sort, fixing them is a win–win proposition: productivity is increased and the true demands of getting the job done are honored, making work more effective *and* more satisfying than before the fix.

The hard design problems, from this perspective, are the ones in which negative effects for people at work are side effects of a deliberate business philosophy or business objective. In these cases, designers experience a tension between promoting the autonomy of system users on the one hand and fulfilling organizational objectives on the other. Charles Richardson illustrates this distinction in his discussion of repetitive-strain injuries (RSIs):

> There are four basic risk factors for repetitive strain injuries: force, awkward posture, repetition, and lack of recovery time. Force and awkward posture are mistakes. They could be called accidents of design. Somebody forgot to think about the person that's doing the job. The current focus on the redesign of work stations according to "ergonomic principles" is aimed at fixing some of the force and awkward posture issues. But repetition and no rest are different matters. Repetition and no rest are in fact design goals of a technology design, of workplace design. (Richardson, 1996)

The fragmentation and routinization of work—leading to repetitive, mind-numbing jobs—is a reflection of how an organization has chosen to respond to economic competition: by creating low-wage, low-skill, replaceable jobs. Furthermore, competitive pressure often leads companies to increase production not by becoming more efficient (producing more without increasing the work required), but rather by intensifying work (shortening or eliminating breaks, increasing production quotas, enforcing a faster pace, and requiring longer hours of work). The negative consequences for employee health and autonomy are a necessary, although not deliberate, byproduct of such a competitive strategy.

Management theorists have begun to question these strategies, suggesting that approaches that decentralize decision making and push it to the lowest levels of the organization are more effective and adaptive in the long term. Total quality management, quality circles, employee involvement, Deming's quality methodologies, and other approaches advocate that managers seek the active and informed participation of the workforce. Design theorists such as Brown and Duguid (1992) describe how to design for learning and innovation, rather than striving to create idiotproof systems that stifle worker initiative.

Even in relatively enlightened organizations, the demands of the organization can still be in conflict with the principles of workplace democracy. There can be situations in which designers are faced with a choice between meeting management's stated objectives and enhancing workers' ability to plan and control their work.

In parts of Europe, the principle of *codetermination* (unions and management making joint decisions on matters that affect the company and the workforce) is well established. Laws ensure consultation with workers and limit negative effects of technology on work. Designers have some legal and cultural basis for making decisions that favor worker autonomy and control, even when doing so conflicts with management directives. In the United States, designers find themselves very much alone, with few places to turn, when confronted by these issues. Although this situation seems unlikely to change drastically in the near future for U.S. designers, there are three relevant precedents that may be helpful.

1. *Workers' bill of rights.* The movement for democratic rights in the workplace has a parallel in the notion that workers should retain their civil rights inside their place of employment. As citizens, workers are protected from unwarranted government interference by the Bill of Rights, but in many ways they surrender their freedom of speech, freedom from search and seizure, and so forth as soon as they enter their place of work. Even though today many corporations are larger and more powerful than were any of the original 13 colonies from which the proponents of the Bill of Rights sought protection, these protections are not extended to cover corporate actions that abridge the civil rights of their employees. Proposals have been made to establish an Employee Bill of Rights; (see Ewing, 1977; International Association of Machinists, 1983). If these rights were indeed established by law, they would constitute a firm grounding for workplace democracy.

2. *Worker participation through unions.* Unions in the United States, in the postwar period, have tended to show little interest in shaping the design of technology. There are exceptions, however. The Machinists' Union's proposed Technology Bill of Rights is one example of union interest in shaping the design and implementation of technology; other unions are working on these issues as well. American workers are at a disadvantage compared to European workers in this respect, because unionization rates in the United States are so much lower. But even with smaller numbers, unions can provide added voice and protection for workers, in aspects that can be valuable to the design process for computer-based systems.

3. *Codes of ethics for designers.* I believe that professional designers, like other professionals, should subscribe to a code of ethics that governs their behavior. Although no consensus yet exists about what should be in a software designer's ethical code, numerous proposals have been made (e.g., Association for Computing Machinery, 1995; Sackman, 1991). There are also proposals for ethical codes that would govern areas of critical social concern, such as the electronic monitoring of employees (Marx and Sherizen, 1989). These codes, coupled with the reflections of the researchers and practitioners discussed in this chapter, can serve as guides for the design professional who recognizes that to design computer-based systems is to make an organizational intervention—an intervention that can have powerful effects on how people work and live.

Suggested Readings

Paul Adler and Terry Winograd (eds.). *Usability: Turning Technologies into Tools.* New York: Oxford University Press, 1992.

Pelle Ehn. *Work-Oriented Design of Computer Artifacts.* Stockholm: Arbetslivscentrum, 1988. (Distributed by Lawrence Erlbaum Associates, Hillsdale, NJ.)

Barbara Garson. *The Electronic Sweatshop: How Computers are Transforming the Office of the Future into the Factory of the Past.* New York: Penguin, 1989.

Harold Salzman and Stephen R. Rosenthal. *Software By Design: Shaping Technology and the Workplace.* New York: Oxford University Press, 1994.

Lucy Suchman (ed.). *Special Issue on Representations of Work.* CACM 38:9 (September, 1995).

About the Author

 Sarah Kuhn is Assistant Professor in the Department of Policy and Planning at the University of Massachusetts at Lowell. In addition to her work on social aspects of workplace computer systems, she has developed courses on software design, including a studio-based course in collaboration with Mitchell Kapor and William Mitchell at MIT.

Profile

14. PARTICIPATORY DESIGN

The field of participatory design grew out of work beginning in the early 1970s in Norway, when computer professionals worked with members of the Iron and Metalworkers Union to enable the workers to have more influence on the design and introduction of computer systems into the workplace. Kristen Nygaard—who was well known for his computer-science research as codeveloper of SIMULA, the first object-oriented language—collaborated with union leaders and members, to create a national _codetermination agreement_, which specified the rights of unions to participate in the design and deployment decisions around new workplace technology.

In the following decades, several projects in Scandinavia set out to find the most effective ways for computer-system designers to collaborate with worker organizations to develop systems that promote the quality of work life. The DEMOS project, conducted in Sweden in the second half of the 1970s, involved an interdisciplinary team of researchers from the fields of computer science, sociology, economics, and engineering. Sponsored by the Swedish Trade Union Federation, its focus was "trade unions, industrial democracy, and computers" (Ehn, 1992, p. 107). Researchers worked with union members at a locomotive repair shop, a daily newspaper, a metalworking plant, and a department store.

In the locomotive repair shop, DEMOS participants were brought in because union members were unhappy with a computer-based planning system being introduced by management. Originally, the call for assistance was motivated by controversy over the amount of time assigned to different work tasks; after working together, however,

Profile Authors: Sarah Kuhn and Terry Winograd

union members and researchers saw that the overall assumptions of the system (that work could be deskilled, and that all planning was a management prerogative) formed the chief issue. As a result, the union conducted its own investigation into production planning, and called attention to significant problems with materials organization, job design, and overall planning that were hindering production efficiency. Insight into the production process and its relationship to computer-system design and job design led the union to formulate a series of principles and positions that it could then use as a basis for bargaining with management (Ehn, 1992).

The UTOPIA project was a collaboration between Swedish and Danish researchers and the Nordic Graphic Workers' Union. It developed and applied a work-oriented approach to the design of computer-based tools for skilled workers. The project team explicitly sought to reinforce and enhance skilled workers' control over process and methods, focusing on computer assistance for page makeup and image processing for newspapers.

Pelle Ehn, a primary participant in the UTOPIA project, describes its design philosophy, which they called the *tool perspective*:

> The tool perspective was deeply influenced by the way the design of tools takes place within traditional crafts ... new computer-based tools should be designed as an extension of the traditional practical understanding of tools and materials used within a given craft or profession. Design must therefore be carried out by the common efforts of skilled, experienced users and design professionals. Users possess the needed practical understanding but lack insight into new technical possibilities. The designer must understand the specific labor process that uses a tool. (Ehn, 1992, p. 112)

Good systems cannot be built by design experts who proceed with only limited input from users. Even when designers and prospective users have unlimited time for conversation, there are many aspects of a work process—such as how a particular tool is held, or what it means for something to "look right"—that reside in the complex, often tacit, domain of context. The UTOPIA researchers needed to invent new methods for achieving mutual understanding so that they could more fully understand the work world of graphics workers.

> Requirement specifications and systems descriptions based on information from interviews were not very successful. Improvements came when we

made joint visits to interesting plants, trade shows, and vendors and had discussions with other users; when we dedicated considerably more time to learning from each other, designers from graphics workers and graphics workers from designers; when we started to use design-by-doing methods and descriptions such as mockups and work organization games; and when we started to understand and use traditional tools as a design ideal for computer-based tools. (Ehn, 1992, p. 117)

The UTOPIA project applied innovative design techniques, such as the use of role-playing scenarios with low-fidelity mockups to give the workers a feel for what their work might be like with new technology. In the end, UTOPIA produced a working system, called TIPS, that was tested at several newspapers, and was eventually sold to a company that developed image-processing systems.

There has been some participatory design in the United States in the Scandinavian style (see, e.g., Sachs, 1995), and widespread use of design techniques that are based on participatory design. Greenbaum and Kyng (1991, p. 4) identify four issues for design:

1. The need for designers to take work practice seriously, to see the current ways that work is done as an evolved solution to a complex work situation that the designer only partially understands
2. The fact that because we are dealing with human actors, rather than cut-and-dried human factors, systems need to deal with users' concerns, treating them as people and not as performers of functions in a defined work role
3. The idea that work tasks must be seen within their context and are therefore situated actions, whose meaning and effectiveness cannot be evaluated in isolation from the context
4. The recognition that work is fundamentally social, involving extensive cooperation and communication

These principles apply in all workplaces, regardless of the specific interactions between workers and management. They are at the root of design approaches that have been developed with names such as *contextual inquiry* (Holtzblatt, 1993), *situated activity* (Suchman, 1987), *work-oriented design* (Ehn, 1988), *design for learnability* (Brown and Duguid, 1992) *situated design* (Greenbaum and Kyng, 1991). An ongoing series of conferences on participatory design, organized by Computer Professionals for

Social Responsibility (see Schuler and Namioka, 1993), has provided an opportunity for participatory-design concepts and practices to move beyond their original settings to a larger community of software designers.

Today, some of the concepts of participatory design are becoming standard practice in the computing industry. The emerging common wisdom in the major software-development companies is that it is important to design *with* the user, rather than to design *for* the user (as highlighted in De Young's account in Chapter 13). Participatory-design researchers have devised a variety of techniques to facilitate the communication of new technology possibilities to workers, to give the ultimate users insight into what it would be like to work with an envisioned system. These techniques include the low-fidelity mockups and role-playing activities of UTOPIA, as well as technology-aided methods such as the use of quick-and-dirty video animation to simulate the patterns of interaction with a new interface (see Muller et al., 1993; Muller, 1993).

In a panel at the 1994 Participatory Design Conference, Tom Erickson of Apple Computer set out four dimensions along which participation by users could be measured:

1. Directness of interaction with the designers
2. Length of involvement in the design process
3. Scope of participation in the overall system being designed
4. Degree of control over the design decisions

The original participatory-design movement was at the high end of all these scales. Designers worked over the full development cycle with a highly involved group of worker representatives. These representatives considered every aspect of the computer system being developed and of the deployment planned for it. They were in a setting where their labor–management agreements guaranteed that they had significant control over the outcome. As Kuhn describes in Chapter 14, the focus was on issues of industrial democracy.

In many software-design settings, the degree of participation along these dimensions may not be uniformly high. The overall principles of participatory design, however, are relevant: The conceptual approach and its repertoire of techniques are applicable across a wide range of products and design settings.

Suggested Readings

Susanne Bodker. *Through the Interface: A Human Activity Approach to User Interface Design.* Hillsdale, NJ: Lawrence Erlbaum Associates, 1991.

Joan Greenbaum and Morten Kyng. *Design at Work.* Hillsdale, NJ: Lawrence Erlbaum Associates, 1991.

Michael Muller and Sarah Kuhn (eds.). Special Issue on Participatory Design, CACM 36:4 (June, 1993).

Douglas Schuler and Aki Namioka, (eds.). *Participatory Design: Principles and Practices.* Hillsdale, NJ: Lawrence Erlbaum Associates, 1993.

Reflection

In the letter of invitation to the workshop that initiated this book, the organizers posed a series of questions for the participants to consider.

1. What is *quality* in software design? How can quality be usefully articulated to practitioners and students?
    *   How can design methodologies lead to quality?
    *   What is good and bad about the conventional software design approach of emphasizing the proliferation of rich functional mechanisms?
    *   What kind of professional training is appropriate? How are people learning the skills today?
    *   What is the role of tools in good design? (especially for prototyping)
    *   How do we design for (with?) new technologies such as hypermedia and virtual reality?

2. Where does software design stand with respect to other disciplines?
    *   What are the lessons (positive and negative) to be learned from experience with other design disciplines, such as architecture and product design?
    *   What are the unique characteristics of the digital medium, and how do they affect the possibilities for design?
    *   What useful parallels are there to the history of other media (for example, print)?
    *   Where does design fit into the academic institutions that deal with more traditional aspects of software and computing?

3. What is *design* in general?
    *   Is there a theory or underlying philosophy at the center of the discipline?

- What is the *design stance* and how does it relate to science and engineering?
- What are the key commonalities of ways of thinking and doing that cut across the design fields?
- How do human values and needs get incorporated into design thinking? Where is this currently done well, and done badly?

As a conclusion to the book, we invite you to pause and reflect on these questions and on the mosaic of answers that have been offered in the preceding chapters. We will not attempt to summarize the many directions and approaches taken by the authors in addressing these questions, leaving the task of integration to be done in the context of understanding for each reader.

The question that we address in this closing section is future oriented: Where do these questions and their possible answers lead us in our ongoing activities in software design?

Toward a Profession of Software Design

In his manifesto (Chapter 1), Mitchell Kapor declared "We need to create a professional discipline of software design." Throughout this book, our authors have described aspects of what such a discipline might encompass, and of how its practitioners might go about their work. Of course, it is possible to have a software industry without a professional discipline of software design. People have, after all, been designing software since the beginning of computing. Some of the software is excellent in one or more aspects of design; some of it is abysmal. At times, even when design is done well, the result is not accompanied by an understanding of what has been done or of how to repeat the success. We stand in awe of a brilliant creation, without grasping its implications for future designing.

In every professional discipline, the magic of creativity is still critical, but it does not stand apart. It is expressed within an identifiable process: a process that enables designers to repeat success and to pass on to new practitioners an understanding of how to succeed. A professional discipline relies on a body of knowledge and techniques, which enable practitioners to make relatively simple what might otherwise be complex, unintelligible, and incomprehensible.

As many of the authors have emphasized throughout the book, design—of any kind—is not an activity that can be reduced to the application of formalized methods, calculations, and standard procedures. We do not ever expect to see a cookbook for software design that enables anyone with proper training to succeed by simply following the rules. Guidelines and formal methods can play an important role: As Crampton Smith and Tabor point out in Chapter 3, such articulations of practice can improve software quality by "making the good better and the bad difficult." But they are only one piece of a larger and more complex picture.

Part of the complexity arises because software design draws on so many other disciplines: software engineering, software architecture, programming, human factors, graphic information design, art and aesthetics, sound production, psychology, and more. Software design, by the nature of what it aims to accomplish, sweeps into its scope all these interests, concerns, and disciplines.

What expertise do software designers need, then? They need to be able to envision, to create, and to develop a representation of their vision that they can communicate. They need to be able to speak the language of all the people involved in the enterprises addressed by software design: the user, the programmer, the graphic designer, the database architect, the marketing specialists, and all the rest. They need to be able to understand each discipline well enough to know when to involve relevant collaborators and how to incorporate the contributions of experts from other disciplines into the software-design visions that they create.

Education for Software Design

Every profession has its standards and institutions for training. A student who wants to become a physician goes to medical school; one who wants to become an interior designer takes a certification course from the American Society for Interior Design. If software design is a profession, it seems appropriate to ask, *How do you train to become a software designer?*

There is, of course, no standard answer. Today, the most common response is, "I was trained to do some other job, but ended up doing software design." The other job may have been programming, graphic design, human-factors analysis, or design management, among others. There are few people today who would say, "I trained in software design." This situation is changing rapidly, however. We can see the pace of change by scanning through the references on software design that are included in the suggested readings and bibliography of this book. Most have been published since Kapor first stated his manifesto in 1990. Many appeared between the time of our workshop in 1992 and the publication of this book in 1996. New teaching programs in software design are emerging in universities around the world (see Profile 9).

There are still questions about whether the most appropriate training environment is in colleges and universities, in special courses and institutes, or on the job. If at least a part of software-design education can be effectively provided in colleges and universities, should it be in departments of computer science, or in interdisciplinary programs that explicitly cross departmental boundaries? Should it be built around traditional courses, around studio work, or as a process more akin to apprenticeship? Should it train students from the beginning of their college careers, or admit students who have already done college-level work in one of the related traditional disciplines?

Answering these questions will require more experiments, more experience, and perhaps another book.

Quality in Software Design

Finally, it is worth taking a moment to reflect on the goals of the software-design profession. What are we trying to achieve?

In the end, we are concerned with the quality of our work—with the quality of the software that we produce and with the quality of the experience for the people who use that software. *Quality* is perhaps one of the most elusive of the terms that we have introduced. The assessment of quality is at once both objective and subjective, personal and political. Criteria for assessing quality range from the statistical precision of Deming's (1988) six-sigma measure to the familiar refrain about art: "I don't know what's good art, but I know what I like." Neither extreme is appropriate for evaluating software design. Software design is neither a science, nor an art; it combines aspects of the two.

In every mature field of design, standards of quality are a focus of attention, even when they cannot be quantified and measured objectively. The community develops a working consensus—even if that consensus cannot be fully articulated—through the ongoing observation and critique of new designs. The standard for this critique is the judgment of designers who have been recognized by their peers for the quality of their work. In teaching programs, experienced practitioners work with students in an ongoing round of trial and critique, as described by Schön (1988). For practicing designers, assessment comes from their clients, and from their peers in the form of design competitions and awards.

At the time of writing this book, we are witnessing the first emergence of peer awards for software design, as distinct from software engineering and research. The *interactions design awards* will be given in 1996, under the auspices of the Association for Computing Machinery (ACM), whose Turing Award and Software Systems Award are widely respected marks of quality in other aspects of computing. The results will appear in *interactions* magazine, one of the new software-design publications mentioned in our introduction. The call that was sent out for submissions for the awards included a description of how entries would be judged.

> This isn't an award for good looks or clever innovations. We aren't going to recognize the fanciest new widget. We aren't looking for the best-selling, the most adrenaline-inducing, or the best use of video. Not that these things are bad—we like an adrenaline-inducing multimedia best seller with clever widgets as much as the next techno-sapiens. But when it comes to awards, we care about quality of interaction. We want to recognize products, services, and environments that enhance people's lives. We're looking for designs that effectively help people work, learn, live, play, or communicate.

Multimedia design competitions, such as *Communication Arts* magazine's Interactive Design Annual (initiated in 1995), are increasingly emphasizing considerations of software design that go beyond good looks and adrenaline induction.

The role played by public assessments of software-design work will be greatly enhanced by the use of new communications media, such as the World Wide Web (Profile 5). Online communication will enable a wide range of people interested in software design to see the results, and to participate in the discussion when design competitions, such the *interactions design awards*, make their entries and results available on the WWW. A group at Lund University in Sweden is going further in making use of the Internet in the *Qualiteque*, which they describe as "the first international and virtual design studio and exhibition on information technology (IT),...[focusing] on the designers' ability to design for quality-in-use."

The Qualiteque will be an interactive medium on the WWW, where structured representations of software designs in use are presented and debated. Design awards are planned for 1997, to be determined by a jury of researchers and software designers who will comment on the contributions. But the assessments by these recognized experts will be the start of the Qualiteque—not the final result. Visitors to the virtual studio will investigate the contributions and comments, try out interactive prototypes of the described artifacts, and engage in a dialog about the contributions and critiques. The result will be a mixture of a publication, a conference, and an open studio, where the larger community of people concerned with software design can enter into the shared discussion of quality: how to assess it, and how to achieve it.

The authors and editors of this book have worked to initiate an interactive dialog as well. Although we have employed the older and less interactive medium of print, we see our words as a beginning rather than as a destination; as a way to engage you as a participant in the ongoing dialog that will shape the profession of software design.

About the Author

Terry Winograd is Professor of Computer Science at Stanford University where he has developed an innovative program in software design. Winograd completed much of his work on this book at Interval Research Corporation, where he is a regular consultant. He is a member of the advisory board of the Association for Software Design, the editorial board of *Human–Computer Interaction*, and the national board of Computer Professionals for Social Responsibility.

Bibliography

Adams, James. *Conceptual Blockbusting: A Guide to Better Ideas* (third edition). Reading, MA: Addison-Wesley, 1986. (First edition, 1974).

Adams, James. *The Care and Feeding of Ideas*. Reading, MA: Addison-Wesley, 1986.

Adler, Paul and Terry Winograd (eds.). *Usability: Turning Technologies into Tools*. New York: Oxford University Press, 1992.

Agostini, A, G De Michelis, M Grasso, and S Patriarca. Reengineering a business process with an innovative workflow management system: A case study. *Proceedings of the Conference on Cooperative Office Computing Systems* (COOCS'93). Hayward, CA, November 1993, 154–165.

Alben, Lauralee, Jim Faris, and Harry Saddler. Making It Macintosh. *interactions* 1:1 (January, 1994), 11–20.

Alexander, Christopher. *Notes on the Synthesis of Form*. Cambridge, MA: Harvard University Press, 1964.

Alexander, Christopher. *A Pattern Language*. New York: Oxford University Press, 1977.

Alexander, Christopher. *The Timeless Way of Building*. New York: Oxford University Press, 1979.

Andriole, Stephen and Peter Freeman. Software systems engineering: The case for a new discipline. *Software Engineering Journal* 8:3 (May, 1993), 165–178.

Apple Computer. *Human Interface Guidelines: The Apple Desktop Interface*. Reading, MA: Addison-Wesley, 1987.

Apple Computer. *Making It Macintosh: The Macintosh Human Interface Guidelines Companion* (CD ROM). Cupertino, CA: Apple Computer, 1993.

Arnson, Robert, Daniel Rosen, Mitchell Waite, and Jonathan Zuck. *Waite Group's Microsoft Visual Basic How-To*. Publishers Group West, 1990. (second edition in press.)

Association for Computing Machinery. ACM Code of Professional Conduct. In Deborah Johnson and Helen Nissenbaum (eds.). *Computers, Ethics, and Social Values*. Englewood Cliffs, NJ: Prentice-Hall, 1995, 598–605.

Baecker, Ronald, Jonathan Grudin, William Buxton, and Saul Greenberg. *Readings in Human–Computer Interaction: Toward the Year 2000* (second edition). San Francisco: Morgan Kaufmann, 1995.

Bang, Mollie. *Picture This: Perception and Composition*. Boston: Little Brown, 1991.

Baran, Barbara and Jana Gold. New markets and new technologies: Work reorganization and changing skill patterns in three white collar service industries. Report of Berkeley Roundtable on the International Economy. University of California at Berkeley. March, 1988.

Baudrillard, Jean. *For a Critique of the Political Economy of the Sign*. St. Louis, MO: Telos Press, 1981.

Bauersfeld, Penny. *Software by Design: Creating People-Friendly Software*. New York: M&T Books, 1994.

Baynes, Ken and Francis Pugh. *The Art of the Engineer*. London: Lund Humphries, 1981.

Bennett, John, Brad Hartfield, and Terry Winograd. Learning HCI design: Mentoring project groups in a course on human–computer interaction. *Proceedings of the SIGCSE '92 Technical Symposium of the ACM*. March, 1992, 246–253.

Bewley, William, Teresa Roberts, David Schroit, and William Verplank. Human factors testing in the design of Xerox's 8010 "Star" office workstation. *Proceedings of CHI'83*, New York: Association for Computing Machinery, 1983, 72–77.

Bieber, Michael and Tomas Isakowitz (eds.). *Special Issue on Designing Hypermedia Applications. CACM* 38:8 (August 1995).

Bierut, Michael, William Drenttel, Steven Heller, and DK Holland (eds.). *Looking Closer: Critical Writings on Graphic Design*. New York: Allworth, 1994.

Blum, Bruce. *Software Engineering: A Holistic View*. New York: Oxford University Press, 1992.

Blum, Bruce. *Beyond Programming: To a New Era of Design*. New York: Oxford University Press, 1996.

Bodker, Susanne. *Through the Interface: A Human Activity Approach to User Interface Design*. Hillsdale, NJ: Lawrence Erlbaum Associates, 1991.

Boehm, Barry. Software engineering. *IEEE Trans. Computers* C-25 (December, 1976), 1226–1244.

Boehm, Barry. A spiral model of software development and enhancement. *IEEE Computer* 21:2 (May, 1988), 61–72.

Borenstein, Nathaniel. *Programming as if People Mattered: Friendly Programs, Software Engineering, and Other Noble Delusions*. Princeton, NJ: Princeton University Press, 1991.

Bravo, Ellen. The hazards of leaving out the users. In Douglas Schuler and Aki Namioka (eds.). *Participatory Design: Principles and Practices*. Hillsdale, NJ: Lawrence Erlbaum Associates, 1993.

Brooks, Frederick. *The Mythical Man–Month: Essays on Software Engineering*. Reading, MA: Addison-Wesley, 1975. (Anniversary edition 1995, with four new chapters).

Brown, John Seely and Paul Duguid. Enacting design for the workplace. In Paul Adler and Terry Winograd (eds.). *Usability: Turning Technologies into Tools*. New York: Oxford University Press, 1992, 164–198.

Brown, John Seely and Paul Duguid. Borderline issues: Social and material aspects of design. *Human–Computer Interaction* 9:1 (Winter, 1994), 3–36.

Bush, Vannevar. As we may think. *Atlantic.* 176 (July, 1945), 101–108.

Card, Stuart, Thomas Moran, and Allen Newell. *The Psychology of Human–Computer Interaction.* Hillsdale, NJ: Lawrence Erlbaum Associates, 1983.

Carroll, John (ed.). *Designing Interaction: Psychology at the Human–Computer Interface.* New York: Cambridge University Press, 1991.

Clement, Andrew and Peter Van den Besselaar. A retrospective look at PD projects. In Michael Muller and Sarah Kuhn (eds.). *Special Issue on Participatory Design. CACM* 36:4 (June, 1993), 29–37.

Coplien, James and Douglas Schmidt. *Pattern Languages of Program Design.* Reading, MA: Addison-Wesley, 1995.

Corbett, J. Martin. Work at the interface: Advanced manufacturing technology and job design. In Paul Adler and Terry Winograd (eds.). *Usability: Turning Technologies into Tools.* New York: Oxford University Press, 1992, 133–163.

Covey, Stephen. *The Seven Habits of Highly Effective People.* New York: Simon & Schuster, 1989.

Crampton Smith, Gillian. The art of interaction. In Rae Earnshaw and John Vince (eds.). *Interacting with Virtual Worlds.* London: John Wiley, 1994.

Dair, Carl. *Design with Type.* Toronto: Toronto University Press, 1952. (second edition 1967).

DeGeorge, Gail and Veronica Byrd. Knight Ridder: Once burned and the memory lingers. *Business Week* No. 3366 (April 11, 1994), 74–76.

DeGrace, Peter and Leslie Hulet-Stahl. *Wicked Problems, Righteous Solutions: A Catalogue of Modern Software Engineering Paradigms.* New York: Yourdon/Prentice-Hall, 1990.

Deming, W. Edwards. *Out of the Crisis.* Cambridge, MA: MIT Center for Advanced Engineering, 1988.

Denning, Peter (1992a). What is software quality? *CACM* 35:1 (January, 1992), 13–15.

Denning, Peter (1992b). Work is a closed loop process. *American Scientist* 80:4 (July–August, 1992), 314–317.

Denning, Peter, Douglas Comer, David Gries, Michael Mulder, Allen Tucker, Joseph Turner, and Paul Young. Computing as a discipline. *CACM* 32:1 (January 1989), 9–23.

Denning, Peter and Pamela Dargan. A discipline of software architecture. *interactions* 1:1 (January, 1994), 55–65.

Denning, Peter and Raúl Medina-Mora. Completing the loops. *ORSA/TIMS Interfaces* 25 (May, 1995), 42–57.

de Sausmarez, Maurice. *The Dynamics of Visual Form.* London: Studio Vista, 1964.

Dijkstra, Edsger. On the cruelty of really teaching computer science. *CACM* 32:12 (December, 1989), 1398–1404.

Dix, Alan, Janet Finlay, Gregory Abowd, and Russell Beale. *Human–Computer Interaction*. Englewood Cliffs, NJ: Prentice-Hall, 1993.

Dunlop, Charles and Rob Kling (eds.). *Computerization and Controversy: Value Conflicts and Social Choices*. Boston: Academic Press, 1991.

Earnshaw, Rae and John Vince (eds.). *Interacting with Virtual Worlds*. London: John Wiley, 1994.

Ehn, Pelle. *Work-Oriented Design of Computer Artifacts*. Stockholm: Arbetslivscentrum, 1988. (Distributed by Lawrence Erlbaum Associates, Hillsdale, NJ).

Ehn, Pelle. Scandinavian design: On participation and skill. In Paul Adler and Terry Winograd (eds.), *Usability: Turning Technologies into Tools*. New York: Oxford University Press, 1992, 96–132.

Ehn, Pelle and Morten Kyng, Cardboard computers: Mocking-it-up or hands-on the future. In Joan Greenbaum and Morten Kyng (eds.), *Design at Work*. Hillsdale, NJ: Lawrence Erlbaum Associates, 1991, 169–195.

Ewing, David. *Freedom Inside the Organization*. New York: E.P. Dutton, 1977.

Fischer, Layna (ed.). *New Tools for New Times: The Workflow Paradigm* (second edition). Alameda, CA: Future Strategies, 1995.

Floyd, Chistiana, H Züllighoven, Reinhard Budde, and Reinhard Keil-Slawik (eds.). *Software Development and Reality Construction*. Berlin: Springer-Verlag, 1992.

Forester, Tom (ed.). *Computers in the Human Context*. Cambridge, MA: MIT Press, 1989.

Gal, Shahaf. Building bridges: Design, learning, and the role of computers. *Journal of Machine-Mediated Learning* 4:4, 1991, 335–375.

Garson, Barbara. *The Electronic Sweatshop: How Computers Are Transforming the Office of the Future into the Factory of the Past*. New York: Penguin, 1989.

Gibson, James. *The Ecological Approach to Visual Perception*. New York: Houghton Mifflin, 1979.

Giedion, Sigfried. *Space, Time, and Architecture: The Growth of a New Tradition*. Cambridge, MA: Harvard University Press, 1941.

Goodman, Danny. *The Complete Hypercard 2.2 Handbook* (fourth edition). New York: Random House, 1993.

Greenbaum, Joan and Morten Kyng. *Design at Work*. Hillsdale, NJ: Lawrence Erlbaum Associates, 1991.

Hammer, Michael. *Reengineering the Corporation*. New York: HarperBusiness, 1993.

Heckel, Paul. *Elements of Friendly Software Design*. Berkeley, CA: Sybex, 1994.

Helander, Martin (ed.). *Handbook of Human–Computer Interaction*. New York: North-Holland, 1988.

Hix, Deborah and H. Rex Hartson. *Developing User Interfaces*. New York: Wiley, 1993.

Holtzblatt, Karen and Sandra Jones. Contextual inquiry: A participatory technique for systems design. In Douglas Schuler and Aki Namioka (eds.),

Participatory Design: Principles and Practices. Hillsdale, NJ: Lawrence Erlbaum Associates, 1993, 177–210.

Horn, Robert. *Mapping Hypertext*. Lexington, MA: Lexington Institute, 1989.

Howard, VA (ed.). *Varieties of Thinking*. New York: Routledge, 1990.

Illich, Ivan. *Tools for Conviviality*. New York: Harper & Row, 1973.

International Association of Machinists. Workers' Technology Bill of Rights. *Democracy* 3:2 (Spring 1983), 25–27.

Johnson, Deborah and Helen Nissenbaum (eds.). *Computers, Ethics, and Social Values*. Englewood Cliffs, NJ: Prentice-Hall, 1995.

Johnson, Jeff, Terry Roberts, William Verplank, David C. Smith, Charles Irby, Marian Beard, and Kevin Mackey. Xerox Star: A retrospective. *IEEE Computer* 22:9 (September, 1989), 11–29.

Jones, Chris. *Essays in Design*. London: Wiley, 1984.

Kapor, Mitchell. A software design manifesto: Time for a change. *Dr. Dobb's Journal* 172 (January 1991), 62–68.

Karagiannis, Dimitris (ed.). *Special Issue on Business Process Reengineering. SIGOIS Bulletin*, 16:1, (August, 1995).

Karasek, Robert and Töres Theorell. *Healthy Work: Stress, Productivity, and the Reconstruction of Working Life*. New York: Basic Books, 1990.

Keen, Peter. *Shaping the Future: Business Design Through Information Technology*. Boston: Harvard Business School, 1991.

Kepes, Gyorgy. *Language of Vision*. Chicago: Paul Theobold, 1969.

Koberg, Don. *The Universal Traveler: A Soft-Systems Guide*. Los Altos, CA: Kaufmann, 1974.

Koberg, Don and Jim Bagnall. *The All New Universal Traveler*. Los Altos, CA: Kaufmann, 1981.

Krol, Ed. *The Whole Internet User's Guide & Catalog* (second edition). Sebastopol, CA: O'Reilly, 1994.

Kuhn, Sarah and John Wooding. The changing structure of work in the United States; Part I: The impact on income and benefits. *New Solutions* 4:2 (Winter 1994), 43–56.

Kuhn, Sarah and John Wooding. The changing structure of work in the United States; Part II: Implications for health and welfare. *New Solutions* 4:4 (Summer 1994), 21–27.

Land, George and Beth Jarman. *Breakpoint and Beyond*. New York: HarperBusiness, 1992.

Landauer, Thomas. *The Trouble with Computers: Usefulness, Usability, and Productivity*. Cambridge, MA: MIT Press, 1995.

Laurel, Brenda (ed.). *The Art of Human–Computer Interaction*. Reading, MA: Addison-Wesley, 1990.

Laurel, Brenda. *Computers as Theatre* (second edition with additional postscript). Reading, MA: Addison-Wesley, 1993.

Lave, Jean and Etienne Wenger. *Situated Learning: Legitimate Peripheral Participation*. Cambridge: Cambridge University Press, 1991.

Marcus, Aaron. *Graphic Design for Electronic Documents and User Interfaces*. New York: ACM/Addison-Wesley, 1992.

Marx, Gary and Sanford Sherizen. Monitoring on the job. In Tom Forester (ed.). "Computers in the Human Context." Cambridge, MA: MIT Press, 1989, 397–406.

McLuhan, Marshall. *The Gutenberg Galaxy: The Making of Typographic Man*. Toronto: University of Toronto Press, 1962.

McLuhan, Marshall. *Understanding Media* (second edition). New York: New American Library, 1964.

Medina-Mora, Raúl, Terry Winograd, Rodrigo Flores, and Fernando Flores. The ActionWorkflow approach to workflow management technology. *The Information Society* 9:4 (October–December, 1993), 391–406.

Microsoft Corporation. *The Windows Interface: Guidelines for Software Design*. Microsoft Press, 1995.

Mitchell, William J. *The Reconfigured Eye*. Cambridge, MA: MIT Press, 1992.

Mitchell, William J. *City of Bits*. Cambridge, MA: MIT Press, 1995.

Moggridge, Bill. Design for the information revolution. *Design DK* 4 (1992), Copenhagen: Danish Design Centre.

Moran, Thomas (ed.). *Special Issue on Context in Design*. *Human–Computer Interaction* 9:1 (Winter, 1994).

Mountford, S. Joy. Tools and techniques for creative design. In Brenda Laurel (ed.). *The Art of Human–Computer Interaction*. Reading, MA: Addison-Wesley. 1990, 17–30.

Muller, Michael and Sarah Kuhn (eds.). *Special Issue on Participatory Design*. *CACM* 36:4 (June, 1993).

Muller, Michael, Daniel Wildman, and Ellen White. Taxonomy of PD practices: A brief practitioner's guide. *CACM* 36:4 (June, 1993), 26–27.

Muller, Michael. PICTIVE: Democratizing the dynamics of the design session. In Douglas Schuler and Aki Namioka (eds.). *Participatory Design: Principles and Practices*. Hillsdale, NJ: Lawrence Erlbaum Associates, 1993.

Mullet, Kevin and Darrell Sano. *Designing Visual Interfaces: Communication Oriented Techniques*. Englewood Cliffs, NJ: Prentice-Hall/SunSoft, 1995.

Nardi, Bonnie. *A Small Matter of Programming: Perspectives on End User Computing*. Cambridge, MA: MIT Press, 1993.

Nass, Clifford and Byron Reeves. *The Media Equation*. Cambridge: Cambridge University Press/CSLI, 1996.

Neumann, Peter. *Computer-Related Risks*. Reading, MA: Addison-Wesley, 1995.

Newman, William and Mik Lamming. *Interactive System Design*. Reading, MA: Addison-Wesley, 1995.

Nielsen, Jakob. *Usability Engineering*. Boston: Academic Press, 1993.

Nielsen, Jakob. *Multimedia and Hypertext: The Internet and Beyond*. Boston: Academic Press, 1995.

Norman, Donald. *The Design of Everyday Things*. New York: HarperCollins, 1990. (Originally issued as *The Psychology of Everyday Things*, 1988.)

Norman, Donald. *Turn Signals Are the Facial Expressions of Automobiles.* Reading, MA: Addison-Wesley, 1992.

Norman, Donald. *Things That Make Us Smart.* Reading, MA: Addison-Wesley, 1993.

Norman, Donald and Stephen Draper. *User Centered System Design: New Perspectives on Human–Computer Interaction.* Hillsdale, NJ: Lawrence Erlbaum Associates, 1986.

Nunberg, Geoffrey (ed.). *The Future of the Book.* Berkeley, CA: University of California Press, 1996.

Nyce, James and Paul Kahn (eds.). *From Memex to Hypertext: Vannevar Bush and the Mind's Machine.* Boston: Academic Press, 1991.

Ong, Walter. *Orality and Literacy: The Technologizing of the World.* London: Methuen, 1982.

Ortony, Andrew (ed.). *Metaphor and Thought* (second edition). Cambridge: Cambridge University Press, 1993.

Parnas, David. Software aspects of strategic defense systems. *CACM* 28:12 (December, 1985), 1326–1335.

Pava, Calvin. *Managing New Office Technology.* New York: Free Press, 1983.

Perlman, Gary, Georgia Green, and Michael Wogalter. *Human Factors Perspectives on Human–Computer Interaction: Selections from Proceedings of Human Factors and Ergonomics Society Annual Meetings, 1983–1994.* Santa Monica, CA: Human Factors and Ergonomics Society, 1995.

Pfleeger, Shari Lawrence. *Software Engineering: The Production of Quality Software.* New York: Macmillan, 1987.

Polanyi, Michael. *The Tacit Dimension.* Garden City, NY: Doubleday, 1966.

Preece, Jenny, Yvonne Rogers, David Benyon, Helen Sharp, and Simon Holland. *Human–Computer Interaction.* Reading, MA: Addison-Wesley, 1994.

Rasmussen, Steen Eiler. *Experiencing Architecture* (second United States edition). Cambridge, MA: MIT Press, 1959.

Reddy, Michael. The conduit metaphor: A case of frame conflict in our language about language. In Andrew Ortony (ed.). *Metaphor and Thought.* New York: Cambridge University Press, 1993, 164–201.

Rheinfrank, John. The Technological juggernaut: Objects and their transcendence. In Susan Yelavich (ed.). *The Edge of the Millennium: An International Critique of Architecture, Urban planning, Product and Communication Design.* New York: Watson-Guptill, 1993.

Rheinfrank, John, William Hartman, and Arnold Wassermann. Design for usability: Crafting a strategy for the design of a new generation of Xerox copiers. In Paul Adler and Terry Winograd (eds.), *Usability: Turning Technologies into Tools.* New York: Oxford University Press, 1992, 15–40.

Rheinfrank, John and Katherine Welker. Meaning. In Michael Bierut et al. (eds.). *Looking Closer: Critical Writings on Graphic Design.* New York: Allworth, 1994.

Richards, Dick. *Artful Work.* San Francisco: Berrett-Koehler, 1995.

Richardson, Charles. Computers don't kill jobs—people do: Technology and power in the workplace. *Annals of the American Academy of Political and Social Science* (in press).

Roberts, Jason. *Director Demystified*. Berkeley, CA: Peach Pit Press, 1995.

Rosmarin, Adena. *The Power of Genre*. Minneapolis, MN: University of Minnesota Press, 1985.

Ruder, Emil. *Typographie*. Teufen, Switzerland: Arthur Niggli, 1967 (text in German, English, and French).

Rumbaugh, James. *Object-oriented Modeling and Design*. Englewood Cliffs, NJ: Prentice-Hall, 1991.

Sachs, Patricia. Transforming work: Collaboration, learning, and design. *CACM* 38:9 (September, 1995), 6–44.

Sackman, Hal. A prototype IFIP code of ethics based on participative international consensus. In Charles Dunlop and Rob Kling (eds.). *Computerization and Controversy: Value Conflicts and Social Choices*. Boston: Academic Press, 1991, 698–703.

Salzman, Harold and Stephen Rosenthal. *Software by Design: Shaping Technology and the Workplace*. New York: Oxford University Press, 1994.

Schael, Thomas and Buni Zeller. Workflow management systems for financial services. *Proceedings of the Conference on Cooperative Office Computing Systems* (COOCS'93). Hayward, CA, November, 1993, 142–153.

Schön, Donald. *The Reflective Practitioner: How Professionals Think in Action*. New York: Basic Books, 1983.

Schön, Donald. *Educating the Reflective Practitioner: Toward A New Design for Teaching and Learning in the Professions*. San Francisco: Jossey-Bass, 1987.

Schön, Donald. The design process. In V Howard (ed.). *Varieties of Thinking*. New York: Routledge, 1990.

Schor, Juliet. *The Overworked American: The Unexpected Decline of Leisure*. New York: Basic Books, 1991.

Schrage, Michael. *No More Teams*. New York: Doubleday Currency, 1995.

Schuler, Douglas and Aki Namioka (eds.). *Participatory Design: Principles and Practices*. Hillsdale, NJ: Erlbaum, 1993.

Searle, John. *Speech Acts*. New York: Cambridge University Press, 1969.

Shaiken, Harley. The automated factory: Vision and reality. In Tom Forester (ed.). *Computers in the Human Context*. Cambridge, MA: MIT Press, 1989.

Shneiderman, Ben. *Designing the User Interface: Strategies for Effective Human–Computer Interaction* (second edition). Reading, MA: Addison-Wesley, 1992.

Smith, David Canfield, Charles Irby, Ralph Kimball, Bill Verplank, and Eric Harlslem. Designing the STAR user interface. *Byte* 7:4 (April, 1982), 242–282.

Strong, Gary. New directions in HCI education, research, and practice. *interactions* 2:1 (January, 1995), 69–81.

Suchman, Lucy. *Plans and Situated Actions*. Cambridge: Cambridge University Press, 1987.

Suchman, Lucy (ed.). *Special Issue on Representations of Work. CACM* 38:9 (September, 1995).

Tanizaki, Jun'ichiro. *In Praise of Shadows*. New Haven: Leete's Island Books, 1977.

Tognazzini, Bruce. *Tog on Interface*. Reading, MA: Addison-Wesley, 1992.

Tognazzini, Bruce. *Tog on Software Design*. Reading, MA: Addison-Wesley, 1995.

Tufte, Edward. *The Visual Display of Quantitative Information*. Cheshire, CT: Graphics Press, 1983.

Tufte, Edward. *Envisioning Information*. Cheshire, CT: Graphics Press, 1990.

Verplank, Bill, Jane Fulton, Allison Black, and Bill Moggridge. Observation and invention: Use of scenarios in interaction design. Handout for Tutorial, INTERCHI'93, Amsterdam, 1993.

Wheelwright, Steven and Kim Clark. *Leading Product Development: The Senior Manager's Guide to Creating and Shaping the Enterprise*. New York: Free Press, 1995.

Winograd, Terry. What can we teach about human–computer interaction? *Proceedings of the CHI90 Conference on Human Factors in Computing*. Seattle: April, 1990, 443–449.

Winograd, Terry and Fernando Flores. *Understanding Computers and Cognition: A New Foundation for Design*. Reading, MA: Addison-Wesley, 1987. (first issued by Ablex, 1986).

Winograd, Terry. Environments for software design. *CACM* 38:6 (June 1995), 65–74.

Yanagi, Sōetsu. *The Unknown Craftsman: A Japanese Insight into Beauty*. Tokyo and New York: Kodansha, 1972 (second edition 1989).

Yates, JoAnne. *Control Through Communication: The Rise of System in American Management*. Baltimore, MD: Johns Hopkins University Press, 1989.

Yelavich, Susan (ed.). *The Edge of the Millennium: An International Critique of Architecture, Urban Planning, Product and Communication Design*. New York: Watson-Guptill, 1993.

Software

The ActionWorkflow Analyst. Alameda, CA: Action Technologies, Inc., 1993.
Director. San Francisco, CA: Macromedia, 1988.
EarthQuest. Palo Alto, CA: Earthquest, 1991.
HyperCard. Cupertino, CA: Apple Computer, 1987.
Kid Pix. By Craig Hickman. Novato, CA: Brøderbund Software, 1991.
Lotus 1-2-3. Cambridge, MA: Lotus Software, 1983.
Microsoft Bob. Redmond, WA: Microsoft, 1995.
Quicken. Menlo Park, CA: Intuit Inc., 1993.
Spelunx. By Cyan Software. Novato, CA: Brøderbund Software, 1991.
Visual Basic. Redmond, WA: Microsoft, 1990.

Credits

Chapter 1 reprinted with permission of *Dr. Dobb's Journal*.

In Chapter 3, Figure 3.1, from *A Guide to Intercity Train Services* 28 May to 23 September 1995, © TRMC for British Railways Board, p. 24. Reprinted with permission of Travel & Rail Marketing Co.

Chapter 10 reprinted with permission of Michael Schrage.

In Chapter 14, "Work at the Interface. . . ," from J. Martin Corbett in Adler/Winograd (eds.), *Usability: Turning Technologies into Tools*, 1992, New York: Oxford University Press. Reprinted with permission.

In Chapter 14, "Scandinavian design: On participation and skill. . . ," from Pelle Ehn in Adler/Winograd (eds.), *Usability: Turning Technologies into Tools*, 1992, New York: Oxford University Press. Reprinted with permission.

Paul Saffo's photograph by Steve Castillo Photos.

Peter Denning's photograph by Neil Adams.

MicroSoft® and Windows® are registered trademarks of Microsoft Corporation.

MicroSoft® Bob™ is a trademark of Microsoft Corporation.

Name Index

Subject Index

Other Books of Interest

BUGS in Writing Lyn Dupré

If you are a person who writes and who works with computers, Dupré's *BUGS in Writing* will show you how to rid your prose of the most common problems that writers face. With simple principles for lucid writing conveyed by numerous, intriguing, and frequently hilarious examples, *BUGS* may also be the first book on English grammar that you will read for sheer fun. ISBN 0-201-60019-6

Safeware: System Safety and Computers Nancy Leveson

We are building systems today—and using computers to control them—that have the potential for large-scale destruction of life and environment. This book, by a leading authority on the subject, examines what is currently known about building safe systems, and provides software engineers, systems developers, and their managers, a guide to preventing accidents and losses caused by technology. ISBN 0-201-11972-2

Computer-Related Risks Peter G. Neumann

Neumann is the moderator of the popular Internet newsgroup, The Risks Forum. In this ACM Press book, he organizes and analyzes problems addressed in that forum, problems involving reliability, safety, security, privacy, and human well-being. ISBN 0-201-55805-X

Distributed Multimedia: Technologies, Applications, and Opportunities in the Digital Information Industry
Palmer W. Agnew and Anne S. Kellerman

A guide for both users and providers of information, this ACM Press book shows how global communications systems are converging into a single, interactive, digital network, and how this convergence is facilitating the conveyance of multimedia information to and from remote locations. ISBN 0-201-76536-5

Interactive System Design William M. Newman and Michael G. Lamming

This textbook and practical reference by well-known authors presents a framework for user-oriented design and a comprehensive guide to modern design techniques. It includes numerous examples based on real-world data, and two in-depth case studies illustrating usability analysis and innovative design. Foreword by Terry Winograd. ISBN 0-201-63162-8

Detailed information about Addison-Wesley and ACM Press books is available from our World Wide Web sites (see the URLs on the back cover). You will find these books wherever technical books are sold, or you may call ACM (members only) at **1-800-342-6626** or Addison-Wesley at **1-800-822-6339**.